THE WRITINGS OF

William Carlos Williams

THE WRITINGS OF

William Carlos Williams

Publicity for the Self

Daniel Morris

UNIVERSITY OF MISSOURI PRESS

COLUMBIA AND LONDON

Copyright © 1995 by
The Curators of the University of Missouri
University of Missouri Press, Columbia, Missouri 65201
Printed and bound in the United States of America
All rights reserved
5 4 3 2 1   99 98 97 96 95

Library of Congress Cataloging-in-Publication Data

Morris, Daniel, 1962-
    The writings of William Carlos Williams : publicity for the self / Daniel Morris.
      p.   cm.
    Includes bibliographical references (p.   ) and index.
    ISBN 0-8262-1002-3
    1. Williams, William Carlos, 1883-1963—Criticism and interpretation.   2. Self
in literature.   I. Title.
    PS3545.I544Z656   1995
    811'.52—dc20   95-7718
                                                                        CIP

∞ This paper meets the requirements of the
American National Standard for Permanence of Paper
for Printed Library Materials, Z39.48, 1984.

Designer: Kristie Lee
Typesetter: BOOKCOMP
Printer and binder: Thomson-Shore, Inc.
Typefaces: Garamond and Mistral

For credits, see page 217.

THIS BOOK IS DEDICATED

to my mother and to the memory of my father,

Irwin Walter Morris.

Contents

Acknowledgments

I WISH TO THANK the many persons who provided information, advice, and encouragement while I was writing this book. My special thanks go to Wendy Stallard Flory, Allen R. Grossman, Daniel R. Schwarz, and Stephen Watt. For their assistance in the final manuscript preparation, I thank my editor, Jane Lago, and the rest of the staff at the University of Missouri Press. I also want to thank my mother, Phyllis, and my two brothers, David and Peter, for their love and faith in me.

THE WRITINGS OF
William Carlos Williams

Introduction

In *The Case for a Humanistic Poetics,* the pragmatic neo-Aristotelian critic Daniel R. Schwarz writes: "If there is a trend that humanistic critics should welcome, it is the returning emphasis in literary studies to the anterior reality which gives rise to imagined worlds and how the process of mimesis renders those worlds. The dialogue between anterior reality and texts . . . is crucial because it enables us not merely to see what texts are about but how they are created."[1] This book directs the "dialogue between anterior reality and texts" and "the creation of the text" toward an American boundary figure. It concerns the stories told about himself by a liminal American poet, a man of diverse ethnic origins and a paradoxical cultural interest that included avant-garde developments in international modernism, celebrity pictorial displays in *Life* magazine, and an allegiance to 1930s movements in social realist documentation of the working poor. I will show how the poet whose name combines both north and south inscribed the meaning of a signature that is hard to forget but that not too long ago was on the verge of being forgotten: William Carlos Williams.

In order to understand how Williams imagined himself in his fictions and then in his long poem *Paterson,* I incorporate into my readings aspects of modern and postmodern culture that have not received adequate attention in previous discussions of his work, concentrating especially on the relationship between modernism and mass (or commercial) culture as they interact in these works. I perform close textual analysis of Williams's writings in a variety of genres: the short poems "Between Walls" (1938) and "The Lonely Street" (1921); the short stories "Old Doc Rivers" (1932), "The Girl with a Pimply Face" (1938), and "A Night in June" (1938);

1. *The Case for a Humanistic Poetics,* 11.

1

the novels *A Voyage to Pagany* (1928) and *In the Money* (1940); prose essays such as "Against the Weather: A Study of the Artist" (1939) and "On Measure—Statement for Cid Corman" (1954); the *Autobiography* (1951); and, finally, the modernist "epic" *Paterson* (published sequentially in five books between 1946 and 1958). Through this close reading, I construct an argument about how, with the style of the writing as well as the content of the narrative representations of the Williams personage, the author created a metanarrative that in each instance and in each literary form situated him as an interstitial or threshold figure. In this way Williams presented himself as able to provide for an unacknowledged social group the dignity of appearance in privileged classes of representation such as the modern poem. In order to make my argument about Williams I situate myself in relationship to two interpretive communities of modern literature, each of which presents theoretical arguments about the production of literature with which I am in sympathy and that in this book I bridge in a fashion that I believe would have pleased Williams.

Tenets of a humanistic formalism allow me to address the question of authorship and the authorial presence of the poet in his own imaginative works in a way that assumes that Williams intended what he wrote, consciously or unconsciously. My argument about the appearance of the poet in *Paterson* takes into account Paul de Man's understanding in "Autobiography as De-facement" of writing as a deadly mediation that produces an erasure of presence to the same degree that the authorial mask becomes apparent. I argue that this representative masking was a performance shaped by Williams's desire for personal renown. The authorial self was designed by Williams for specific purposes that in the end produced a complex kind of presence-making that can best be identified through a critical approach such as the "humanistic formalism" defined by Schwarz:

> A revitalized humanistic criticism would discard such New Critical orthodox-ies as the biographical fallacy and the shibboleth 'exit author' and discover how to speak of the author as a formal presence in the text in ways that go beyond equating the omniscient narrator, or implied author, with the bio-graphical author. . . . In the process of reading we respond to an *imitation*, a *representation* of the real creator of the text. He is in the imagined world as a distortion—at times, an idealization, a clarification, a simplification, an obfuscation—of the creating psyche.[2]

2. Ibid., 6.

My argument about Williams's fictions, and especially about *Paterson* book 5, takes into account "the author as a formal presence" while offering a recovery of a New Critical attitude toward literature as separate from anterior reality in a way that liberates the author to participate in the world of others who exist outside the literary text. Williams's insistence in book 5 on the poem as a work of art unrelated to his substantiation in the poem as a figure of renown or to his community's sense of its "living history" triggers an affirmation of, and a respect for, participation with other citizens outside the poem. While diminishing his authority as a representative speaker, Williams's refusal to identify the poet with the poem, as described in *Paterson* book 3, part 2, in the scene dramatizing a 1902 fire that destroyed the Danforth Library, defers the tragic (de Manian) logic of self-creation as disfiguration. By the end of *Paterson* he no longer authorizes the poem through claims to the heroic central-ity of the modernist poet as an orphic or world-making legislator. He can, however, play a less ambitious, but survivable, role on the margin of cultural affairs in the world outside the poem. In *Paterson* book 5, Williams in effect registers a refusal to submit to what Allen R. Grossman terms "semantic actualization." Instead he favors a desire to return to the privilege of organic life. By turning away from his massive construction as King Paterson, Williams in the end refuses to adhere to what Grossman calls "the most familiar moral spectacle of Western representation . . . the exchange of being for meaning."[3] He reverses a hierarchization of value in which symbolic leadership (displayed in the figure of King Paterson) is privileged over organic life (displayed in the figure of Dr. Paterson). Williams accepts the poem as an act of serious play that affirms his tem-porary presence through the act of making art, and through the act of teaching others to make art. He does not have to appear in *Paterson* as a character like Sam Patch, the legendary nineteenth-century daredevil who leaps to his death in the Passaic Falls—which is to say, as a subject made into a sacrificial object.

By accepting the design of the poem as distinct and other to the self, Williams in book 5 returns to a position about the relationship between poetry and self-fashioning that he had held, implicitly, in earlier lyrics such as "The Lonely Street." In that poem, as I believe is the case in book

3. "Why Is Death in Arcadia?: Poetic Process, Literary Humanism, and the Example of Pastoral," 162.

5, the poet's consciousness, his lyric "I," is suggested through attention to craft (as in the invocation in *Paterson* of the three-stepped line, for example). The reader's attention in terms of the poet's presence, however, is directed outward to the scene described, which is the appropriate site for interpersonal sharing and commitment. By focusing on the poem as an object of interpersonal mediation, Williams establishes a relationship between artist and object and, more important, between artist and subject that Terence Diggory has recently described as an ethical act. Diggory argues that, like the painter Pieter Brueghel, Williams is able to convey, through his passion and investment in his medium, his experience of being a part of the world while eschewing appropriations and possessions of it.[4] By considering the appearance of the person as "made" through the transformative process of a series of fictions that stand between art (symbol) and life (organic process), Williams's fictions of the self may themselves be designated as the ritual liminal phenomena that produce the outcome of Williams's practice in book 5. Mircea Eliade would call that outcome the initiation into "the status of human being" which leads to "a socially responsible and culturally awakened being."[5]

The second literary-cultural approach that informs this study has been described by Kevin J. H. Dettmar in *Rereading the New* as a third moment of modernist criticism:

> Modernism, we are now beginning to see, is as much a strategy of read-ing as it is a style of writing. . . . [T]he modernists were more successful than any preceding group in forging both a *literary* and a coherent *critical* practice—creating and disseminating the interpretive paradigm by which they would be read. . . . Surely one component of what we have learned to call Modernism is only a recuperative habit of "interpreting" texts, whereas the most enduring of those "Modernist" texts, read in another spirit, in another age, look strikingly postmodern. Perhaps, then, we are just beginning to appreciate what was apparent to the Modernists all along—that the edifice of Modernism was always vulnerable, and that the best Modernist writing always betrayed the artifice of its construction in ways we have begun to call postmodern—that the monuments of High Modernism already contained within them the seeds of their own de(con)struction.[6]

---

4. *William Carlos Williams and the Ethics of Painting,* 1–13.

5. See Eliade's *Rites and Symbols of Initiation: The Mysteries of Birth and Rebirth* (New York: Harper and Row, 1958), 3.

6. *Rereading the New: A Backward Glance at Modernism,* 13–15.

In reassessing Williams's interpretations of his own relationship to modernism through his telling of stories about his role as a public figure and, implicitly, about his role as a poet sensitive to the needs for representation of a dispossessed group of urban immigrants living on the eastern seaboard, I focus on the middle to late phase of Williams's career (1928–1958). This period was bound by the publication of his first conventional novel, *A Voyage to Pagany* (1928), and of *Paterson* book 5 (1958). Written after the falling out of print and out of memory of his first six books of poems, Williams's autobiographical fictions were attempts to integrate the poet into the community of ordinary American readers to which he returned after his visit to Europe in 1924. I examine how and try to imagine why Williams looked back at his personal and literary past in *A Voyage to Pagany* in a way that effaced or at least imagined in a new way his original allegiance to European modernism. In so doing, his task was to create an identity as a poet in the American grain of processual authors (such as Emerson and Whitman) who also incorporated into his own practice a shadowed or syncretic relationship to atavistic formal cultural and religious practices established in Europe.

In 1935 Williams wrote that he was looking for "some more simple, some shrewder, inventive method" of getting his work into print other than a full-blown political revolution toward communism, such as was advocated by Gorham Munson and others at the American Writers Congress. One inventive method that Williams embraced was to apply conventional strategies of marketing to poetry that allegedly opposed commercial art. To promote the first edition of *Collected Poems* in 1934, for instance, he allowed Wallace Stevens to write the introduction, and he hired a literary agent named Maxim Lieber as "the first step in [my] selling campaign."[7] A second method was to control how his work would be inserted into the culture of renown by casting his own literary identity within the fictions.[8] Williams's desire to mount a "selling campaign" on behalf of his poetry,

---

7. Paul Mariani, *William Carlos Williams: A New World Naked,* 378, 338.

8. From the start of his career as a published poet, Williams was interested in how to advertise his poetry. His autobiography recalls his meetings between 1910 and 1920 with a personal friend of his father's who was, Williams tells us, a professional ad man. At these meetings his literary name, "William Carlos Williams," was decided upon. Williams's father was himself a salesman, and he met Williams's mother on a business trip to Puerto Rico. As early as 1906 Williams was aware of the mnemonic powers of the advertising jingle to inscribe the name and the messages of a product upon the minds of consumers. He recalls in his autobiography walking at the Penn green and

coupled with his perception that his innovations in modern poetic forms were being slighted or forgotten after he had invested three decades on literary experiment, animated his shift toward prose, which was designed to relay the news of his renown to an audience of ordinary readers.

In his fictions of the self, Williams was looking back at his past at a time when the national economy had shifted to what Fredric Jameson refers to as Late (consumer or symbolic) Capitalism.[9] Williams's fictional simulations of his first literary acts mirror and reflect the shift in emphasis in the national economy from the production of goods to innovative ways to sell them. His fictions were promotional in the sense that they were professionally driven simulations and reinterpretations of the historical past through narrative representations; they were Williams's forum for reading, interpreting, and disseminating his place in modern American letters. As my readings of the reviews of Williams's books that appeared in *Time* magazine after 1938 will show, Williams's fictional versions of who he was as an American boundary figure became absorbed by ordinary readers to the point that the image of the author challenged in importance (and in a sense became) the commodified literary thing itself.

According to John Guillory, T. S. Eliot was able to lead southern New Critics such as Cleanth Brooks to do the work of domesticating and containing his poetry. Thus, Eliot's work became accessible to a popular audience through its interpretation by the gatekeepers of the newly established canon of modern letters in the English departments of American universities.[10] Situating himself as a maverick on the edge of literary power in New York, London, and Paris, Williams lacked such a close relationship to influential members of an official cultural apparatus. He had been, in his own view, "cast out" of the seat of authority of High Modernism during his visit to Paris in 1924. He therefore needed to develop a personal iconography as an American poet that could distinguish his contribution to modern letters from that of other poets whose reputations were far more secure than his own as the High Modernist phase drew to a close just prior to World War II. Williams shaped his image as a poet in the popular imagination through his narratives and, in this sense, reimagined his contributions to American letters and modern literature through the fiction.

---

witnessing a group of fraternity boys singing a popular song that parodied (but also enforced) the alleged healing powers of Lydia Pinkham's vegetable tonic.

9. "Postmodernism, or the Cultural Logic of Late Capitalism."

10. See "The Ideology of Canon-Formation: T. S. Eliot and Cleanth Brooks."

In his own domesticating and sense-making narrative constructions, Williams hoped to benefit from his first sustained publication contract with James Laughlin's fledgling New Directions Press. The Williams-Laughlin relationship began in 1937 with the publication of the first of the Stecher Trilogy of novels, *White Mule*. The other fictions he published with New Directions—such as *Life along the Passaic River* (1938), which contained many of the "Doctor Stories" collected under that title by Williams's student Robert Coles; *In the Money;* and the narrative sections of *Paterson*—aligned Williams's own story as a literary renegade with the plight of ordinary citizens who perceived themselves to be outside the privileged systems of public acknowledgment, whether these systems were economic, medical, or literary.

My affiliation with Dettmar's third generation of postmodern critics of modernism centers upon my interest in what Dettmar calls "a consideration of the vexed, complex, perplexing relationship of Modernist writing to popular culture."[11] Critics such as Dettmar, Lawrence S. Rainey, and Jennifer Wicke, as well as Lawrence Levine and Andreas Huyssen, have tried to reread and reassess modernism from a perspective that is sensitive to the intense cultural tensions and ideological shifts that informed and helped to shape both the modernist canon as we have come to know it and the design and content of the modernist texts themselves.[12] These critics have begun to understand or at least to investigate how many modernist writers constructed their relationship to the emerging mass culture. This investigation seems especially prescient in terms of the contemporary cultural and political situation. As we live in a period of resistance to aesthetic enactments by totalizing structures that in high modernity tended to naturalize references to what were essentially oppressive systems of power and control, a dialogic critical imagination should be fostered in order to create an enhanced tolerance for difference. At the same time, we should remain sensitive to aspects of divergent cultural practices that can converge to produce a social text. To attempt to articulate the modern through the popular is a particularly intriguing critical intervention to make. I say this because the first generation of modernist critics and

11. *Rereading the New,* 16.
12. Wicke, *Advertising Fictions: Literature, Advertisement and Social Reading;* Huyssen, *After the Great Divide: Modernism, Mass Culture, Postmodernism;* Levine, *Highbrow/Lowbrow;* Rainey, "The Price of Modernism: Reconsidering the Publication of *The Waste Land."*

many of the canonical modernist writers (some of whom were themselves among the first generation of modernist critics, as was the case with Henry James, Pound, Eliot, and Wallace Stevens) were often in possession of the loudest voices in opposition to mass culture. They were among those who chose to see the modern as a reaction against the popular.

Recent critics such as Ellen E. Berry, however, have attempted to show a convergence between ordinary (mass) and extraordinary (avant-garde and modernist) cultural practices. In her work on Gertrude Stein, Berry has shown that modern writers besides Williams refused to sort out cultural products hierarchically and into categories of modern art as a privileged site of creativity, imagination, and subjectivity, versus what members of the Frankfurt School called the "culture industry," which produced repetitive copies of everyday life. Berry demonstrated how mass media forms and new technologies contributed to the speed and nonlinearity of Stein's "camera style." As was the case with Ernest Hemingway and Williams (as Cecelia Tichi and Lisa Steinman have pointed out), according to Berry the speed of the car and the transmission of information through the radio and cinema influenced the "rapid transit moment," the sudden shifts, in Stein's formally mimetic style.[13] While a study such as Berry's captures the Jamesonian (schizoid) postmodern sensibility of an author such as Stein who did away with the conventional notions of character, story, events, and linear narrative in her most recognizable works, Berry has less interest in thinking about how modern writers attempted to appeal to a wider audience by "making" themselves into reproducible symbols of public trust.

Williams could be perceived as a conservative or atavistic figure (in comparison, say, to Gertrude Stein) if one were to consider only the form he employed to recuperate in midcareer his personal image. He turned to conventional forms of nineteenth-century narrative to portray characters, stories, and events in his fiction and in the prose sections of *Paterson*. It is, however, also important to stress that Williams's retention of a connection to existing narrative and poetical conventions and to generic expectations was, throughout the middle period of his career, subverted, or rotated, in order to present his affiliation to dispossessed social groups, especially

13. Berry, "Modernism/Mass Culture/Postmodernism: The Case of Gertrude Stein"; Steinman, *Made in America: Science, Technology, and American Modernist Poets;* Tichi, *Shifting Gears: Technology, Literature, Culture in Modernist America.*

those of his region. Edward Said's notion of "nativism" or a "new territoriality" in his essay "Yeats and Decolonization" will help to explain further my sense of Williams's relationship to his "region of affiliation."

Williams's desire in *Paterson* is to recover the geological ground of Paterson, New Jersey, as meaningful in terms of the story of Paterson's (the giant-poet's) search for his relationship to its meaning. Williams's quest for recognition of a place previously unacknowledged as significant in literary modernism would be construed by Said as the first step in defining a decolonized identity for an oppressed social group, in Williams's case the immigrant poor of urban New Jersey. Said writes:

> With the new territoriality there comes a whole set of further assertions, recoveries, and identifications; all of them quite literally grounded on this poetically projected base. The search for authenticity, for a more congenial national origin than that provided by colonial history, for a new pantheon of heroes, myths, and religions, these too are enabled by the land. And along with these nationalistic adumbrations of the decolonized identity, there always goes an almost magically inspired, quasi-alchemical redevelopment of the native language.[14]

Paradoxically, in the case of the archetypal American poet here under consideration, the relationship to "Eurocentric" culture as a universalist conception resembles the relationship to imperial power found in the liberational work of contemporary resistance writers in Third World countries. As Said points out, the first stage in a resistance to imperialism involves what he calls a "nativistic" agenda for writing. Although the concept of "nativism" (or an interest in representing the speech, customs, and history of an ethnic group that is being overwhelmed by a more politically powerful "outsider") risks becoming a source of oppression and exclusivity as it becomes "nationalistic," the nativist impulse for writing occurs as a liberationalist response toward another culture's nationalism; nativist writing is an attempt to overcome the source of oppression.

Williams emphasizes in *Paterson* the history of the local place, identifying with this place through the mythologization of the self in prosopopoeiac form. Paterson's history was inscribed in local media such as the *Rutherford Advertiser*, Charles Pitman Longwell's *A Little Story of Old*

---

14. "Yeats and Decolonization," 79.

Paterson and *Historic Totowa Falls.*[15] It was also transmitted through an oral tradition of mythologies about Paterson and the immigrant poor who migrated there at the turn of the twentieth century. Williams's historical localism can be viewed as a form of resistance against a European culture that, while not physically in control of the northeastern seaboard of the United States, still controlled the means of evaluating the worth of life there. Writing about this consciousness of place among contemporary African, Caribbean, Irish, Latin American, and Asian poets, Said describes the emphasis in their works on the recovery of the land as developing "out of a desire to distance the native" from the master:

> Before this [distancing] can be done, however, there is a pressing need for the recovery of the land that, because of the presence of the colonizing outsider, is recoverable at first only through the imagination. Now if there is anything that radically distinguishes the imagination of anti-imperialism it is the primacy of the geographical in it. Imperialism after all is an act of geographical violence through which virtually every space in the world is explored, charted, and finally brought under control. For the native, the history of his or her colonial servitude is inaugurated by the loss to an outsider of the local place, whose concrete geographical identity must thereafter be searched for and somehow restored.[16]

In *Paterson,* Williams identifies the prestige of his "manifestation, on the level of the referent, of a linguistic structure"—to use the words of Paul de Man—with the symbolic value of the inhabitants of Paterson, New Jersey, primarily those whose lives are damaged by poverty and a lack of recognition by those in political power, and who are not represented in prestigious forms such as the poem that is epic in scope.[17] Williams's strategy in the short poems as well as in the story of Dev Evans's quest in *A Voyage to Pagany* was to access literary power by inverting the accepted signs of empowerment toward a disqualified account of the world. This strategy of inversion had been employed before him by nineteenth-century American women writing "sensational" novels, as described by Jane Tompkins.[18] In Williams's case, structures of established authority

15. Mike Weaver, *William Carlos Williams: The American Background,* 203.
16. "Yeats and Decolonization," 77.
17. Paul de Man, "Autobiography as De-facement," 71.
18. "The Other American Renaissance," 34–58.

are to be found in the mythopoetic imagination of T. S. Eliot and James Joyce as this imagination informs Williams's novel *A Voyage to Pagany,* in the "insider" knowledge of the corporate manager in *In the Money,* in the knowledge of medical technology the "Doc" learned in Switzerland and at the University of Pennsylvania in the "Doctor Stories," and in the speaker's ambitions to majority in *Paterson.* Like other "syncretist" authors, Williams accessed systems of representation with the intention of recognizing the stature of those American citizens who James Agee said belonged to "a portion of unimagined existence."[19]

A populist and anti-fascist liberal, if not a political revolutionary, Williams expressed his moral imagination in the interplay between free and traditionally ordered sorts of discourse. This formal interplay suggests his own interstitial relationship to institutions and to organized sources of power and authority, whether these be the medical establishment, the church, the university, the world of consumer capitalism, the modernist literary establishment, or the traditionally ordered line of the English poem. Williams's position in American culture as an interstitial or threshold figure, or as one who shuttled between more than one interpretive community, positions him as an ideal figure to study if one's area of interest is the relationship between ordinary and elite culture, between poetry and prose genres, and between a conception of modernism as autotelic and as a more inclusive literary practice that was a part of a larger social text. These broader cultural concerns are inscribed in the formal properties of Williams's signature poetry, in his prosody in particular, and in the formal narrative structure of *A Voyage to Pagany,* which combines the syntax of the relatively unmediated and virtually immediate diary entry with the synchronic form of a "rite of passage" tale.

I locate Williams in a tradition of literary radicalism through his inversion of narrative forms for purposes that work against an affirmation of the political status quo. Williams's narrative representation of his own first accomplishments and identity as a modern American poet should not be interpreted as a straightforward and unproblematic project in terms of literary radicalism, however. How are we to evaluate the later prose works of an author whose earlier books of poetry themselves illustrated a radical breakup of linear discourse (think of the modern pastiche of *Kora in Hell* [1920] and *Spring and All* [1923]) and a deconstruction of the lyric "I,"

---

19. *Let Us Now Praise Famous Men,* xiv.

which has been attacked (most recently by members of the Language poetry movement) for being an assertion of "bourgeois naturalism" implicated in the preempting of the voice of the other?[20] We now associate works such as *Kora in Hell* and *Spring and All* with a High Modern poetic discourse that attempted to separate experimental literature from more popular forms. These early works were designed by Williams to decenter a repetitious and, at least according to such European modernist critics as Theodor Adorno and Walter Benjamin and to such modernist critics in New York as Dwight Macdonald and Clement Greenberg, *inauthentic* mass culture formed through technological reproduction. Williams's fiction after 1928, from this point of view, was a conservative rendering of his earlier poetry; it reduced his poetry to an easily consumed commodity and attempted to reestablish the continuity of the authorial subject. Like all criticism, his fictions of the self were in competition with the wildness of his own first literary efforts, a domestication and reduction of his "pure products of America."

Williams's project in the fiction he published with New Directions, like the critical project of the New Critics, or the notes that Eliot included at the end of *The Waste Land,* or the outline to the mythical design of *Ulysses* that Joyce leaked to Stuart Gilbert, was to control and to reorder the initially subversive or stylistically difficult first poetry—in his case, by associating it with the author's struggle to attain his majority against, in Williams's own term, a "gang" of literary insiders who he felt wished to sabotage his accomplishments as a literary renegade. This story of a writer who broke away from what he saw as the hegemonic establishment of literary modernism ruled by Eliot and Pound was, paradoxically, told through old-fashioned (nineteenth-century, linear, coherent) narratives that were postmodern only in the sense that they were second-order simulations of an unrecoverable real moment. By focusing on a charismatic figure of public trust whose image was designed to be associated with a literary product of another kind, the New Directions prose was structured in ways involved in the consumption, rather than the production, of a product of limited use but of wide symbolic import. Can Williams, in turning his attention away from poetry to more popular generic forms and to the placing of his image in popular American periodicals such as *Time* and *Life,*

20. My understanding of the politics of the resistance to the lyric "I" in experimental American poetry is indebted to an unpublished essay by Joseph Lease.

be accused of reifying his own personal identity in order to make his work a popular commercial production? And if this is the case, to what degree should we praise Williams for breaking down what Andreas Huyssen refers to as "the great divide" between "mass" and "high" culture in order to make way for a decentered, pluralistic environment? Should we question the meaning of this transformation from a focus on the poetic "thing itself" to a concern with the work of making a public self? As my *Paterson* chapter shows, these are the questions that Williams asked of himself as he developed autobiographical fictions that were really a demonstration of a process of becoming with no final or fixed point of finish.

I treat my subject in five main chapters devoted to Williams's works as well as in an afterword that discusses a story by James Laughlin entitled "A Visit" (1978). My first chapter shows Williams as a reader of images of the novelist Ernest Hemingway and of the painter Charles Sheeler, as the iconography for each of these American cultural workers appeared in *Life* magazine in 1938 and 1941. In my fourth chapter on *In the Money*, I suggest Williams's motivation for promoting his work through a rhetoric of persuasion that is sublimated within his fictions. We might intuitively align the graphic presentation of the imagistic poem with the designs of contemporary advertising. The appearance of the word *soda* surrounded by asterisks in "The Attic Which Is Desire," for example, absorbs into the poem a commercial marker. During Williams's New Directions phase, however, the poem became the material artifact that was given its "symbolic" or "sign" value—its cultural weight as well as its economic value in a consumer context—in stories. Thus, one set of cultural constructions— the late prose—in effect introduces and encodes another set of cultural constructions—the earlier poetry. In order to read Williams's fiction as notarizing artifacts, I have examined his publication history, paying specific attention to his professional relationship with the only publisher dedicated to a sustained issuance of his work—James Laughlin, the founder of New Directions Press. My claim is that Williams's needs for the New Directions series differed from Laughlin's and that this conflict influenced the matter and form of the prose Williams wrote for New Directions until 1950.

I will examine two types of promotional fictions from the New Directions phase. In my third chapter, I read "Old Doc Rivers," "The Girl with a Pimply Face," and "A Night in June"—all so-called Doctor Stories that were collected in 1932 and 1938. I show Williams attaching an eclectic therapeutic function to his poetry by combining aspects of contradictory codes of American medical healing. These codes, which were the subject of a debate between "kitchen style" and "university professional" doctors in the nineteenth century, become sources of a productive alignment for Williams, as word man and as medicine man, to systems of value found inside and outside his region of identification. *In the Money*, the subject of my fourth chapter, presents the Williams personage in the mask of government printer and money manager. In the novel, Williams explores the relationship between intellectual work as the production of the tools for exchanging and mediating the symbolic commodities of the mind and the work performed by those who deal with a substance of mediation in the sphere of finance, the money order. Joe Stecher, the renegade printer of *In the Money*, leaves the corrupt firm of Wynnewood and Crossman in order to form his own firm. I align Stecher's rebellion to Williams's professional break in the 1930s away from an identification with the international avant-garde led by Eliot and Pound, a break made manifest when he began to publish with New Directions. As was the case for Williams as poet, Stecher concentrates upon the streamlined production of a public form of value and exchange in a way that suggests that Williams deserved a form of Social Credit through Laughlin's faith in him as a careful author.

The issues of literary authority and literary origins, or how we trust an author's account of the world as bearing truth, are related to the economy of literary dissemination. My chapter on Williams's first conventional novel, *A Voyage to Pagany*, addresses the problem of access to a version of poetic authority associated with another class of poetic speakers. His syncretic and interstitial relationship to this European version of literary authority might appear to counteract our notion of Williams as the poet who "stayed at home" or Robert Lowell's assessment of him as the modern poet who "loved America, excessively." The heroic quest of his surrogate, Dev Evans, enhances rather than contradicts Williams's American theory of poetic legitimacy based on the Emersonian values of immediacy and unmediated perception through references to traditional institutions of the management of human affairs and a narrative structure associated with an archetypal quest romance. In Evans's story, Williams displays his wish to contact European sources of power, much as he wanted to "embrace the foulness" of the lower-class life of the immigrant poor whom he served as poet and physician in Paterson and Rutherford, New Jersey.

In the fifth chapter, I turn my observations about the making of Williams's self in language back to his poetry, his main form of literary identification. I examine *Paterson* in light of the way I have read his fiction as a means toward public dissemination of his work to an audience different from the small group of readers who had earlier gained access to his poetry through privately printed editions. *Paterson* was Williams's most significant effort in poetry after his conversion to didactic fiction. The kind of "hidden critique" of other poets that I have been able to detect in the fiction is a constituent feature of Williams's long poem as well. *Paterson* may be understood as Williams's attempt to mediate within the poem his competing moral claims. He displays the modernist aesthetic antithetical to market concerns while offering, covertly, a desire to make his signature known through the language of publicity, which was, after all, the rhetorical contribution of his region of affiliation. Besides serving as an address to his intended audience about how to evaluate the poem, *Paterson* is also a commentary on the problematic outcome of the desire to make coincidental the completion of the personal story (a project made preliminary in the prose fictions) and the completion of the poem. Chapter 5 ends with a reading of *Paterson* book 5. Past seventy and suffering from strokes and depression, Williams lets go of his identification with Paterson as culture hero. He accepts instead the restricted role of a teacher who can enable the literary production of a younger generation of poets such as Allen Ginsberg. Book 5 also describes the poet's experience of the pleasure of reality found outside representation, an embrace of the real that was blocked, paradoxically, by his massive struggle for acceptance from his local community through his appearance in story and in *Paterson* itself.

Instead of focusing on Williams's gorgeous later lyrics, I close by paying attention to how the same economic and cultural tensions that produced Williams's fictions also produced a late textual intervention and moving testimony of friendship and love in Laughlin's "A Visit." For just as the commercial possibilities produced in Williams a distancing of himself from himself as he created a series of fictional masks that were intended to objectify and to stand in for the natural man in order to gain notoriety for his poetry, "A Visit" reveals that the publisher had to his regret also dismissed the significance of Williams's life as an ordinary citizen. Laughlin admits in the story that his professional ambitions as a young man going into business for the first time blinded him to Williams's struggles as a professional author. In the late lyrics Williams had returned to a commitment to an individual love relationship with Flossie—the journey to love—that had little to do with his grandiose ambitions toward becoming the totalizing monster of *Paterson.* "A Visit" shows that the publisher, too, at the end of Williams's life came to see how the costs of publicity for the authorial self weighed against his own ability to honor the humanity of the man, Williams, whom he admits he had viewed primarily as literary merchandise during the early years of their stormy professional alliance. In the story, Laughlin comes to terms with what his surrogate, Marshall MacDonald, calls the two "halves" of the poet's identity, the impersonal and larger-than-life persona constructed by the author in and through his literary designs and the natural man whose trace I claim appears in book 5 of *Paterson.* Facing the poet's dying body, MacDonald turns his attention away from the imagination of the literary giant. Instead of this fiction, he privileges the natural life of the maker, whose identity, formed in fictions, has now been separated out and allowed to come through in moving ways in a dialogue with those in the world closest to him, as was the case with Williams and his great companion, Flossie, as well as Laughlin himself.

One

"Geeze, Doc, What Does It Mean?"

Reading Williams Reading *Life*

Although William Carlos Williams did receive in the last decade of his life the professional accolades and the public renown he had sought for many decades, he was not satisfied with the way his main publisher after 1937, James Laughlin, publicized his writing for New Directions upon initial publication. In reading the correspondence between Williams and Laughlin, one is struck by the degree to which Williams, who once claimed he set his writing against "the calculated viciousness of a money-grubbing society," pushed Laughlin to publicize his work through techniques associated with the commercial culture he claimed to oppose.[1] In this chapter I will contextualize my chronological treatment of Williams's promotional fictions (*A Voyage to Pagany,* the "Doctor Stories," and *In the Money*) by examining letters from Williams to Laughlin that describe the poet's relationship to publicity. Williams's interest in the promotional displays on behalf of Charles Sheeler and Ernest Hemingway that appeared in *Life* in 1938 and 1941 will provide a context for my first interrogation of the paradox he faced as a modernist who wished to introduce through fiction his stylistically innovative writing to an audience of ordinary readers unaccustomed to the techniques of modernism. A central argument

---

1. Hugh Witemeyer, ed., *William Carlos Williams and James Laughlin: Selected Letters;* hereafter cited in the text as *SL.* Also see William Carlos Williams, *The Autobiography,* 158; hereafter cited in the text as *A.*

throughout this book will be that the tension between wanting to write the difficult modern poem and a contradictory desire to honor his democratic impulse through being understood and embraced by a wide audience of ordinary readers informed the generic choices Williams made as he began to publish with New Directions in 1937. The democratic impulse that informed his concern with creating a socially intelligible personal image attractive to the citizens of Rutherford also stimulated him to write fiction that identified him as an urban American poet who shared the status of cultural outsider with the poor people of his city.

Williams's intermediate relationship to elite and popular cultures is inscribed in his publication history. Here, after all, was a poet who wanted to resuscitate his career by appearing in a promotional photographic display in a mass-circulation pictorial weekly while, at the same time, he was publishing his writing with New Directions, a house whose founder, James Laughlin, was unabashedly opposed to a blurring of the distinction between the profane literature of "pulp" and the sacred literature of "contemplation." In his letters to Laughlin, Williams, in effect, attempts to break down the difference between two cultures—one of art and one of commerce. These two cultures were understood by critics in the 1940s to require opposite strategies for bringing renown to the literary work. Although *Life,* the magazine spearheaded by the conservative pub-lisher Henry R. Luce, did promote the careers of Sheeler and Hemingway through pictorial displays, Luce and his editors did so by altering the polit-ical content and aesthetic values of each artist's work. Sheeler's paintings and Hemingway's prose were interpreted and reinscribed by *Life*'s editors as a celebration, rather than a critique, of American business interests and the attendant consumer culture. Williams responded to *Life*'s interest in Sheeler and Hemingway with a mixture of delight and chagrin, perhaps because of the compromise he had had to make with his own sensibility as a modernist author. In any case, Williams, as involved as he was with finding ways to promote the neglected figures in modernism with whom he identified himself, ignored in his commentary to Laughlin the ways in which *Life* assimilated Hemingway's most politically radical novel (*For Whom the Bell Tolls*) and Sheeler's aestheticization of American industrial culture into celebrations of American business interests.

Williams's situation within the literary culture of the late 1930s in-fluenced how he managed his public image in the period leading to *Paterson.* Books that are considered today to be landmarks of high modern pastiche—*Al Que Quiere* (1917), *Kora in Hell* (1920), and *Sour Grapes* (1921)—were all printed at Williams's own expense. In his *Autobiography* Williams recalls that he "never received a penny, on sales" (*A, 159*). *Spring and All,* originally printed in 1923 in an edition of three hundred copies, was, according to Robert von Hallberg, "virtually unseen in the United States because most of the copies were lost on the dock of New York; any book coming from Europe around World War One considered suspect." In *I Wanted to Write a Poem,* Williams recalls that *Spring and All* had "no circulation at all," and, as Linda Wagner has noted, during the late 1930s Williams reached a "plateau of inactivity" that she claims lasted until 1943.[2] By 1934, the date of *Collected Poems, 1921-1931,* Williams could expect almost no audience for his poetry. Not receiving "a penny for sales" now seemed to him like a fatal judgment on the quality of his work, rather than the badge of genuine dedication to vanguard experimentation that it might have seemed in the 1910s and 1920s. In *I Wanted to Write a Poem,* he described the offer by Objectivist Press to produce *Collected Poems* as friendly, but useless: "a lovely gesture from my own gang." He continued, "Needless to say, it didn't sell at all."[3] I call the period from 1937 to 1950, when Laughlin agreed to publish anything new Williams wrote, as well as anything old he wished to collect or reprint, the "New Directions Phase." Williams believed that New Directions could provide the commercial exposure to reverse his standing as a neglected poet, especially considering the privileged background of his new publisher, James Laughlin IV.

James Laughlin, who was born in Pittsburgh on October 30, 1914, was the son of Henry and Marjory (Rea) Laughlin. Henry Laughlin was an executive for and heir to the Jones and Laughlin Steel Company, which was founded in 1846 by Benjamin Franklin Jones (1824-1903). The company became known as Jones and Laughlin Steel in 1857 when the publisher's grandfather, James Laughlin (born in Belfast, Ireland, in 1806; died in Pittsburgh, December 18, 1862), became a partner in the firm with which he had been associated since 1854. The firm converted from a partnership to a corporation in 1902, when it was the second largest steel producer

2. von Hallberg, *American Poetry and Culture, 1945-1980,* 12-13; Williams, *I Wanted to Write a Poem: The Autobiography of the Works of a Poet,* 36; Wagner, *The Poems of William Carlos Williams: A Critical Study,* 15.

3. *I Wanted,* 52.

in Pittsburgh, with a capital stock of $20 million. Although the firm was, according to Gertrude G. Schroeder, the "least inclined of all the major companies to get involved in merger maneuvers," Jones and Laughlin was nonetheless, by any measure, among the longest lived and most successful of the Pittsburgh steel companies.[4] As of 1950 Jones and Laughlin ranked fourth among the Pittsburgh companies in production of steel tonnage, and by 1982 its plants were the only steel mills remaining in Pittsburgh. The story of Laughlin's ancestors does not illustrate the mythic rags-to-riches background embodied by the atypical story of Andrew Carnegie. Like most of the leading Scotch and Irish steel magnates of Pittsburgh, Laughlin's parents came from wealth, and they wished to further assert the professional status their families had established in the United States before the Civil War.

In spite of the financial status of his ancestors, Laughlin's cultural identification was as the grandson of an immigrant who stood outside the centers of institutional legitimacy, such as the university. In a study of the cultural background of the Scotch-Irish steel giants, John Ingham writes, "[W]hat happened in Pittsburgh in the late nineteenth century was less the rise of a group of individuals from poverty origins to wealth, than it was the rise of men and families—already wealthy and part of the upper-class social system in that city,—to positions of relative parity with seacoast elites in cities such as Philadelphia." Families such as that of Laughlin's father had by the turn of the century already begun to achieve mainstream respectability. Their desire was, according to Ingham, to win "acceptance at [society's] uppermost levels."[5] The task that Laughlin's parents set for him was to make further gains for the family in terms of establishing a cultural legitimacy to match its great fortune. Laughlin studied literature with Dudley Fitts at Choate and attended Harvard, beginning in 1933. Disappointed at the English faculty's reluctance to study modern writers (such as Pound and Eliot) whose work Laughlin had been introduced to at Choate by Fitts, he wrote a letter to Pound in August 1933: "Could you and would you care to see me in Rapallo? . . . I am an American, now at Harvard, said to be clever, and the whiteheaded boy of Fitts, [Sherry] Mangan, etc." Pound said yes, and Laughlin, taking a leave from Harvard, traveled to Paris and Italy. In 1935, Pound told Laughlin to "do something

---

4. *The Growth of Major Steel Companies, 1900–1950*, 54–55, 134.
5. *The Iron Barons: A Social Analysis of an American Urban Elite, 1874–1965*, 6, 7.

useful" by publishing neglected writers of experimental poetry in the United States. With the financial support of his family, which he describes as stemming from "the generosity of my father," Laughlin was able to begin New Directions, a name suggested by Gorham Munson, the Social Credit advocate whose theories about economics were influential to Laughlin.[6]

Williams in 1937 had entered into a steady publishing contract with this heir to the Laughlin and Jones Steel fortune. Williams hoped New Directions, named by a Social Credit theorist, could prove to be *his* chance to receive social credit for the neglected but expert work he had already done in the field of experimental modern letters in the United States. In a letter written in August 1940, Williams told Laughlin that he wished to try his hand at writing a potentially lucrative gangster story with a New Orleans writer whom he had heard about from Fred Miller: "I'd like to get my hands into such a book," Williams wrote. "I bet that collaborating with [Fred Miller's friend] I could make that stand up like nobody's business" (*SL*, 53). Williams's desire to gain from his placement in the New Directions catalog a significant "taste of fortune" (which was the original title he had in mind for his "gangster" novel of 1940, *In the Money*) was perhaps fanciful. His desire to turn Laughlin's commitment to him into a forum for contesting and then reshaping public opinion about his identity as a poet, however, was more a realistic expectation for the outcome of his narrative project. First, though, Williams had to solve a problem that stemmed from his paradoxical situation as a key author at New Directions: how to gain this "taste of fortune" while maintaining his image as one of Laughlin's literary saints, one of those, in Laughlin's words from the preface to the *New Directions in Prose and Poetry* annual for 1936, who set his work against commercial literature in order to foster a "new," presumably less acquisitive, "social order":

> It is hard to conceive of a new social order except by revision of verbal orien-
> tation. And it is the writer alone who can accomplish that reorientation. But it
> will not be the slick paper writers who cater to inferiority complexes, or the
> editor who will print nothing "unfamiliar to his reader" or the commercial

6. James Laughlin quoted by Rockwell Gray, "Relentlessly Clever: Ezra Pound's Correspondence with Publisher James Laughlin," *Chicago Tribune,* Sunday, August 14, 1994, section 14, 5; in an interview with Susan Howe and Charles Ruas, however, Laughlin claims that his parents stopped sending him money because they were upset he had not returned to Harvard from Italy. See Howe and Ruas, eds., *The Art of Literary Publishing: Editors on Their Craft.*

> publishers' hair-oil boys. It will be men like Cummings or Carlos Williams who know their business well enough to realize the pass to which language has come and are willing to endure obscurity and poverty to carry on their experiments.

By contrast, here is Williams in a letter to his publisher about the publication of his *Complete Collected Poems (1906-1938)*: "So, in the end, make your arrangements for distribution as complete as possible, especially make more detailed arrangements for advertising my stuff than you did with *White Mule*. I think inadequate management of sales cost us plenty that time" (*SL,* 28). The paradox at the core of the relationship between Williams and Laughlin informs both Williams's interest in the promotional displays in *Life* and his attention to telling stories about the author in his own New Directions writings, most notably in the "Doctor Stories," the *Autobiography,* the Stecher Trilogy of novels, and *Paterson*. Williams wanted to enter his work into a marketplace other than the prestigious but decidedly *unpopular* little magazines. Laughlin, the son of a manufacturer, had spent his twenties in pursuit of a more rarefied culture than he could have found near the blast furnaces of Pittsburgh. The task that Laughlin's parents set for him, by placing him at Choate and at Harvard, was to gain a cultural legitimacy that existed above market interests. Thus, Laughlin, who in his early twenties had an idealistic relationship to vanguard writing, wanted to publish modern literature for reasons of spiritual or cultural identification, not commercial gain. Laughlin understood (or misunderstood, as I believe) Williams to be a member of a unified community pursuing a spiritual activity outside the demands of the marketplace, as this comment from Laughlin to Williams dated March 6, 1943, suggests: "The hell with reputations, making money, poets' jealousies, ambitions, wars, struggles of all kinds, and mostly anything that impinges on the effect in life of a good art form" (*SL,* 89). Laughlin's comment does not take into account the contest for renown that led Williams in the 1930s and 1940s to look toward *Life* for cues about how to appear before a readership other than as one of Laughlin's "literary saints."

The Charles Sheeler display that caught Williams's eye appeared in the August 8, 1938, issue of *Life*. It was prompted by the publication of Constance Rourke's book-length study, *Charles Sheeler, Artist in the American*

Tradition. Rourke's book was part of her contribution to the development of a criticism specifically about what she called the "special native fiber" of American arts and letters. Her work, which included studies of John James Audubon and of American folk humor, is an important gauge of the climate into which Williams inserted his poetry through didactic fiction. Williams knew that Rourke's project was the recovery of an American aesthetic tradition opposed to a culture based in Europe. She rejected the notion, proposed by John Fiske, of a "transit of civilization" in which American artists were simply "carriers" of pieces of European culture, and so always lagged behind the old world masters. "The seeds of influence may fall," Rourke wrote in an essay called "The Roots of American Culture," "but they may not germinate. Works belonging to other cultures may stir the imagination but not the creative imagination." As Van Wyck Brooks put it in his introduction to Rourke's posthumously collected essays: "[She] explored our possession of native characteristics of folk culture, architecture, early American theater, music, old Shaker colonies, Negro folklore." Rourke did not advocate a revival of colonial American folk culture in the twentieth century. Instead, she admired Sheeler for his modernist recognition of the severe geometric, almost cubist, beauty of Shaker homes, barns, and hay silos in Bucks County, Pennsylvania. Although Sheeler did borrow ideas from architectural styles found among the homes of English Protestants as well as from developments in European modernism such as cubism, Rourke was interested in him because he had concentrated his attention on the American landscape. In her work, she asked whether or not it was true that "we [Americans] had failed to produce a culture in which the arts could flourish." In her discovery of "the arts as common utility" in the diffuse cultures of New England, Pennsylvania, and the American West, Rourke claimed that this "uncentralized" cultural pattern was itself "a pronounced cultural trait." Judging from his desire to provide Rourke with access to his short fiction, it appears that Williams wished to be Rourke's example of a modern writer from whose work could "be derived fresh beginnings, from half-formed yet vigorous new directions."[7]

Considering Williams's position as a professional author in 1938—his first self-proclaimed "winner" (*White Mule*) was published the year before

7. Constance Rourke, *Roots of American Culture, and Other Essays*, 49, ix, vi, 53, 51.

by New Directions, and his second collection of short fiction, *Life along the Passaic River,* had just reached the bookstores—we can understand why he expected free publicity in *Life* for his own career. His career appeared to be on the upswing, as Paul Mariani notes: "That was a golden moment for Williams, an interlude he would remember for the rest of his life, a time when he could plan the *Collected Poems,* plan his novel, plan for years of writing with his newly found publisher."[8] We can also understand why Williams projected his own desire for recognition onto his old friend Charles Sheeler, whom Williams had first met in 1923, and with whom he would remain friends throughout their maturity. Both Sheeler and Williams were born in 1883. Furthermore, the physical resemblance between the two men was uncanny. The half-page photo of Sheeler that appeared in the *Life* display looks very much like the photograph Sheeler took of Williams that eventually appeared on the softcover editions of the poet's autobiography, as well as beside reviews of Williams's work in the pages of *Time* after 1938.

In the picture of Sheeler in *Life,* the American artist is depicted as an ordinary (read: masculine) citizen with his gaze focused directly into the eye of the camera in a way that contradicts the romantic iconography of the artist looking away for inspiration into a transcendent and decidedly antisocial space (such as might be found on a cliff by the sea). Sheeler in *Life* and Williams in the Sheeler photograph are figured as good gray professional men, not bohemian outcasts. Although both Sheeler and Williams through their association with *Time* and *Life* were involved in counteracting what T. J. Jackson Lears has called "the central modernist project: the attempt to disengage the autonomous work of high art from the corrupting embrace of mass culture" in order to claim essential authenticity for their work, their images as masculine producers enforce the modernist discourse of authenticity that Lears says "was without question rooted in masculine anxieties about the emasculating effects of mass culture." Descended from an Anglo-American Protestant tradition that according to Lears located "public virtue in plain speech and plain living" and that celebrated "the leather-aproned 'producer' as the ultimate embodiment of republican reality," Sheeler is cast as an authentic male producer and not as the "effeminate parasite" associated with the deceitful

8. *A New World Naked,* 434.

face of commercialism.[9] He is thin-lipped and wears horn-rimmed glasses and a jacket and tie; his neatly trimmed hair is gray and thinning. Such an image of the professional cultural worker was precisely the way Williams hoped he had come across to fellow townspeople, as he suggested to Walter Sutton in a 1961 interview: "The reception of poetry by the general public is very much better than it used to be. It used to be that when I attempted to read poetry they could not understand what I was talking about in the first place. And any man who dealt with poetry must be effeminate. And therefore he must compensate. But that's entirely in the past. I'm accepted by the ordinary people I know, my friends, in my town. They have come to accept me."[10] *Life* claims that "at 55 Sheeler looks more like a college professor than artist," and this image of the artist as a steady and wise community elder, and not a decadent outcast surviving on the fringe of mainstream society, could certainly be said to be shared by Williams.

The two men had also developed similar programs for American arts and letters. Each attempted to find "beauty in the commonplace" through a concentration on precise formal displays that suggested the "strength" and "reality" of the urban industrial landscape, as the *Life* headline ("Sheeler Finds Beauty in the Commonplace") correctly suggests. In his introductory note to the 1939 Museum of Modern Art catalog *Charles Sheeler: Paintings, Drawings, Photographs,* however, Williams also identifies the subversive, anticorporate nature of Sheeler's paintings. In this introduction, Williams applauds Sheeler's modernist project of removing the images of the everyday landscape from their context of "conglomerate normality."[11] The new context provided by Sheeler, according to Williams, allows aesthetic criteria to replace economic criteria when judging the value of an object. Williams's understanding of Sheeler's task of defamiliarization in the Museum of Modern Art catalog essay therefore contradicts the way *Life* understands Sheeler's work as an unequivocal celebration of large-scale industrial capitalism and its leading figures.

In a letter to Laughlin, Williams described his spirited reaction to the Sheeler display:

9. "Sherwood Anderson: Looking for the White Spot," 14, 15.

10. Linda Wagner, ed., *Interviews with William Carlos Williams: "Speaking Straight Ahead,"* 50.

11. Introduction to *Charles Sheeler: Paintings, Drawings, Photographs,* 8.

Inside news, keep it under your hat as confidence! Constance Rourke, one
of the best, has done a noteworthy book on Charles Sheeler, the painter and
one of my best friends. It's a pip, text and illustrations combined. Flash! On
August 18 [*sic*], *Life* is running six pages of illustration in color advertising
the book. Fer Gawd's sake now don't spill that to anybody. The book appears
August 11, Harcourt, Brace & Co. It's right down our alley. (*SL*, 32–33)

Williams's response to the publicity display is strongly approving in tone
("It's right down our alley"). He is pleased with the montage style of
Rourke's book ("text and illustrations combined") and not at all critical of
how his friend's image and art have been so obviously appropriated in *Life*
to suit the conservative business and political interests of Henry Luce, who
promoted the presidential candidacies of Wendell Willkie and Thomas
Dewey in *Life*'s pages and who by no means unequivocally supported
Franklin Roosevelt's New Deal.[12]

The *Life* display interprets Sheeler's project to be a celebration of the
careers and economic structures developed by such American monopo-
lists as John D. Rockefeller and Henry Ford, as well as such institutions
as Harvard University. *Life* values Sheeler's photorealist paintings as com-
modities. They are valuable pieces of private property owned either by
wealthy industrialists or by private museums such as Harvard's Fogg. Self-
described in the copy as being "like any day laborer," Sheeler becomes a
propagandist working on behalf of the value of the institutions controlled
by the American ruling class. One picture shows Sheeler painting a cover
for *Fortune* magazine (another Luce publication) of a water tower at the
Ford Plant in Detroit. Emphasizing the commercial identity of this Ameri-
can artist, rather than his identity as a social critic of a corporate ideology,
the copy tells us that "he took commercial pictures of fashion models
for 'Conde Nast Publication.' " The intricately patterned painting of the
Ford plant at River Rouge is depicted as the clearly celebratory summary
of "Sheeler's ten-year reflection on U.S. industrialism." The kitchen of the
Governor's Palace in Virginia is described as "Sheeler's favorite building
in the Williamsburg restoration built by Rockefeller money." Sheeler, char-
acterized as "the consistent realist," is everywhere cast as the chronicler

12. For details of how Luce used *Life* to express support for American business and
to oppose communism in China, Europe, and the Soviet Union, see W. A. Swanberg,
Luce and His Empire, and Dorothy Schmidt, "Magazines, Technology, and American
Culture."

of sources of American business power and success. Sheeler's cultural function is to instruct viewers in how to take pleasure in the formal qualities of machines in a way that will bring praise to men such as Rockefeller, who have restored a sense of a proud American historical past by renovating places such as Williamsburg into a colonial heritage park. Both Rockefeller's re-creation of a site of American origin at Williams-burg and Sheeler's shining pictorial simulation of the contemporary auto plant in Detroit function in this scheme to applaud American progress from a colonized state into a wealthy superpower without questioning the history of racial oppression, class stratification, and environmental exploitation that enabled the very few to achieve economic domination.

Another part of the 1938 letter from Williams to Laughlin might help to explain why Williams understands this display as "right down our alley" and not as a part of "the calculated viciousness of a money-grubbing society" that he opposed in his autobiography: "Read the enclosed [Rourke's letter], the last part of it, though it's no news to you. Damn it! ain't there some way so that sort of thing doesn't have to happen" (*SL*, 32). Sheeler's display in *Life* had been prompted by Rourke's book on Sheeler. We learn in the letter that Williams had been told by Rourke in another letter from 1938 that she had looked for, but had been unable to obtain, a copy of Williams's second story collection, *Life along the Passaic River*, in the New York bookstores of Doubleday and Scribners. Williams's logic becomes clearer once we situate his response within the context of an author caught between two cultures—one of art, one of commerce—each with different strategies for gaining professional legitimation. If Rourke had only seen his book, Williams reasons, she would have written about her response to it, as she had done about Sheeler's paintings. Her words, in turn, might have led to the visual appearance in *Life* that Williams desired. Williams's excitement for Sheeler has turned into a criticism of the distribution practices of his publisher, James Laughlin.

Since we live in the aftermath of Andy Warhol and Norman Mailer, and in the age of celebrity artists such as Cindy Sherman and Madonna who simulate the appearance of celluloid heroines from the past, we need to be reminded of how radical an idea it was for Williams, in 1938, to be looking to a promotional display in *Life*, and not to a conventional book review by Rourke, as the medium through which he wanted his work to be publicized. Compare, for example, Williams's interest in *Life* to Robert Hughes's description of how strange it seemed to contemporaneous artists and critics for Jackson Pollock, one of the first beneficiaries of Luce's wish to replace Paris with New York as a center of modern art, to appear in the same publication:

> Publicity had not been an issue with artists in the forties and fifties. It might come as a bolt from the philistine blue, as when *Life* made Jackson Pollock famous; but such events were rare enough to be freakish, not merely unusual. By today's standards, the art world was virginally naive about the mass media and what they could do. Television and the press, in return, were indifferent to what could still be called the avant-garde. "Publicity" meant a notice in *The New York Times,* a paragraph or two long, followed eventually by an article in *Art News* which perhaps five thousand people would read. Anything else was regarded as extrinsic to the work—something to view with suspicion, at best an accident, at worst a gratuitous distraction. One might woo a critic, but not a fashion correspondent, a TV producer, or the editor of *Vogue.* To be one's own PR outfit was, in the eyes of the New York artists of the forties or fifties, nearly unthinkable—hence the contempt they felt for Salvador Dali.[13]

Williams's hankering for a visibility and popularity similar to that of others who had achieved, in Hughes's phrase, "the state of being well known for well-knownness," is again evident in a January 6, 1941, letter to Laughlin about Hemingway's display in *Life.*[14] Williams's response to this display is different from his reaction to Sheeler's, however. Now there is an ambivalent tone that was not apparent in his discussion of Sheeler and *Life* three years earlier. I will, in a moment, try to explain how developments in Williams's career might account for this difference in judgment. For now, let us say that Williams's eye was again trained on a high-culture figure whose public image was being celebrated and shaped through photographs in *Life.* The "jealousy" over Hemingway's fortune that the poet mentions in his letter to Laughlin must be interpreted, in part, as his own wish for publicity in the pages of the magazine.

Part of a three-page spread in the January 6, 1941, issue entitled "The Hemingways in Sun Valley: The Novelist Takes a Wife," the picture on which Williams comments in his letter shows Hemingway "at work and play" with his third wife, the politics writer for *Collier's* magazine, Martha Gellhorn, whom Hemingway had married on November 21, 1940.[15] The

---

13. "The Rise of Andy Warhol," 48.
14. Ibid., 56.
15. See Daniel Morris, "Ernest Hemingway and *Life:* Consuming Revolutions."

image is described as one of eight "intimate pictures of a great American at work and play" taken by war photographer and "intimate friend" Robert Capa. Captioned "Under a barbed-wire fence," the picture does not enhance the image of "literary tough" that Hemingway, whose personal fame by 1940 outweighed his literary eminence, might have liked as an advertisement for his new best-seller, *For Whom the Bell Tolls*. It shows the Hemingways pheasant hunting, a classic representation of Hemingway in one of his favorite roles. But here, the message is less than favorable because he is evidently too out of shape to perform the hunt, and this, we shall see, bothers Williams. Martha Gellhorn must lift up the top strand of a barbed-wire fence so that the novelist, no longer the rugged ambulance driver that he proclaimed himself to be during the First World War or the guerrilla soldier with steel nerves of the Spanish Civil War, can crouch under the fence and enter into a pasture while continuing to wield his "double-barreled Winchester model 21 shotgun."

In his letter to Laughlin about Hemingway's new novel, Williams writes that it has taught him about the value of inserting "NEWS" into his prose fiction. "NEWS," he realizes, is the "MESSAGE!" and the "Something to say" that Pound had told Williams throughout their friendship was the secret to making literature. Williams's discussion then shifts away from the novel's qualities and toward a fascination with the *Life* depiction of Hemingway:

> In a word you got to go and be where the news is happening and then dish it. But I'm glad it wasn't I whom they [*Life*] blazoned on the pages shooting with my third wife. That made me a little sick to my stomach. They needed a little touch of John Barrymore to make it convincing. Poor ol' Hem and his guts trying to get under the barbed wire while she held it up for him, so to speak. . . . Just jealous! (*SL*, 61)

Williams is not wholly enthusiastic in his response to Hemingway's "emblazoning." Seeing this display makes Williams "jealous," but also "a little sick." The sickness may stem from seeing Hemingway receive the kind of publicity that Williams himself desired, but it may also have to do with the genuine pathos of seeing Hemingway turned into an unsuccessful version of the already established Hemingway image ("ol' Hem and his guts") and of witnessing Hemingway's private life being exposed for the purpose of selling a novel as a consumer good. Each of these reactions would have been consistent with Williams's fears about his own position in 1941 as an aging writer whose attempts at self-fashioning—the novels and stories, the contract with Laughlin, the attempt to write the long poem that he described to Bob McAlmon in 1943 as "a psychological-social panorama of a city treated as if it were a man, the man Paterson" (*SL*, 216)—had not yet significantly changed his status as a writer.

However unsure Williams was about how well the photographs of Hemingway served to promote *For Whom the Bell Tolls*, he understood *Life*'s dramatization of the artist as being promotional in intention, rather than reportorial.[16] That Hemingway had been the object of a "blazon" meant that his life and character had been heralded publicly, that he had been abstracted—othered—from himself. He had been objectified as the sign of value for something else, in this case the sign of the author as American culture hero to be associated with *For Whom the Bell Tolls* and, more important from the point of view of *Life*, to be associated with the benefits afforded to Hemingway as a producer, and as a product, working in a popular entertainment medium. Hemingway's novel, *Life* was pleased to announce, had just been sold to Paramount for $100,000 plus 10 cents for every copy of the book sold up to 500,000, "the highest price ever paid for a novel."[17] *For Whom the Bell Tolls* is described in the *Life* copy as "reconfirm[ing Hemingway's] place in American literature" because the novel had "already sold over 400,000 copies" and "is moving at the rate of 50,000 a week." *For Whom the Bell Tolls,* the political novel based on Hemingway's engagement with the Spanish Loyalists in the late 1930s, is presented as a mass-produced, massively promoted and distributed entertainment item.

We can interpret the values Williams thought Hemingway meant to embody—instead of parody—by attending to the subject matter of the photographs. These settings accentuate the myth of Hemingway as sportsman, the master of a preindustrial capitalist good life. Such an image was useful to advertisers who claimed that the products of the new culture of leisure allowed for the reproduction of roles from an earlier period in American life: the ruggedness, violence, and survival instincts of the hunter, the sexual male of insatiable desire, as well as the good father, as suggested in the photo of "Papa" at the "hunt dinner." The problem with "ol Hem," according to Williams, is not that his images are being used, in the words of John Raeburn, to give readers "cues about the good and

16. Mariani, *A New World Naked*, 471.
17. "The Hemingways in Sun Valley: The Novelist Takes a Wife," 52.

satisfying life, [while] they provide us with a vicarious enjoyment of rich and dramatic personal experience," but that the values his figure is meant to suggest are imperfectly embodied.[18] Williams writes that Hemingway, as he appears in the article, lacks dramatic flair. Even if Williams is only suggesting that Hemingway inject more flair into his presentation ("a little touch of John Barrymore") and not that a professional actor should play Hemingway, the emphasis is on managing the image of the artist in a popular medium, an emphasis that is then reinforced by the reference to a second popular medium, film (with Barrymore as Hemingway).

I find it striking that Williams paid attention to Hemingway's honeymoon in *Life* but was silent about *Life*'s lack of attention to Hemingway's activities in the late 1930s on behalf of the Spanish Republicans, a movement toward which Williams felt sympathy, as attested by his tender homage to Federico García Lorca, which originally appeared in *Kenyon Review* in 1939. Unlike Luce, who supported Franco in the pages of *Time* and *Life,* Hemingway, of course, was at least until 1940 a supporter of the Loyalists, as his biographer Kenneth Lynn has noted:

> All told, he would pay four visits to the war-stricken country, in the spring and fall of 1937 and the spring and fall of 1938. From his reports from the front and his other activities on behalf of the Loyalist cause that appeared while serving as correspondent for the North American Newspaper Alliance in Spain, as well as his preachment of social solidarity in a new novel, *To Have and Have Not* (1937), he would emerge in the eyes of the world as a man of strong leftist sympathies.[19]

Williams was not satisfied with Hemingway's emblazoning in *Life* because he projected his own desires for popular approval onto Hemingway. With his focus on the popular image of the maker, rather than on the aesthetic or political criteria through which *Life* judged Hemingway, he ignored aspects of *Life*'s version of Hemingway that distorted the politically and aesthetically radical aspects of the novel and that replaced the special

18. *Fame Became of Him: Hemingway as Public Writer,* 11. Raeburn makes the point that Hemingway's 1936 series of letters in *Esquire,* which described Hemingway as a connoisseur of everything from which beer to drink on a fishing trip to what to order when in Paris, fit exactly into *Esquire*'s desire to offer copy that promoted the "leisure" style of life also being applauded in the paid advertisements.

19. *Hemingway,* 442.

graphic qualities of Hemingway's prose style with a filmic sequence of eighteen Robert Capa photographs that present the actual settings where Hemingway's novel takes place.

I have said that Williams hoped to make money from the publication of *In the Money.* It was the second installment of the Stecher Trilogy, following the modest success of *White Mule.* The critical and commercial reception of *White Mule* at first pleased Williams, but finally disappointed him. While it sold out of an initial run of 1,500 copies, it could not be reprinted in time to take advantage of favorable reviews because, the poet complained in a letter to Laughlin, his publisher was away on a characteristic ski trip to New Zealand. As he set about to write the follow-up to *White Mule,* Williams was angry with Laughlin for failing to make "more detailed arrangements for advertising my stuff." He believed that Laughlin treated New Directions as a hobby, and not as a means for Williams to survive as an author: "Inadequate management of sales cost us plenty that time" (*SL,* 28). Williams wanted to write a best-seller, but his New Directions contract did not initially create an enormous demand for his writing. The time between 1938, when he was optimistic about the potential of *In the Money* to increase the audience that he had begun to attract through *White Mule,* and 1941, when he became disappointed with *In the Money*'s ability to change his public standing, was a sobering period in terms of Williams's attempt to reach ordinary readers by using commercial appeal. His disappointment with New Directions is registered in his different responses to the two displays in *Life.*

I have so far presented Williams as a writer whose work lacked publicity. This is not to say that he failed to achieve any recognition in popular American periodicals during his relationship with New Directions. It is also not to say that by the end of his life, the image of Williams as the trustworthy doctor-poet, the Henry Ford–style tinkerer at poetry, and the ordinary American citizen who identified with the cultural dispossessed had not seeped into the imaginations of ordinary readers through the pages of popular American periodicals. As my third chapter on the "Doctor Stories" will show, after 1938 Williams's work was consistently reviewed in *Life*'s sister publication, *Time,* as well as in the *Saturday Review of Literature* and in *Poetry.* These reviews were indeed based on the conception of Williams as a figure of public trust, as this figure was constructed by Williams in the narrative fictions he published with New Directions in the late 1930s and 1940s.

Time accompanied its reviews of Williams's work with photographs of the writer. These photographs, however, were modest when compared to the pictorial celebrations of Hemingway, Sheeler, and Pollock in *Life*. All but one of the Williams pictures that ran in *Time* were one column by three inches, and all of them were subordinated to the reviewer's text. Unlike the *Life* displays that caught Williams's attention, these mug shots were not intended to replace the significance of Williams's texts with glamorous simulations of the writer as a Hollywood-type celebrity, as was the case when *Life* displayed Hemingway on hunting and fishing vacations with the likes of Clark Gable. While the book reviews in *Time* did advertise the poetry by pointing out the intriguing connection between the man who delivered thousands of American babies and at least as many poems in a fresh, new "American idiom," their function is directed toward helping uninitiated readers obtain and better understand the poetry and fiction under review, which is often quoted and discussed in the reviews. *Time,* in other words, belongs to print culture in a way that *Life* never did.

I do not think that Williams's interest in *Life* was arbitrary or eccentric. With its power to form public opinion; its enormous circulation (*Life* was first published in a run of 466,000 copies on November 19, 1936); its blurring of news and publicity features; its emphasis, when analyzing world affairs, on the role played by individual "great men" who shaped history; and, most important, its focus on pictures over words, *Life,* for Williams, was a tantalizing forum for implementing his plan to shorten the distance between poet and ordinary citizen.[20] Williams's ambitions for publicity, however, often outweighed his actual progress at reaching out to a new audience for modern literature. His two appearances in *Life,* for instance, were inconsequential, one occurring within a story marking Harriet Monroe's celebration of the fortieth anniversary of *Poetry,* the other coming posthumously and, ironically, without a photograph, in a 1966 review of M. L. Rosenthal's *William Carlos Williams Reader* by Webster Schott.[21] His desire to appear in *Life,* however, remains significant in terms of Williams's challenge of elitist assumptions about the economics of modernism, its patrons, its intended audience, and its relationship to mass-produced forms of culture that we have seen in the quotations from

20. See Swanberg, *Luce and His Empire,* 142, for the publication history of *Life.*
21. See "A Birthday for 'Poetry' " and Webster Schott, "A Gigantic Poet Who Wrote American."

Laughlin's letters to Williams and from his preface to *New Directions in Prose and Poetry.* The same issues informed the following comment in an essay by Wallace Stevens: "Time and time again it has been said that [the poet] may not address himself to an elite. I think he may. There is not a poet whom we prize living today that does not address himself to an elite. The poet will continue to do that. . . . And that elite, if it responds . . . will thereafter do for the poet what he cannot do for himself, that is to say, receive his poetry."[22]

As his interest in the photographic displays in *Life* shows, Williams not only refused to turn his attention away from the subject matter of common experience—and thus, like Stéphane Mallarmé, Paul Valéry, and Stevens, to concentrate exclusively upon the medium of his own craft—but also, in terms of finding new audiences for his poetry and new ways to distribute it, fought against the estrangement from popular culture felt by many avant-garde writers and critics by turning toward the mass-circulation weeklies in order to shape his public image and create a new market for modernism. Unlike Stevens, who distrusted ordinary people and abhorred the crowd, Williams tried to control the meaning and value of his writing through resources found *within* the commercial culture of the United States, the means being the promotion and dissemination of the image of the maker through commonly distributed and easily obtained forms of publicity. While Williams's desire to extend the reach of modern letters to ordinary readers through the mass-circulation pictorial weekly *Life* can be applauded as an attack against the aristocratic assumptions about literary patronage that inform such comments as Stevens's, we have also seen that his insight into the democratization of letters through publicity caused him to be blind to troubling political and aesthetic aspects of entering modern work into a medium over which he held no editorial control.

In the 1940s and 1950s, Williams continued to publish stories about the self in his poetry and narrative prose. Williams appears in the mask of Dev Evans as a fastidious Americanist working against the restraint of European notions of cultural origination in *A Voyage to Pagany* (first published in 1928 but reprinted in 1949 as part of New Directions's Classics in American Literature series) and in his most overt celebrations of himself as a constructed cultural giant in *Paterson* and the *Autobiography.*

22. "Art as Establisher of Value," 219-20.

Although Williams continued to experiment with the structures of verse in *Paterson* and, through his development of the three-stepped line, in *The Desert Music* (1954) and *A Journey to Love* (1955), his first years with New Directions were marked by an emphasis on telling stories about the maker, on packaging his earlier work in a uniform edition (*Selected Poems* was published by New Directions in 1949), and, as we have seen, on examining popular American periodicals in order to gauge how other, more prominently displayed, artists and writers were faring in their effort to reach an audience in a country that Williams believed had rejected and ignored his contribution to letters. At the end of the preface to the 1855 edition of *Leaves of Grass,* Walt Whitman wrote that "the proof of a poet is that his country absorbs him as affectionately as he has absorbed it."[23] The rest of this study will concentrate on how Williams employed narrative forms in order to facilitate and to confirm his absorption into American culture as a poet.

23. Preface to *Leaves of Grass* (1855), ed. Malcolm Cowley, 24.

Two

"Flow New under the Old Bridge"

The Quest for Poetic Authority
in *A Voyage to Pagany*

I.

Before examining how an Americanist's account of the world based on individual perception was raised to the power status of representation through the use of traditional European literary tactics in William Carlos Williams's first conventional novel, I wish to present a signature lyric from 1938 that displays Williams's mature formal style as an interstitial poet:

> Between Walls
>
> the back wings
> of the
>
> hospital where
> nothing
>
> will grow lie
> cinders
>
> in which shine
> the broken
>
> pieces of a green
> bottle[1]

---

1. William Carlos Williams, *Selected Poems* (1969 ed.), 84.

In "Between Walls," and in other poems that repeat stanzas formed out of lines of variable length, such as "The Red Wheelbarrow" (1923) and "Proletarian Portrait" (1935), Williams has made a unique gesture. He has imposed an abstract design on a sentence fragment that seems trivial—a description of a drab scene of material reality—when considered outside the poetic space. Because it exists behind the public facade of human caring, the city hospital, this material would be neglected if it were not for the poem. "Between Walls," however, is a characteristic sentence for Williams to recover in the design of a poem. Although it almost appears to be a complete statement, it lacks punctuation and is syntactically a fragment, even if we allow the title to sink into the body of the poem. Here is the sentence of "Between Walls" prior to its formation into the abstract poetic design of its two-line stanzas: "Between walls the back wings of the hospital where nothing will grow lie cinders in which shine the broken pieces of a green bottle." Through his attention to its formal constituents, Williams unifies experience in the poem, which is ordered, however, without a return to the accentual syllabic line of ten positions. Williams ignored the line of ten because he believed it was inappropriate for a poet writing in a democratic country to employ a line whose greatest practitioner, William Shakespeare, used it to describe a feudal world.

Although "Between Walls" resists accentual syllabic measuring, the poem is not informal or free of prosodic restraint. Through the modulation of its alternating longer and shorter lines, the patterning of lines into stanzas, and the use of enjambment that predicts and then retracts the placement into the poem of an object believed to be of value in a hierarchical sorting of the world, Williams has raised to the status of representation this trivial observation about the facts of material reality. Through his attention to the small units of meaning—the unprecedented strangeness, for instance, of his decision to construct a line that consists only of the parts of speech that concern relationships between things ("of the")—Williams revitalizes and enlarges our aesthetic experience of the kind of trivial site that the poem describes. His recovery of the object in the poem is what makes the green bottle "shine." Williams has shown that traditional poetic resources such as the line are not empty shells of a gentlemanly art. If the poem includes elements that contradict elitist conceptions of what belongs there, the resources of poetry can become part of what Edward Said refers to as a "culture of resistance." The poem may transform what readers consider to be valuable. "Nothing"—the zero term, the opposite of what we expect to find in a form supposed to confer value to dignified things—is found "growing" between the back wings of the hospital. The lyric "I" also does not appear in the poem. The maker's desire to demand attention for disqualified terms where we might expect to find exclusive ones, however, allows the poet to invest his subjectivity in the poem, which is understood as an artificial construct.

A poem may be defined as a structure that records and preserves what is considered valuable to some members of the human community. By the employment of this structure, which is not mimetic of the material world, "Between Walls" draws our attention to something in the world outside the poem that we may have wished to ignore in the past, but that we are now invited to think about as consistent with earlier examples of material suitable for poetic representation. Williams's creative impulse is to compose the world through the visual properties of his poem. This understanding of his poetics contradicts a sense of Williams as a writer in the Emersonian grain of American authors interested only in capturing "reality" on paper through an unmediated "leap" into experience and into perception. My statement about the artificiality of Williams's poetics contradicts the early and influential position taken by J. Hillis Miller in *Poets of Reality* about the isomorphic relationship between signifier and signified in Williams's poetry. Miller in that study described the Williams anti-aesthetic as one in which no difference is made between the words in the poem and the facts of the world. My claim is that it is Williams's attention to the designed—or, in Stevens's term from "The Idea of Order at Key West," "made"—aspects of poetry that allows the facts of the world outside the poem to be displayed with the Benjaminian "aura" that demands our attention.[2]

In the third stanza of "Between Walls," Williams's poetic technique emphasizes the word "cinders." Readers concentrate their attention on "cinders" because the word is placed in one of the poem's few positions

2. As both Terence Diggory and Brian Bremen have pointed out, Miller's positions on Williams have, in Bremen's words, "moved from presenting him as an exemplary 'poet of reality' to a writer whose work embodies the 'linguistic moment' " (*William Carlos Williams and the Diagnostics of Culture*, 4); see also Diggory, *Williams and the Ethics of Painting*, esp. 6–13. For more on the contradiction between Williams's adherence to the formal properties of the poem (the poem as a recuperative act of mind) and the argument for a poetry of reality, see Henry Sayre, *The Visual Text of William Carlos Williams*.

of syntactical power, occupying the second line of a couplet in which the first line, because enjambed ("will grow lie"), sets the reader up to expect a value-bearing term in the second. The reader familiar with past instances of the lyric will expect to find . . . what? . . . a bouquet of beautiful flowers? . . . a romantic couple at a picnic? These romantic scenes are not what the poem delivers. Nothing but cinders and broken glass lie behind the hospital walls. "Nothing," "cinders," and "the broken" all occupy their own lines, lines where the payoff to the expectation for a greatly promised object is structurally appropriate.

In "Between Walls," the world of value appears in the margin (between) and in the hidden space (behind), instead of where care and attention are usually found (the hospital); the poem therefore redirects the honor of the reader's gaze away from where it is traditionally directed. Instead of depressing our expectations for a show of value, however, the poet proclaims the discarded items themselves to be worthy of a reader's attention: the broken green bottle is strange and "shines" with value like currency. The static, inorganic place (such as the poem as art object, where "nothing grows") is a place where the traces of significant human action have been able to endure, even if the makers and the breakers of the bottle are nowhere to be found in the poem. Cinders in terms of concrete building blocks imply an attempt at building a place for human dwelling. Cinders as ashes, not blocks, suggest burning, and burning, in this case, implies an imaginative activity to satisfy a basic human need. Knowing what we do about the community Williams served for forty years as a physician, we can imagine hospital workers who have discarded the remains of the hospital's oven heating system. Or, perhaps, we can imagine a group of poor persons creating a fire for warmth behind Passaic General. The broken bottle becomes the trace of the struggle among those forgotten by the rulers of an economically depressed society to forge a sort of community, which is evidenced by these basic signs of human dwelling.

Williams intended to make subject matter out of ordinary facts of the world, although the medium he chose to represent daily life is extraordinary. By taking a "ready-made" or trivial statement of fact into the context of art through a consistent formal patterning that operates from stanza to stanza, Williams accepted the traditional way of acknowledging value through a disciplined arrangement of language. Williams's acceptance of the discipline of poetry, however, serves to alter the reader's opinion about the terms a poet may consider to be legitimate material for the elevated (because additionally restrained) discourse of the poem. One of the reasons we trust Williams to speak with authority about how to account for the world has to do with his attention to the least visible (morphemic) aspects of poetic grammar. Readers are aware of Williams in the poem as a distinguished technician of poetic formation. He is an ordinary person who knows through his extraordinary practice how to bring dignity to terms and persons often left out of the exclusive equations of elite conceptions of art.

II.

In "Between Walls," Williams has employed the discursive structure of a prestigious form of representation to display neglected materials in a way that provides these objects with the distinction of appearance in the carefully arranged poetic account. In his first conventional novel, *A Voyage to Pagany,* Williams addressed the problem of how an author interested in representing the experience of underprivileged groups in the United States might make use of a European version of poetic authority that was associated with another class of poets. He accomplishes this task in a way that might appear to counteract our notion of Williams as the poet who is described in *Paterson* book 1 as having "stayed at home," or Robert Lowell's assessment of him as the modern poet whose poetry "is a Dantesque journey, for he loves America excessively, as if it were the truth and the subject; his exasperation is also excessive, as if there were no other hell. His flowers rustle by the superhighways and pick up all our voices."[3] In *A Voyage to Pagany,*Williams in effect puts exclusive cultural and religious structures that Camille Paglia associates with the Apollonianism of an aristocratic order (law, history, tradition, the dignity and safety of custom and form) to the transgressive purpose of bringing to light an account of the world as seen through the eyes of a Dionysian figure of energy, ecstasy, promiscuity, and emotionalism.[4] The Emersonian theory of poetic legitimacy based on experience and on the perception of the poetic speaker is enhanced, rather than contradicted, by a reference to the traditional institutions for the management of human

3. "William Carlos Williams," 157.
4. See Camille Paglia, *Sexual Personae: Art and Decadence from Nefertiti to Emily Dickinson,* 97.

affairs that existed prior to the world that Williams's surrogate, Dev Evans, finds during his journey to Pagany (Europe).

The critical problem of maintaining an authoritative account of the world based strictly on human perception (without access to the inhuman other who can see everything all at once) is a continuing one in American poetics. Individual perception was the method of creative legitimation for Walt Whitman in "Starting from Paumanok": "As I have walk'd in Alabama my morning walk, / I have seen where the she-bird the mocking-bird sat on her nest in the briers hatching her brood." It was an aesthetic principle also for Ralph Waldo Emerson in "Self-Reliance": "Great works of art have no more affecting lesson than this. They teach us to abide by our spontaneous impression with more good-humored inflexibility than most when the whole cry of voices is on the other side." And for Henry David Thoreau in "Sounds": "No method nor discipline can supersede the necessity of being forever on the alert. What is a course of history or philosophy, or poetry, no matter how well selected, or the best society, or the most admirable routine of life, compared to the discipline of looking always at what is to be seen?" This tradition has been continued in the twentieth century, as, for example, by Wallace Stevens in his late poem "The River of Rivers in Connecticut": "the mere flowing of the water is a gayety, / Flashing and flashing in the sun."[5] The unmediated perception of the common facts of the world is a method of representational legitimation for writers consistent with the principles of a democratic policy of social government. Perception is an inclusive and primordial, rather than an exclusive and feudal, sort of legitimacy. Unlike personal memory, it is not based in loss; unlike cultural memory (as in Homer or Shakespeare), it is not a scarce resource, but perhaps, as in Whitman's "Crossing Brooklyn Ferry," the most abundant resource in the world.

Perception, however, is a fragile way to authorize poetry if one wishes to distinguish poetry from experience in order to allow the poem to point toward the significance of experience outside the brackets of the poem. "Looking always at what is to be seen" is weak authorization for the poem because the question can be asked: how is anything significant if every-thing is to be seen and everybody can see it? Williams's version of authority is like Whitman's in that he claimed attention for his poetry through having

5. See Whitman, *Leaves of Grass,* 17; Emerson, *Essays,* 40; Thoreau, *The Portable Thoreau,* 363; Stevens, *The Collected Poems of Wallace Stevens,* 533.

noticed facts that, because they are a part of human experience, should be known by others. This brand of authority is also what left him in a crisis of authority from the point of view of poetic custom. The burden of gaining the authority to speak accurately about the contemporary situation while maintaining a relationship to past models for describing reality becomes heavy when the modern poet is also determined to identify his or her claims for relevance as an American poet. I use the term *American poet* advisedly here, as it has been used to signify a secular or humanist poetics in a number of reviews of Williams's work. Williams's American style has been linked by Thom Gunn and Louis Simpson to his emphasis on perception, by Leslie Fiedler to his empiricism and detection through seeing without being seen, by Marianne Moore to his "new eyes," by Kenneth Burke to his mastery of the "glimpse," and by Thomas Whitaker to his "attention to the here and now" through poems that are a "record of a continuing act of attention."[6] This chapter addresses how *A Voyage to Pagany* pointed the way toward the contexts of regulation or authoritative trust that Williams wished to invoke and then to dismiss in his general project of honoring a country that was still felt by contemporary critics of American writing like Irving Babbitt and Randolph Bourne to be weakly represented in poems.

In *A Voyage to Pagany,* Williams in part relies on his own journal entries from 1924 to present the travel narrative of a doctor-poet from New Jersey (like the author) named Evans Dionysious Evans (or Dev). The novel bears generic resemblance to a number of works by other writers in the 1920s. For example, like the novel *Les Dernières Nuits de Paris* by the French surrealist Philippe Soupault that Williams translated into English in 1929 as *Last Nights in Paris, A Voyage to Pagany* presents an observer-hero who is, in the words of Linda Wagner, "intrigued by, and subsequently involved in, the mysteries of Paris."[7] The novel also reflects Williams's interest in

6. See Kenneth Burke, "Heaven's First Law," 47; Thom Gunn, "William Carlos Williams"; Louis Simpson, *Three on the Tower: The Lives and Works of Ezra Pound, T. S. Eliot, and William Carlos Williams;* Leslie Fiedler, "Some Uses and Failures of Feeling"; Marianne Moore, "A Poet of the Quattrocento," 43; Thomas Whitaker, *William Carlos Williams,* 17. Allen Grossman refers to Williams's form of poetic authority as based on the "peculiarly American epistemologies of immediacy." See his "On Management of Absolute Empowerment: Nuclear Violence, the Institutions of Holiness, and the Structures of Poetry," 271-72.

7. *The Prose of William Carlos Williams,* 79.

how writers from the past claimed access to literary authority in Europe. Although Williams said he had not read much of Henry James, the novel has been compared to early James in its depiction of the experiences of a provincial American who is at first overwhelmed in a confrontation with European culture. The novel's expositional commentaries on art history, on the sources of poetry, and on international versus American nativist positions about art place it in line with Williams's experimental mixed-genre works such as *Spring and All.* The novel has been compared by critics to a travel diary, but also to the mythographic structuring of everyday experience such as was found in *Ulysses* (1922), a novel Williams admired. Williams himself said that his prose work amounted to "Joyce with a difference. The difference being greater opacity, less erudition, reduced power of perception." More recently one critic has compared its system of poetic initiation to that found in the narrative poem "The Eve of St. Agnes" by John Keats.[8] While Williams admired Soupault, as his translation of the novel about the wandering French prostitute Georgette suggests, he was uncomfortable with the bizarre, dreamlike, and illogical accounts of the world produced by French surrealist or "automatic" writers. In *A Voyage to Pagany,* Williams reveals a desire to suggest a Soupault-style dreamscape. His difference from Soupault and other surrealist writers, however, is that he also wished to use the abstract form of the mythographic quest romance to establish the difference between his account and either natural experience or the relatively unmediated discourse of the travel diary.

8. William Carlos Williams, *The Great American Novel,* in *Imaginations,* 167. For the comparison to Keats, see Stephen Hahn, "Williams' Homage to Keats in *A Voyage to Pagany."* See also Wagner, *The Prose of Williams,* 79. Wagner notes that while Williams worked with his 1924 travel diaries, the events from that trip gave way to "romantic re-creations of place and mood" and to "somewhat overly symbolic characters." See also Vivienne Koch, *William Carlos Williams,* 196, as well as a November 29, 1928, unsigned review in the *Times Literary Supplement* in which *Pagany* is described as a "record of spiritual growing" (quoted in Charles Doyle, ed., *William Carlos Williams: The Critical Heritage,* 115). In "Williams' *A Voyage to Pagany:* The Impossible Search for It," Anne Bowers applies Julia Kristeva's theories about the desire and repulsion of a return to the "preverbal, non-individuated, maternally dominated, infant state" known as the "semiotic." Bowers speaks of Evans's hero as "on a quest for more than aesthetic views of Europe" (40). In "William Carlos Williams and Europe: The Trans-Atlantic Construction of America," Bryce Conrad sees Evans's commitment to medicine as the formal system of arrangement that "saved him from the annihilation that he felt 'letting go' entailed" (7).

In "Between Walls" Williams emphasized the value of disqualified terms by placing them where we might expect to find objects associated with an elitist conception of art. It was through a denial of this expectation that the conversion of the poetic line toward honoring these terms took place. Similarly, the reader anticipates a meaningful journey for Dev Evans. We expect him to enter into the "Great Code" of the European discourse about art and religious culture through a series of meetings with men and women already familiar with that society. The novel, however, disappoints narrative expectations. To cite two movements within the story, Evans fails to receive initiation into the Left Bank literary community, and he also fails to win the approval of any of the expatriated American women, or figures for the "European Muse" (as both Linda Wagner and Harry Levin have called them), whom he admires as much for their aristocratic sensibility as for their liberated sexual attitudes.[9] The narrative of failed attempts to gain access to a "European muse" that in the end affirms the character's initial creative strength provides a clue to Williams's relationship to traditional structures of poetic authority. As in "Between Walls," a reference to poetic or narrative custom that belongs to a system of evaluation that is in disagreement with the author's moral plan produces enough contrast with his initial experience of failure to allow for that experience to appear as significant, as available to shape and story.

The bankruptcy of the old theological systems of feudal authority is, in the novel, beneficial to Williams's project as an American poet. But this is so only in that it creates a structure for what in *Paterson* will be described as "the roar of the present" to be isolated as a significant time and place for the production of a poetry based in an erasure of prior world accounts, an intense and unmediated perception, sensual vigor, and contact with the natural world. By reevaluating Florence as "the City of Arno" rather than "the City of Dante," by erasing the Christian meanings of the Santa Croce church in Florence and reinvesting the church with what Evans calls the meaning of "Pure Italy," a land that is "tall, spare, severe, colored,

---

9. This analysis is in keeping with remarks made by Hahn in "Williams' Homage to Keats." Hahn notices that figures containing the mysterious empowerment of the "other" for Evans in the novel are variously a woman, a goddess, or a sublime work of art. If the novel is patterned accurately after the traditional hero's quest, these figures of empowerment must be transcended by the quester for the journey to be successful. Hahn argues that Evans must renounce, finally, all the enticements offered to him in this realm of "magnetic powers" in order to accomplish his return.

flowerlike," Williams supplements the traditional authority of an orthodox sanction with a prehistoric force that he associates with a natural source of abundance available in the United States. In another crucial inversion of the "rite of passage" quest narrative, the novel ends with Dev Evans ready to *begin* his journey back to the United States. We presume he will become a legitimate poet with the value of "existence as such" superseding feudal life sortings. In the novel, the Christian God dies, and the power of the European cultural past recedes, but not before Dev Evans can carry with him back to the United States the memory and the experience provided by his contact with the chthonic force of the European ground.[10]

A Voyage to Pagany is more severely organized than an incidental travelogue can be. It is also presented as a ritual conversion narrative detailing Evans's initiation into an elevated and exclusive state of being. To borrow the anthropologist Victor Turner's phrase for such tales that tend to be used as evidence on behalf of one cultural direction over another at moments of political crisis, the narrative structure of the novel suggests that Williams was attempting to compose a "processual drama." Turner writes: "Social dramas are in large measure political processes, that is, they involve competition for scarce ends—power, dignity, prestige, honor, purity—by particular means and by the utilization of resources that are also scarce—goods, territory, money, men and women."[11] Evans's being "set apart" or separated out from the central group in Paris, his banishment from the practices of the "secret society," which in this case is the Anglo-American literary and artistic circle on the Left Bank, resonates with forms of "banishment rites," in which the expulsion from the group is itself a part of the successful crossing from novitiate to initiate. My suspicion is that Williams was familiar with the works of anthropologists such as Marcel Mauss, Henri Hubert, and Sir James Frazer at the time he composed *A Voyage to Pagany.*[12] It is clear that the stages that Stephen Hahn has identified in *Pagany* are identical to the process of separation, transition, and incorporation involved in "rites of passage" described by Victor Turner's

10. For one evaluation of "American" poetry as a form that resituates the world spiritually through a renewed sensual attention to it, see Gunn's "William Carlos Williams."

11. "Social Dramas and Stories about Them," 148.

12. In *Paterson,* Williams says "You also, I am sure, have read / Frazer's Golden Bough" (74).

teacher, Arnold Van Gennep, in his *Rites of Passage*.[13] The three funerals, the three prohibited marriages, the discussion of the Parisian avant-garde as a "secret society" to which Evans tries unsuccessfully to gain entrance, Evans's literal and figurative "gate crossing" at his old school in Geneva, and the central movement of the novel, the sea voyage from the pragmatic world of American medicine and middle-class life in New Jersey to the exotic world of the mysterious erotica of Paris nightlife, followed by the anticipated return to the medical office in New Jersey, all mark the novel as one with claims to an archetypal weight. That the novel is, indeed, styled as a quest with what Williams called "an elevated theme" is suggested also in the section titles: "Outward Bound," "At the Ancient Springs of Purity and of Plenty," and "The Return." The last chapter, in which Dev refuses to stay in Paris in spite of the pull of his sister, Bess, who Vivienne Koch correctly calls "a projection of one aspect of Dev's complex sensibility,"[14] is called "Off to the New World."

Williams's ambivalence about entering his story into a rhetorical system established as privileged before his engagement with it is registered in two distinct types of discourse. Ezra Pound's 1928 review of *A Voyage to Pagany* in the *Dial* is perceptive on this point. Pound noticed that the novel seemed at once to be a not very rigorously structured travel diary and a story such as was found in *Ulysses*, in which the immediate experience of the persona is patterned against a prior narrative account. Pound does speak of the novel as having "not very much to do with the 'art of novel writing.' " He notes, "Its plot-device is the primitive one of 'a journey', frankly avowed. Entire pages could have found a place in a simple autobiography of travel." However, Pound also links *Pagany* with *Ulysses* in terms of its use of an "inner monologue" as well as the effort Williams makes in it to bring "Joycean method inventions into a form." The dual vocality Pound finds in a novel that is "a simple autobiography of travel" and also a work imbued with attention to what Pound calls "plot, major form, or outline" suggests Williams's will to simultaneously

---

13. For an account of the rites necessary to gain the status of magician or shaman in Australian tribes—these rites bearing a resemblance to Evans's journey in that they involve ritual movements that simulate dying and resurrection, as well as a dream voyage to the other world in which the shaman acquires the knowledge necessary for subduing evil spirits and obtaining assistance from good ones—see Marcel Mauss and Henri Hubert, *Sacrifice: Its Nature and Function*.

14. *William Carlos Williams*, 205.

appropriate and repel stories of authority that disavow or repudiate the value of immediate experience outside the text.[15]

By listening to these two types of discourse in passages from *A Voyage to Pagany*, the reader can perceive Williams's ambivalence about recording his experience as a traditional quest romance. Here is an example of the relatively unmediated diary style: "Now he knew he would never see Grace again. Why else had she thrown him off? . . . Fool. You should have clung to her. . . . Furious jealousies overcame him. But what in the world have *I* to be jealous of, from her?"[16] The following passage provides an example of attention to archetypal narrative form: "In his room he seemed to be sinking back through imprisoning circles of dark light as through the center of a flower, back to some dimly remembered past, Indian games—mad escapades. Back, back to a lost grace—his own early instincts, perfect and beautiful. Scale after scale dropped from him—more than he had known it to happen under any previous condition in his life before. He never felt less voluptuous, but clarified through and through, not the mind, not the spirit—but the whole body—clear, clear, as if he were made of some fine material strong yet permeable to every sense—opening, loosening, letting in the light" (*VP*, 189). In the first passage the narrative voice is private, perhaps subvocal. It refers to an experience from the speaker's personal history concerning his anxiety about his romantic life. The language, like that found in much of John Ashbery's poetry, is equivocal in its claims to be speaking on behalf of more than one consciousness. The second type of language is more ambitious in terms of its claim to public significance. The second passage invites the reader to expect that Evans's trip to Europe is related to literary issues of national importance through language that suggests that the novel's movement bears a shadowy relationship to an internalized quest romance.

The unmediated quality of the first passage is identified through the rapid changes in the forms of the pronoun address. The pronoun shifts from "he" to "you" and, a few pages later, to "I," with no announcement to prepare the reader for the shift. Evans's sense of "self" is fluid. The "self" is presented as situated between a "linguistic marker" (or a self that has been "othered" into language, to borrow from Roland Barthes's and

15. "Dr. Williams' Position," 34, 35.
16. William Carlos Williams, *A Voyage to Pagany*, 192, 194; hereafter cited in the text as *VP*.

Paul de Man's formulations of the way autobiographical representation necessitates the death of the author), and an "I" that is presumed by the author to signify a real presence with a close relationship between the speaker and his word. The narrator in the first passage is not conscious of (because not worried about) whether the textual self is an accurate documentation of the thoughts and feelings of an actual person, because the travel diary is a class of writing that is closely linked to the living body of the author. Although language is always to some degree conventional, the diary form of the self thinking to and about itself on paper with no expectation or desire for anyone other than the self to listen in is, relative to an internalized romantic quest narrative, a sincere form directed toward the living presence of its author. Anaïs Nin has written:

> As D. H. Lawrence once said, the greatest problem of fiction was how to transport the living essence, the living quality of experience into a prearranged art form, and the danger in this transposition, this carrying of experience into fiction, was that it might die in the process. Now in the diary, no such death takes place because there is no distance. The living moment is caught, and in catching this by accumulation and by accretion a personality emerges in all its ambivalences, contradictions, and paradoxes, and finally in its most living form.[17]

The author of a diary is aware of himself or herself as an active consciousness in the process of thinking, feeling, and simultaneously documenting this process. The third-person point of view is rendered very nearly as a first-person account in the first of the two passages from *Pagany*. By leaving the traces of this autobiographical voice within the texture of a ritualistic initiation narrative, Williams registers his ambivalence about accepting without question a kinship to an orthodox account of the poetic commission. The novel does present Evans as experiencing a ritual death of the body as a necessary precondition to his assumption of literary significance. The "live" tone of voice that I have here tried to describe, a tone that appears even during the scenes of schematic ritual initiation, suggests, however, that Williams was experimenting with ways to gain authority without canceling the possibility of a return to a state of affairs that transgresses upon the accepted domain of representation. This abandoned state of affairs was later recovered through formal design in "Between Walls," "Proletarian Portrait," and "Classic Scene."

17. "The Personal Life Deeply Lived," 157.

In the passage that illustrates the second type of discourse, Evans is aware that his experience, however hesitant, discordant, or subject to revision upon new information, is also subject to an archetypal class of expanded meaning. The passage describes a ritual journey outside chronological time and into a cosmological space of transhistorical significance. Although it is a description of a ritual journey, this passage maintains a sense of speed and phenomenological "nowness"; it also implies Williams's ambivalence about maintaining access to privileged sources of creative power inscribed prior to the action of his presentation. The gerund ("sinking") and the use of the dash as punctuation mark create the feeling of actual time proceeding as the narrative unfolds, rather than of this being an account of experience organized through a previously conceived narrative design. The material described here involves a journey toward primordial origins in the United States; beyond this, it is a journey toward first sight at the beginning of things. Recovering his imaginative life in a European climate that is denying his creativity as well as his relationship to a prestigious literary inheritance, Evans dreams that he journeys back into a prehistoric space and time. He journeys past a scene of aboriginal American Indian culture toward a primitive, aquatic life form ("scale after scale dropped from him"). He is able to gain, through a paradoxically "dark" (Dionysian lunar) light, a sense of seeing things clearly and at first hand.

Williams's description of Evans's deevolutionary journey toward his own creativity by returning to "some dimly remembered past, Indian games" is symptomatic of the widespread and troubling ways such modernist artists as Paul Gauguin and Pablo Picasso and such novelists as Joseph Conrad and D. H. Lawrence viewed nonwhite and non-European cultures. Such passages are symptomatic of the work of contemporaneous ethnographers such as Bronislaw Malinowski, whose work, including *The Sexual Life of Savages* (1929), helped form what Marianna Torgovnick has called "the basic grammar and vocabulary of primitivist discourse." However much such a discourse of "primitivism" is used by Williams to subvert traditional European aristocratic authority, it remains fundamental to the Western sense of self and other. As Torgovnick has written of the crossing of Western myth and nonwhite or non-Western people in the works of a modernist writer such as Freud, in the myth of a white Atlantis in Africa, and in the Tarzan novels of Edgar Rice Burroughs, such yokings "create a never-never land of false identities or homologies. . . . The tropes and categories through which we view primitive societies draw lines and establish relations of power between us and them, even as they presuppose that they mirror us. . . . For Euro-Americans, then, to study the primitive brings us always back to ourselves, which we reveal in the act of defining the Other."[18]

Williams's moral imagination is expressed in the interplay between free and traditionally ordered forms of discourse. The stylistic interplay suggests his own interstitial relationship to organized sources of power and authority, whether these be the medical establishment, the church, the university, the modernist circle in Paris, or the line of the poem. My ability to perceive this display of a moral imagination as it is inscribed in the text hinges upon a sensitivity to formal textual matters—the attention to technique and its relation to meaning.

III.

Dev Evans, the middle-aged physician-poet from New Jersey, journeys in a ritual space (described as a world of incident, not of archetype) from the eastern seaboard to Paris, Italy, Vienna, and back to the United States, where his role as an authentic poet can "begin again" with a heightened sense of the worth and originality of the American literary project. Evans is making a return visit to Paris in order to test what he is "made of" in terms of his literary skill (*VP,* 14). In a limited third-person voice that suggests a first-person narrator speaking to himself (a voice that has access to Dev's thoughts and feelings but to no one else's), the narrator says that Dev "wanted to be let in" (*VP,* 22), that "he wanted to write" (*VP,* 15), and that he feels "he must break through" (*VP,* 14). Like the other expatriate writers with whom he wants to be associated, Evans has left the United States because he does not believe it to be worthy of representation. What separates Evans from the others is that he is also concerned with the question of "return" to literary and social activity in the United States (*VP,* 15).

In the first third of the novel, through his former associate in business and literary matters, Jack Murry, who has left New York to marry a rich woman in Paris, Evans is introduced to leading figures in the vanguard arts community in Paris. Evans is worried that Jack, no longer interested in "rescuing life from the thicket where it is caught in America," has become

18. *Gone Primitive: Savage Intellects, Modern Lives,* 8, 11.

a traitor to the "Others" group of American nativist writers in New York and is now an emissary to the enemy (Eliotic) camp (*VP,* 20).[19] In "The Supper" (chapter 5), Evans, on his third day in Paris, tries to gain the respect of the leaders of what he describes as a "wild tribal village," the literary and artistic elite of the Left Bank. At a dinner and dance given in his honor by Murry, Evans is presented with the opportunity to make a speech that might display his eloquence to the group. However, at the dinner Evans "said something stupid [that] he never forgave himself for saying, and Jack heard it" (*VP,* 42).

Evans fails this initiatory test, as he will fail another test later in the evening when trying to impress a sophisticated expatriate, named Delise, with his skills at dancing. "The Supper" thus presents one of Evans's expulsions from a privileged site that, paradoxically, by the last third of the novel, will allow him the freedom to distinguish himself from the other modernist contenders before returning to the United States. His inability to impress Delise, the European "muse," in this scene prefigures a series of failed attempts at romantic affiliations with three American women who behave as if they were sophisticated European women. In chapter 6, when his sister, Bess, leaves Paris for Marseilles, a woman named Lou Martin resists Evans's interest in her. In Vienna it is Grace Black; and, finally, before returning to America, it is Bess whom Evans must renounce because of her contact with the Eliotic "Poet A," as well as her attempt to persuade Evans to stay in Europe to do his writing. Evans perceives the women he meets in Europe as obstacles who affirm the direction of the male poet's desire for access to literary authority. Evans's voyage away from the expatriate Grace Black, from Lou Martin,

19. Later in the novel, in a strange and telling moment when the line marking the difference between fictional conflicts and Williams's imagination of a true-to-life conflict becomes permanently blurred, T. S. Eliot is explicitly mentioned as a competitor to Evans. Evans's sister, Bess, tries to convince Evans not to go "back to that [American] desert" but to stay on in Paris. Although still attracted to his sister's new inheritance, Evans affirms that "I am not of this club" and that "Europe is poison to us Americans—delicious—distressing." After Bess tries to convince Dev to "quit your cash job and study it out," Dev bewilders his sister with a remark that is not intelligible within the frame of the novel. He brings from out of the submerged allegory the name of the true rival: "Like Eliot?" Dev says (*VP,* 241). Bess responds with understandable perplexity because "Eliot" is not a character within the domain of the story: "Who is Eliot?" she says.

and, in the novel's penultimate chapter, from Bess does not imply the death of his desire, but a repression of desire displaced onto his formation of an American version of what Lauren Berlant refers to as the National Symbolic. With elite European versions of literary power denied to him, America becomes the supplying female, the previously neglected site of female authority that is also the accessible object of his desires. In the narrative movement of this novel, female characters represent and literally mark out the space that the hero—a figure for the male subject in relation to desire—will cross. Teresa De Lauretis's description of the role played by male desire in driving narrative pertains to the role played by Evans in relation to the female "muse" figures in *A Voyage to Pagany:* "That movement is the movement of narrative discourse, which specifies and even produces the masculine position as that of mythical subject, and the feminine position as mythical obstacle or simply, the space in which that movement occurs."[20]

Throughout "Outward Bound," the first section of the novel, Evans doubts his ability to overcome his own lack of confidence in his originality. Doubt leads him to feelings of rejection, self-loathing, and a hatred for the lower-middle-class life back in the United States that he is supposed to want to embrace in his poetry. Evans's distaste for urban American life might come as a surprise to readers who do not expect Williams to sponsor a character uninterested in preserving the dignity of such lives: "He grew furious at the damned stupidity of his [U.S.] people" (*VP,* 43). When he learns of Lou Martin's engagement to a rich Englishman, "Evans dreamed bitterly of his life. He saw them taking what he loved away from him and he could not open his mouth. They were degrading him" (*VP,* 48). With Lou Martin, and later in Vienna with Grace Black, who rejects his marriage proposal, he feels elated and impressed by their lack of taste for American life. In chapter 10, Evans's "warming love" enables Lou to feel "nearly freed from everything that had been America" (*VP,* 70). Grace Black argues that "the only hope" Americans have is "to give up their democracy . . . to generate . . . an aristocracy, a small haven not of brains but of understanding, some few who understand, who do not postpone and hope" (*VP,* 163). Evans, to the surprise of many Williams readers, fails to disagree with her. Before returning to America, Evans must

20. Berlant, *The Anatomy of National Fantasy: Hawthorne, Utopia, and Everyday Life;* De Lauretis, *Alice Doesn't: Feminism, Semiotics, Cinema,* 143.

learn to transcend these American-born figures, suggestive of the classical muses, who discount the value of a poetics based in ordinary life in the United States.

Lou Martin's rejection of Evans in chapter 8, "The Riviera," is among the first places where his story acquires the tone of a myth that will enable the narrative reversal toward his American origins to take place in the last third of the novel: "Evans constructed a more conscious symbolism as they rode along by the sea.—So this is the new life, he said to himself. What would Bess think of me now?" (*VP,* 61). By the last third of the novel, in chapter 33, "Good-by Vienna," Grace Black's denial of Evans will lead him to repress his initial desire for the European sanction in an act of willed forgetfulness that affirms his concentration on the essential facts of the world, a phenomenological attentiveness that has been understood by Hillis Miller, Whitaker, and many others to be Williams's contribution to American modernism. Forgetting such personal defeats as Grace Black's refusal of his marriage proposal will become a principle of the celebrated Williams aesthetic, which is the focus on a contemplation of objects, here presented as a displacement of feeling away from a focus on the disappointing personal and historical past: "My life is an effort to avoid memory; an escape. Fasten I will upon the thing, there outside the window, that lives without pain and without memory. It were idle now to remember. She is gone" (*VP,* 224). Williams's development of an imagistic poetics ("Fasten I will upon the thing") is described in fiction as a repression of the outcome of a disappointing contact with a narrative system designed to confer legitimacy on the authorial surrogate, Evans. The fictional self Williams constructed, one who Lowell said "loved America excessively," is revealed to be the outcome of a willed act of amnesia, the forgetting of a desire "to generate . . . an aristocracy" that had become apparent to Williams against the failed conversion narrative and the European backdrop.

On his tour Evans visits a series of cathedrals, first in Paris, and later in Florence and Rome. Evans respects these places as sources of cultural privilege, but this respect does not diminish his conviction that the world is valuable without theological preconditions. At first, Evans finds the grandeur of the cathedrals to be both oppressive and intimidating. He criticizes Notre Dame for making everything else seem, by comparison, "dead" and "static . . . stopped that is." At the same time he cannot deny experiencing a "chill" at the austere, formal beauty of the place (*VP,* 34). Although Notre Dame represents a "northern gloom" that contradicts his pagan or Dionysian "southern spirit," he is aware of it as a place of authority that, he says, all great political leaders have had to visit prior to their conquests:

> Dev was always cast into a spirit of awe by cathedrals. . . . The pagan strength is in them. When the Christian spirit conquered the world, the pagan gods were turned into these stone images. Oak leaves, acorns, the faces of the people of the streets in the forms of devils and angels. Such was it all. It was the power of those racial stocks that built them, gone to sleep there—to go on, to go on, undefeated. He thrilled always at that thought.
>
> It is like a tomb. Here the sun never comes. When they want to do anything that will last they come here. Or they used to. They come here to the early gods masquerading in these stones, for power. Napoleon came here to crown himself. Here the Kings are afraid. The naked spirit has taken this inexplicable shape right from among fauns and shepherds. (*VP,* 34)

Evans here denies the Christian and Apollonian origins of creative strength, control, and lucidity. This insight comes to him in a Catholic church that is paradoxically described as a Dionysian space: "Here the sun never comes." The church is, in his syncretic reading of it, the space of lasting access to Dionysian experience (the place of fauns and shepherds, of pagan gods). The church is also the institutional structure that can contain his view of the inhuman forces of perceptual enhancement. It is the ground for his access to uncultivated or organically shaped ("naked") spirit. As in "Between Walls," Williams gains access to a form of representational power from "behind" the facade of a traditional situation of authority. Behind the conquering Christian spirit, Evans claims to discover in the "stone images" the chthonic source of spiritual abundance. These stones themselves are invested with sacred meaning, for inscribed on them are images of gods that existed prior to the Christian era. The stones also present images of "the faces of the people on the street," whom he describes as the "racial stock" that built the monuments that signified the power of their rulers. By locating the power of the cathedral in the hidden force of its nameless builders, Evans affirms an alternative version of European cultural authority that is in keeping with Williams's desire to assert control over the site of value (the poetic space) on behalf of the social group whose claims to value are suppressed by the dominant group.

In the second part of the novel, "At the Ancient Springs of Purity and Plenty," Evans begins to secure a reorientation toward his own vision of how to connect with parts of a European past that is in keeping with Harold Bloom's conception of the internalized quest romance of the Romantic poet. Bloom writes that "the internalization of the quest-romance made of the poet-hero a seeker not after nature but after his own mature powers, and so the Romantic poet turned away, not from society to nature, but from nature to what was more integral than nature, within himself. The widened consciousness of the poet did not give him intimations of a former union with nature or the Divine, but rather of his former selfless self."[21] According to Bloom's model of poetic initiation, the ephebe must undergo a symbolic death or rejection in order to chart a new course toward his own imaginative strength. This type of ritual death as a passage into an Emersonian transcendence of the difference between subject and object occurs to Evans in chapter 13, as he travels by "the engine of his own train" (*VP*, 85) to Italy: "This time he was going through. . . . He had sallied out from his body where it sat slumped in the corner of the compartment, numbed to rest, while, in imagination at least, he enjoyed a freedom to come and go as he would, even in the running train, a sense split from feeling . . . he himself slid forward—he alone— trainless—the world existed in his eyes" (*VP*, 85–86, 88). The enactment of a ritual death of the body in order to submit to what Allen R. Grossman calls "semantic actualization . . . the exchange of being for meaning" allows a paradoxical renewal of sensual experience and the preliminary authority of the unmediated perceptual account to take place: "the world existed in his eyes."[22] Williams has contracted the artificial narrative structure of the internal quest romance to authorize a humanist (antitheological, per- ceptually sorted, and sensually based) as well as an American romanticist account of the world as safely constrained through aesthetic mediation: "Impossible to live . . . therefore the arts have authenticity. All attempts at directness end in stupidity" (*VP*, 86). Evans's failed attempt to gain access to the authorized culture of Europe is coupled with his protest against that culture in a way that affirms his own originality and that renews his respect for the culture of his birth.

IV.

In part 1 of the "Delineaments of the Giants" section of *Paterson,* the local genius is described as a monumental figure, a prosopopaeia, made of

21. "The Internalization of the Quest-Romance," 15–16.
22. "Why Is Death in Arcadia?" 162.

stone. Paterson's imagination is said to infuse desire into the "automatons" who live in the nearby cities. The stone giant is himself fed by a water source, the Passaic Falls and River, which is said to be a female power:

> Paterson lies in the valley under the Passaic Falls
> its spent waters forming the outline of his back. He
> lies on his right side, head near the thunder
> of the waters filling his dreams!
> . . . .
> Immortal he neither moves nor rouses and is seldom
> seen, though he breathes and the subtleties of his
>   machinations
> drawing their substance from the noise of the pouring
>   river
> animate a thousand automatons.[23]

In *Paterson,* the force of the Passaic Falls represents a subterranean and limitless source of creativity located in the United States. It represents as well a source of economic power (an aspect of it understood in *Paterson* by Alexander Hamilton) that might drive a national center for the textile industry in Paterson. In chapter 15 of *A Voyage to Pagany,* "The Arno," Evans juxtaposes the rapid power of the Arno River in Florence with the value of French painting, placing them in competition. Each is considered as a contending model for the anticipated rebirth of culture in the United States. Williams anticipates the reliance he will place in *Paterson* upon the physical abundance of the United States by arguing that the natural French, Italian, and Swiss landscapes, a physical endowment equal to that of the United States, are the real treasures of Europe, rather than its prestigious artifacts:

> Flow new under the old bridge.
> He was jealous of French painting and he was backing the river against it.
> Make new. (And the river meanwhile was getting broader and going about its business.) One can put the best painting beside you and judge it by the place where the small stream joins your cool body. It is there! Nothing is more ordered, more certain nor more flexible, more passionate, yet chaste. (*VP,* 96-97)

23. Williams, *Paterson,* 6.

After boldly discounting Renaissance cultural accomplishment by say-
ing "he did not care for history," Evans restricts his knowledge to grounds
prior to the development of European Renaissance culture:

> He knew only a river flowing through March in the sun, making, making,
> inviting the recreators—asking to be recreated.
>   It is the river god singing, that I hear, singing in the morning, asking if all
> making is ended. What to do? (*VP,* 97)

Williams turns the Arno River into an abundant source of perceptual
legitimacy mirroring Whitman's view of the Hudson River as the unlimited
source of perception for the "dumb, beautiful ministers" in his poem
"Crossing Brooklyn Ferry." After the paragraph describing this act of ap-
propriation, the narrator, in a tone of bewilderment over his own audacity
(and with some hesitation about the propriety of his act), discusses Evans's
revision of the elements of a power discourse: "And all the time he was
going to Florence, Dante's city, city of the old bridge, city of 'the David,' of
Raphael—and a faint pang of worn beauty struck him. He wanted to say
Giotto—Instead he called it: City of the Arno, and the Arno before there
was a city, teaching from the fields of Proserpine, the fields of the Vernal
gods" (*VP,* 97).

In the chapters that follow, Evans sets the stage for what will be his
prescription for an enhanced version of American nativist poetics. He
turns away from Florence as the Dantean city of the Paradise to an image
of it as the setting for an American pastoral. By chapter 19, "South to
Naples and Return," the area of Amalfi, where the church is linked to "the
peasant and the growing fields," also "might have been a rocky pasture in
Vermont." Even when confronting the art of Italian masters, Evans feels
the security to quote from Whitman's superb statement of the posture of
comfort and easy receptivity to the physical world of sensations: "I sing
and loaf at my ease" (*VP,* 97). The project here is to publicize American
property as a worthwhile ground for making world literature, as suggested
by an observation made by Evans that appears one paragraph before the
Whitman quotation and follows the passages in which Evans decides to
"make new" the old scene. He is aware of himself as a salesman of a
singular kind of poetic perception inscribed as an American product, like
shoes or any other commercial good: "If I were an agent come here to sell
American shoes, or ploughs, that would be a common reason" (*VP,* 97).

Many of the conflicts that Evans faced in the first part of the novel are presented in concentrated form in an emotionally charged meditation about the Santa Croce church. This meditation, appropriately, takes place on an Election Day in Florence. In contrast to the "northern gloom" that Evans perceived at Notre Dame, Santa Croce refreshes his sight. The place is beautiful, but its authenticity is derived from its proximity to the earth beneath the monument, to the folk who created it, and to the frescoes designed by unknown painters. The frescoes are described as works composed by nature, rather than by the hand of an individual artist. Because of the spare design, Evans understands Santa Croce as a structure that mediates between his grasp of the past and the present without calling attention to itself as an ornamental work of art. Alcoves are described as "sharp-edged . . . undecorated." After he witnesses this place, Evans's vision is said to have been "purified past the walls of any church" so that "a beauty shone through its Christian disguises" (*VP,* 104, 105). Evans feels he has accessed a "Greek beauty—a resurgent paganism, still untouched" (*VP,* 105). Evans's view of the Santa Croce church is part of his subjective reinscription of the monuments of a European past as they are put in the service of his revision of his personal and cultural past. His vision of the church differs from typical considerations of it as a structure that was a fundamental expression of the mathematical precision of its architect, Brunelleschi.[24]

Finding a Christian culture occupied by his rivals and outraged by his own country's storylessness, Evans has tried to divorce Santa Croce from its Christian meanings and return it to what he calls "Pure Italy," a land that is "tall, spare, severe, colored, flowerlike" (*VP,* 101). Such a land could be located anywhere, even in the United States, where what is traditionally considered to be "least" appropriate for representation—the broken green bottle from "Between Walls," for instance—becomes enhanced in this inverted perspective on power relations. Evans thinks that "there must be in Rome a greater thing, inclusive of the world of love and of delight, unoppressive—loosing" (*VP,* 116). Evans recovers from this "Pure Italy" a chthonic force. *Chthonic* comes from the Greek word for "earth" and is associated with the English word *humble,* which comes from the French for "low." It is also related to the Latin word *infernal,* meaning "situated

24. H. W. Jansen, *History of Art,* 388-93.

under."[25] Evans's effort to shake the ground from under the cathedrals and palaces of Rome is evident in the following passage: "He was conscious of the strange Christian influence in everything; he felt it with disgust, with despair. He tried to separate out Italy, the power itself, to tear it from this moss. The incense belonged to Apollo. They had copied their politics from Plato. It all worked so marvelously well, so smugly well. It had drawn in even the makers, warped them to its confounding delicacy" (*VP*, 101).

Evans continues to feel the pull of the old world "enchantment" that he would "never cease to recall thereafter as long as he should live—nor to enjoy" (*VP*, 103). However, unlike his response to the earlier seductions by the Left Bank community and by the "European Muses," Lou Martin and Delise, when he would gladly have renounced the "American" heritage that will differentiate him from the expatriate authors by the end of the novel, Evans now realizes the "need for escape" from Europe. As long as he can understand that the value of the church differs from the values of High Renaissance classicism, Evans can proclaim his access to the cleansing power of direct contact with a religious source without losing a sense of his own creativity. By chapter 17, "To Rome," the transformation in his opinion about the Italian monuments has taken place: "beaten by his oppressive thoughts—he sat down and began to write. It was in Rome, in fact, during these days, that he most made a wife of his writing, his writing—that desire to free himself from his besetting reactions by transcribing them—thus driving off his torments and going often quietly to sleep thereafter" (*VP*, 108-9). Through writing about his failures, Evans feels he has gained the power to control his emotional life and to return to confidence in his creativity. Writing becomes a relief from the pain of rejection and from the loss of contact with those he loves. Through his writing he comes to feel "free," and the ability to sleep returns. Writing also becomes a displaced form of erotic fulfillment. This transformation from representational impoverishment toward an insurgent account of the world based in the abundance of what can be seen will be secured as Evans travels to Geneva before his return voyage by ship to New Jersey.[26]

25. In his introduction to the 1970 New Directions edition of the novel, Harry Levin suggests that the Venus, associated with chthonic power, eludes Evans (xvi).

26. Williams again examines such a transformation in *The Build-Up*, when Charlie Bishop renounces his desire for the Viennese-trained pianist Charlotte Herman and accepts marriage with her younger sister, Flossie, whom he had previously ignored

V.

In the last chapters of *A Voyage to Pagany* (chapters 26–32), Evans leaves behind Grace Black and Vienna. They represent his final temptations to maintain contact with that "rich ground" and "profound heritage" without also establishing what we might call his "subaltern consciousness." In Vienna, Evans is still in awe of the Spanish Imperial Horses, the Yeatsian "chiefest pieces of living beauty left in the world"; a performance of a Bach opera could still make Dev "sure he had heard the Christ speaking, but not repeating a rôle" (*VP*, 178). After he leaves Vienna, able to contact the force of the monuments of prestige although access to them has been withheld from him, Evans renominates European scenes as American grounds. In chapter 35, set at Lucerne and Interlaken near the Jungfrau in the Swiss Alps, Evans locates a brewery: "All about it were the fields of long grass filled with flowers. It boiled up in his mind—America!" (*VP*, 229). In the next chapter, Evans has a rendezvous with his sister, Bess, in Geneva, which he again connects with his home. "Now he was no longer in a foreign country. The hotel was redolent of Bess. He had come definitely under a new influence which unconsciously he had been waiting now to test, to see what there was, as he had never done before, to see if it would do. Now at last he realized fully what he had been looking forward to. He had come to Bess" (*VP*, 233).

The final section of the novel, "The Return," is cast as the postliminal stage of a ritual "rite of passage" ceremony. Evans has distanced himself from his original position as an American poet divorced from the authority of an older tradition of representation. He has also removed himself from the exclusive forms of authority that would prevent access to the immediate world of activity upon his return home. Only the return or conversion to his home with a new vision informed by the personal gains made during the trial period is left in anticipation as the novel ends. Although Williams has maintained the equivocal style of the notes from his 1924 journal, he has revised that document into a purposefully shaped linear narrative. *A Voyage to Pagany* has a beginning, a middle, and an end: "He fled now with a purpose to the next step. Eagerly now he felt the end of this slow journey" (*VP*, 231).

---

because he thought she was uncultivated. The consequences of a model in which sexual prowess is linked with poetic empowerment are displayed in Williams's play *A Dream of Love* (1948), reprinted in *Many Loves and Other Plays*.

In Geneva, Evans returns to the old schoolhouse where he spent a year as a boy: "There was the old gateway with the enormous horse-chestnut trees over the entrance. But the school had ceased to exist, the town had taken it for a City Hall" (*VP,* 233). This school "where as a boy of thirteen he had gone" is described as a symbolic space, a threshold. The schoolhouse is an archetypal space in which transformative crossings take place. Yet the school of Evans's boyhood "had ceased to exist." The town "had taken it for a City Hall." Evans has crossed a familiar threshold that, through its transformation from a site of instruction to a site of political and social governance, links his adolescent experience to his adult concerns about authority in the public sphere. The consequences of this crossing have changed as they have gained in public significance. Williams has left obscure the difference between Evans's adolescent contention for growth toward adult maturity (a psychosexual issue), the literary contention, and the political valence that is contained in shadowed form within the literary issue of telling stories about the control of signs of power. In contrast to trying to make "the first team, when they told him they would pass the ball to him, left forward, at the kick-off" (*VP,* 232), which Evans says was the agony of his year as a boy in Switzerland, the agony of accomplishment now has taken on the weight of municipal importance: "the town" had taken the school "for a City Hall" (*VP,* 233). Although the boundary between private and public conflicts has been blurred, Evans has been able to return to a time of adolescent "torment and delight." He is in a position to work through his fears that "the spell will not work" and that Geneva will remain a "foreign country" to him. He leaves Geneva confident that the "new influence" that he "had been waiting now to test" (*VP,* 233) was a sufficient resource of imaginative strength.

At the end of the novel, after a scene of erotic flirtation with Bess, who has been initiated into the European circle through her sexual relationship with the "Poet A," whom her brother considers a dangerous emissary for the expatriate side, Williams presents Dev Evans as having negotiated a quest. He has overcome physical desire in order to overwhelm nature with his imaginative vision. Granted the marks of a diffident style that I have already commented upon, Evans has made what Harold Bloom would refer to as the solitary and sublime crossing into narrative significance. He releases himself from his sister's offer to help him with his "instinct for writing." He then offers her an argument that I consider to be Williams's own statement of his purpose for presenting the story of his literary contention in veiled fictions. "Keep your dirty fingers off that," Evans says to Bess: "A wave of anger swept over him. . . . How to find a way to do it and not to be beaten off, driven off or beaten or dirtied. Yes, that's my life, he replied" (*VP,* 250). To a degree, Evans accepts experiential loss, displaced onto the loss of his sister, who has also been viewed by Vivienne Koch as an earlier version of himself, in order to make a rhetorical gain. At the cost of the loss of his bond with his sister he has been able to achieve a reintegration into his previous environment with the difference of consciousness.[27]

In order to carry out the reformist idealism of empowering the lives of ordinary citizens back home in New Jersey, Williams chooses a persona in the fiction that places limitations on his subversion of an elite form of the power relations in Europe. Throughout *A Voyage to Pagany,* Williams presents a debate between nativist Americanist and international modernist versions of literary authority. This debate is figured in terms of a contest among male poets for possession of a woman. Evans's repudiation of his desire for authorial legitimation in Europe is figured in the repression of his desire for Lou Martin, Grace Black, and, finally, his own sister, Bess. Authority to construct the American version of the national symbolic is presented as a blocked or repressed fulfillment of sexual desire. In "Seine Sister," the novel's penultimate chapter, Bess becomes for Dev a source of bliss (her familiarity) and confusion. To assert the singularity of his vision as an American poet, Evans must repel his sister (and the inadmissible transgression of his own attraction to her) by converting her into the self which is Other. Bess becomes the female body as obstacle that, in Evans's view, has been dirtied or made abject through her relationship with the Eliotic "Poet A." Ironically, although Williams has been read as a post-romantic poet of reality who asserted no difference between signifier and signified, the fiction of the authorial self returning from Europe to America is figured as a displacement of prohibited sensual experience onto the level of access to discursive empowerment, Evans's ability to conceive of the American ground as a worthy site of representation in poetry. To illustrate his change of status from a minor figure of international modernism into a uniquely inspired poet of the American idiom, Williams's surrogate, Dev Evans, figures his writing as a chosen site for representation against the erotic allures of the female American body held captive in Europe.

27. See Harold Bloom, *Agon: Towards a Theory of Revisionism,* 225.

Three

The Power of Healing

The Medical Fictions from the 1930s

By 1932, when Williams published *The Knife of the Times,* his first collection of short stories that included medical fictions such as "Old Doc Rivers," the formation of an identity bound to be trusted through the association with American medicine required a careful negotiation between two classes of healing. The descendants of both the "low" tradition of oppositional self-healing, typified by Samuel Thomson's kitchen cure of the nineteenth century, and the "high" tradition associated with the dangerous "emetic" curer Dr. Benjamin Rush of Philadelphia and the medical "normals" who had been sanctioned by the American Medical Association since 1847 maintained, through advanced forms of publicity, increasingly powerful claims on the public trust. The "Doctor Stories" represent a complex type of promotional fiction because they serve the twin purposes of authorizing at once both a medical and a literary practice.

As in his portrayal of Dev Evans in *A Voyage to Pagany,* Williams presents the character he calls Doc as a liminal or threshold figure. Williams's fictional surrogate is situated at the margins between ordinary and extraordinary discursive systems. In the stories, the authority to heal others has as much to do with the caretaker's selection of appropriate linguistic and interpersonal responses to a medical crisis as with any scientific insight he might possess. In attempting to recover his personal and professional history in the "Doctor Stories," Williams focuses on creating a productive alignment with the American poet about whom he felt the most ambivalence—Walt Whitman—who is represented in the "Doctor Stories" as the wild teacher of charismatic healing, Old Doc Rivers. Williams's ambivalence about Whitman's contribution to American poetry is recovered and made productive to his own poetry in "Old Doc Rivers," which is the first of the three medical fictions I will discuss in this chapter. In the two other "Doctor Stories" examined here, "The Girl with a Pimply Face" and "A Night in June," both from the 1938 New Directions collection *Life along the Passaic River,* Williams returns with the mediational difference of his professional training to the nativist style of care associated with Rivers's charismatic practice. Williams's fictional surrogate, Doc, is figured as an eclectic combination of the charismatic healer, the university-trained medical professional, and the purveyor of hygienic goods available through commercialized medicine.

In "The Girl with a Pimply Face," Doc performs the role of social agent for a teenage girl with a skin disease. Her facial appearance is made to conform to mainstream social expectations through his initiation of her into the uses of medical products and consumer goods differentiated by brand name. After discussing the implications of Doc's concern for altering the appearance of the girl's face through the application of brand-name goods, I examine how Williams's own representation of himself as Doc, an action that is mirrored in the story by Doc's sensitivity to how the girl looks, became assimilated into popular American culture through a mass-circulation weekly, *Time,* after 1938. In "A Night in June," Doc worries that he has, over the years, come to accept without discrimination the modern faith in commercial medicine that was his primary form of cure for the teenage girl's skin disease in "The Girl with a Pimply Face." He attempts to reaffirm his commitment to the generative localism embodied by Rivers while accepting, with discrimination and alteration, the commercial products that were displayed in "The Girl with a Pimply Face."

The "Doctor Stories" suggest Williams's desire to assert, if not economic superiority, then claims to ethical, moral, and technical superiority over his medical peers. Williams constructs (as well as conceals) an analogy between the members of the corrupt medical establishment found in these stories and the literary insiders whom he felt were blocking his access to an intended audience of ordinary readers. The legitimation of Williams's *oppositional* medical practice appears to readers, paradoxically, through an inversion of the authority of the institution against which he wishes to rebel, the medical establishment being, arguably, the most mystified and exclusive sort of authority available in the twentieth century in the United States. Williams's 1906 graduation from Penn Medical School and his residency at Rutherford General and the "Hell's Kitchen" children's hospital in New York City are the well-publicized signs of his "normal" institutional legitimacy.

I. Without Valid Restraints: Old Doc Rivers and the Charismatic School of American Healing

The "I" of "Doc" and "Old Doc Rivers"

"Old Doc Rivers" is a memoir about the relationship Doc had with Rivers while serving as his seventeen-year-old apprentice. The ethics of the medical care performed by Doc are compared favorably to the unrestrained and egoistical style of care administered by his charismatic teacher. Rivers was trained in nineteenth-century American homeopathy and charismatic healing; he does not know a lot about the techniques of advanced medical science that a younger physician such as Doc would have learned at university medical schools such as Penn just after 1900. The younger Doc is sympathetic to and allied with Rivers, who is the initiating shaman figure the new practitioner will displace with his own eclectic form of medicine in the first decades of the twentieth century. Williams presents Doc as embracing Rivers's empathy for poor patients while swerving away from his iconoclastic tendency to cure members of the dispossessed community at great cost to his own health and endurance, and at the cost of life to other members of the community. The story shows that Rivers, a figure of self-reliance, disintegrated because he lacked a relationship to a professional institution outside the self to support his ambitions to heal. Doc, telling the story from the point of view of an adult practitioner in the 1930s, wishes to show readers he has avoided Rivers's unrestrained egoism through his professional training. Doc has developed his own eclectic medical style through a productive alignment with a quintessentially American type of alternative medicine—Rivers's charismatic school. He has coupled this knowledge of kitchen medicine with contemporary advances in medical science such as would be approved of by the American Medical Association.

Williams's "Doctor Stories" were originally published in collections in 1932 and 1938.[1] This was the period during which Williams, virtually out of print and unappreciated when compared to his modernist rivals,

---

1. The first collection, *The Knife of the Times and Other Stories,* was published prior to the New Directions contract by The Dragon Press of Ithaca, New York, in

attended to the display of his literary reputation through a series of recuperative fictional self-creations that appeared in a uniform edition from New Directions, beginning with *White Mule* in 1937. "Old Doc Rivers" should be read as an example of these promotional fictions. It should especially be read as Williams's attempt in fiction to claim the professional knowledge to re-form his literary heritage as an American poet through a displaced portrayal of the reputation of a gigantic influence on his own poetry, Walt Whitman. In *A Voyage to Pagany*, Williams expressed a shadowed relationship to European origins; in "Old Doc Rivers," he offers a displaced allegory of a poet's nativist American literary origins. The story of the young Doc's wish to conserve his former master's reputation while leaving room for his own contributions as a professional clinician reflects Williams's commentary in essays about Whitman, his primary precursor in poetry. In a 1955 essay to mark the centennial of the first edition of *Leaves of Grass*, for example, Williams described Whitman as "the man [who] had his hands full with the conduct of his life and couldn't, if they had come up, be bothered with other matters."[2] This characterization of Whitman as a problematic, but necessary, literary origin for Williams as poet mirrors Doc's representation of the erratic Rivers. The conservative literary sensibility that informs Williams's belated criticism of Whitman's line of "free sense" during the period when Williams was imagining his own relationship to his past is evident in Doc's ambivalent relationship with a medical precursor whose native power he encouraged, but whose authority he wished to check in his own practice as a professional clinician.

Williams was pleased that Whitman had contributed to a sense of an American identity in poetry, but he also felt that Whitman's line needed reform in order to reflect contemporary developments in science such as

---

an edition of five hundred copies. "Few books were sold," Williams recalled in his *Autobiography* (298). These stories were later re-collected, together with those from *Life along the Passaic* (an original New Directions title from 1938), by New Directions in 1961 as *The Farmers' Daughters: The Collected Stories of William Carlos Williams*, using the Random House plates of *Make Light of It* (the 1950 collection of Williams's stories). The first run of the paperback edition of *The Farmers' Daughters* was ten thousand copies. Although Williams left Laughlin to publish with Random House in the 1950s, he returned to publish with Laughlin in the last three years of his life. I am indebted to Emily Wallace's bibliography of Williams for the publication history of these collections.

2. "An Essay on *Leaves of Grass*," 903.

Albert Einstein's theory of relativity and Marie Curie's discovery of radium. By understanding poetry as an imaginative action that when applied to an "inert mass" of material recharged it with renewed value, Williams was employing the same language he had used to describe the discovery of radium: "The imagination uses the phraseology of science. It attacks, stirs, animates, is radio-active in all that can be touched by action. Words occur in liberation by virtue of its processes."[3] Williams persistently discussed his modernist theories of prosody through the technical language of the scientific expert. Rational understandings of the sciences of engineering and physics, rather than belated forms of a nineteenth-century Romantic inspiration, became the point of legitimation for Williams's poetic constructions:

> Relativity gives us the cue. So again, mathematics comes to the rescue of the arts. Measure, an ancient word in poetry, something we have almost forgotten in its literal significance as something measured, becomes related again with the poetic. We have today to do with the poetic, as always, but a *relatively* stable foot, not a rigid one. . . . Only by coming to that realization shall we escape the power of these magnificent verses of the past which we have always marveled over and still be able to enjoy them.[4]

Williams's references in his critical writings to physics (his theory of the "relative" measure), to chemistry (Curie's experiments, which Williams describes in *Paterson* as "the radiant gist"), and to anatomy (the "skeletal" nature of Gertrude Stein's poetry described by Williams in his 1935 essay "A 1 Pound Stein") were among his most persistent analogic strategies for claiming the contemporary quality of his poetic lines.[5] When juxtaposed to his essays about prosodic measure and his commentaries about Whitman, "Old Doc Rivers" appears to be an ironic text, an allegory of Williams's literary heritage in the form of a story about his medical lineage. The story is a type of documentary expression about medical technology in 1932 as well as a proud reclaiming of American medical folkways. However, I want to discuss it primarily as a literary promotion for Williams as a nativist type of modern poet who was concerned with securing through

3. *Spring and All*, in *Imaginations*, 149.
4. William Carlos Williams, "On Measure—Statement for Cid Corman," in *Selected Essays*, 340.
5. See Stephen Cushman, *Williams and the Meanings of Measure*.

technically advanced means and in the distinguished form of the avant-garde poem the language and experience of a dispossessed social group.

The story is told through the point of view of an experienced and prudent Doc, who is engaged in explaining why he values Rivers's service and why he also has come to have reservations about it. The narrator presumes his listeners will be skeptical about his interpretation of Rivers as a legitimate source of medical knowledge. As we come to trust Doc's perceptions and feelings about Rivers, however, the authorial hope is that readers will also come to accept Doc's view of Rivers as trustworthy. The story enforces our faith in Doc's authority as an interpreter (or diagnostician) of American communal myth and folk history rather than our faith in Rivers's legend. Having reached his prime level of practice in the 1890s, Rivers is from an earlier generation of physicians than Doc. Doc wants to recover (as well as to resist) the old man's practice in order to prevent it from being erased altogether from communal memory as a local folk legend. Doc, now a hospital staff physician, knows about Rivers through four means of gathering information: personal observation; folk legend; checking records at St. Michael's Hospital, particularly the ledgers of the years between 1905 and 1908; and interviewing other doctors who worked as interns during Rivers's most active years.

From the beginning of the story, what happened to Rivers is not a mystery: until his body and mind withered away from drink and drug abuse, Rivers healed some patients and lost others. Other physicians attacked Rivers's methods and judgment, but they failed to unseat his authority before a community of those who believed in him in spite of, or perhaps because of, his wild excesses. Instead of reading for the plot, our interest in reading about Rivers's character consists in discovering what Rivers means *to Doc*. We are interested in how Doc, now a mature physician in his own right, chooses to read, and, by reading, to reconstruct, the Rivers myth. The struggle for medical and, because he is the storyteller and the reader of the past, *literary* authority belongs to Doc, not to Rivers.

To be sure, Rivers does achieve a form of transcendence through impersonal means, but his path to transcendence is personally annihilating. Among Rivers's problems are his addiction to morphine and opium.[6] He

6. In assigning a relationship between Whitman and Rivers, I obviously am not attempting to claim that every aspect of Rivers's personality will match Whitman's biography. The connection between Whitman and Williams and Rivers and Doc results

takes these drugs to relieve the burden of his role as a healer with only the myth of his own accomplishments to sanction his activity. His reliance on his powers of healing, magnetic but unchecked, wears Rivers down in the end, in mind and in body.[7] Rivers's style of care lacks the decorum of the contemporary medical professional or even of the homeopathic healer. At times his risky, bravado performances place him in the tradition of the dangerous (and often misogynistic) "heroic" school of bloodletters and purgers, the emetic curers of whom Benjamin Rush was the best-known American practitioner prior to 1900. Nineteenth-century medical reformers such as Lucretia Mott would have been justified to criticize Rivers's repugnant boasts of violent action against the female body: "It is said that he had made the remark that all a woman needed was half her organs—the others were just a surgeon's opportunity. Half the girls of Creston were without the half of theirs, through his offices, if you could believe [the] story."[8] Rivers's vices, however—his drinking, his drug abuse, his emotional instability (it is known that he has been in and out of the mental hospital), his errors of judgment in the heat of his ambulatory sort of practice—all these "flaws," paradoxically, contribute to his legend in the town:

> In reality, it was a population in despair, out of hand, out of discipline, driven about by each other blindly, believing in the miraculous, the drunken, as it may be. Here was, to many, though they are diminishing fast, something before which they could worship, a local shrine, all there was left, a measure of the poverty which surrounded them. They believed in him: Rivers, drunk or sober. It is a plaintive, failing story. . . . They believed in it and it was so. . . . People sought him out, they'd wait months for him finally—though

from the way Williams situated himself in a nativist American tradition that he needed both to access and to repel. In terms of poetic structures, this figure, time and again, is Whitman. In terms of Williams's heritage as a medical healer, this figure is Rivers. In "An Essay on *Leaves of Grass*," Williams refers to Whitman as "a symbol of indiscriminate freedom" (905).

7. Williams suggests Rivers's lack of control through a favorite metaphor, the driving of an automobile. In "To Elsie" (1923) Williams employed the metaphor to discuss problematic social governance ("no one / to witness / and adjust, no one to drive the car"). Here, "Rivers would often take out in the car with him on his calls [his pet dogs], holding them on his lap, for in those days he himself never sat at the wheel" (*FD*, 105).

8. William Carlos Williams, "Old Doc Rivers," in *The Farmers' Daughters and Other Stories*, 100; hereafter cited in the text as *FD*.

> he did, of his own volition, give up maternity cases toward the end. When
> everyone else failed, they believed he'd see them through: a powerful fetish.
> He would save them. (*FD*, 104)

Rivers is cherished as a local genius because his experience of vio-
lence, despair, and internal chaos mirrors fundamental aspects of the
townspeople's perceptions of themselves as violent and despairing. He
is viewed by the townspeople as a metonymic embodiment of Creston,
a "pure product" able to cure through an empathetic identification with
those in pain, like with like. Doc's presentation of Rivers's experience as
a structure ("local shrine") and measure ("a measure of the poverty which
surrounded them") that reflect in their form "a population in despair, out
of hand, out of discipline" parallels Williams's claim that the unbridled
measure of Whitman's line was an inadequate response to nativist despair
because his line presented no difference between the facts of the world
as they are available to experience and the poet's imagination of experi-
ence as manageable through a form of technical restraint, the aesthetic
construction of the poem as an artificial, well-made thing.

Rivers opposes the style of rational medicine imported by the university-
trained physicians who were not raised in the town of Creston and who
hold its poor residents in contempt. Even after his all-too-human abuses
cause him to lose the respect of some members of his community, Rivers
remains a celebrated healer based solely on the legend of his reputation:

> Of course, [the opiates] got him finally; he began to slip badly in the latter
> years, made pitiful blunders. But this final phase was marked by that curious
> idolatry that sometimes attracts people to a man by the very danger of his
> name. It lived again in the way many people, not all, still clung to Rivers the
> more he went down and down.
>
> They seemed to recreate him in their minds, the beloved scapegoat of
> their own aberrant desires—and believed that he alone could cure them. He
> became a legend and indulged himself the more. . . .
>
> How did he get away with it?
>
> It is a little inherent in medicine itself—mystery, necromancy, cures—
> charms of all sorts, and he knew and practiced this black art. Toward the last
> of his life he had a crooked eye and was thought to be somewhat touched.
> (*FD*, 100–101)

Rivers is known in the town for being an individual greater than, and
therefore free from, any system of support that might inhibit his un-
orthodox style. Through the disorientation of the self associated with

drug abuse and with mental illness, he is presented as if in touch with a healing power that originates in forms that subvert a patriarchal religious explanation for mysterious phenomenon: witchcraft and magic. Although one of Doc's informers tells us that Rivers "went to Europe, to Freiburg to study with Seibert, the pathologist (I don't think he studied very much)," he is always also characterized as an average man, one of the crowd. The townspeople can identify with his problems; hence they assume he can understand and share in their problems.

> Sunday mornings were the times. It was a regular show. Because most of his patients were poor people and they could come only on Sunday. I'm telling you you never saw an office like it. He had the right idea, he was for humanity—put it any way you like. They'd be sitting all over the place, out in the hall, up the stairs, on the porch, anywhere they could park themselves.
>
> When it was somebody that didn't know me, he'd say I was a young doctor. I was just seventeen then. He'd give me a white coat and tell me to come on. Jesus! Naturally I thought he was great. And I'll tell you in all those four months I never used to see any of those butcheries they'd talk about. Everything he did was O.K. I suppose I'd think different now, but then I thought he was a wonder. (*FD*, 95)

Doc supports what he calls Rivers's Sunday morning medical "shows" because, in the informer's words, Rivers "was for humanity." Doc claims for himself a kinship, as well as a reformative stance, to the home-based tradition of his master's unrestrained medical ethics. The mature narrator wants his readers to know that he has gained insight from having as a young man beheld Rivers's mysterious practice. He does not, however, want himself to be known as inhabiting Rivers's sublime position. As we saw in *A Voyage to Pagany,* and as we shall see again in *Paterson,* Williams wants to avoid an absolute relationship to creative sources of empowerment such as the unconscious in order to preserve his sense of a social self.

Just as Williams would prefer his identification with the dispossessed social group to be as a word man, Rivers's empathy for the welfare of the "have-nots" is what Doc wants to integrate into his mature practice as a medicine man. Because Rivers cured patients by encouraging them to have faith in his reputation as a shaman, however, everyone's attention was turned toward the magnificence of the healer rather than the constituency being served. This egoistical aspect of Rivers's performance is what the mature Doc believes needs to be checked and re-formed in his own practice through his affiliation with established institutions of medical care such as Rutherford General Hospital. Rivers's authority to heal hinged upon his powers' being known to citizens through an oral transmission of his feats before he began his esoteric work; his "deed took the popular fancy and the rumor of them spread like magic" (*FD*, 103). The experienced narrator is able to revise the version of the story his younger self understood by presenting Rivers's claim to heroism with an ironic detachment. A beneficiary of belatedness, Doc is in possession of a critical distance that allows the significance of his own contributions to show through.

Rivers's sensitivity to the polyglot American language in its vernacular form is perhaps the most endearing and persuasive of all the aspects of his practice. His avoidance of the discourse of the medical regulars helps us to identify him as a Whitmanic "ur" figure of American language who will provide Williams as poet with a way to establish a relationship to the American soil while maintaining the "discipline" of the literary specialist. Rivers's willingness to speak the local slang is an important part of his homeopathic appeal, of his ability to cure from the inside of the culture. A drinking man, Rivers knows how to employ the local figures of speech heard at the pub. He is, therefore, trusted as an "insider" by other members of this community of marginal persons: "This is how he practiced. . . . Come in, Jerry—making a pass at him with his open hand—How's the old soak?" (*FD*, 78). Rivers's practice is a form of linguistic or psycho-linguistic therapy that builds upon a trust and identification between healer and patient. The narrator is proud to claim that Rivers "knew them all" (*FD*, 77). Being "known" by an exalted figure such as Rivers who possesses extraordinary abilities but who speaks like an ordinary man is part of the cure. The list that the narrator includes in his summary of the occupations of Rivers's hospital clients reads like a catalog from Whitman's "A Song for Occupations": "And who were they? Plumber, nurseryman, farmer, saloonkeeper (with hob-nail liver), painter, printer, housewife, that's the way it would go. It was a long and interesting list of the occupations of the region from tea merchant to no occupation at all" (*FD*, 81–82). The difference between Doc's relationship to the local slang and Rivers's is that Doc will, in the stories about his mature practice such as "The Girl with a Pimply Face," call to the patient's attention that he can communicate with other doctors and pharmacists who have access to medicine and medical techniques that might provide safe alternatives to the heroic style of Rivers's practice.

I can now secure my analogy between the way Doc validates the local idiom by coming to hear it with the authority of a disinterested expert and Williams's arguments on behalf of his method of poetic construction as precise and efficient professional work. In Williams's essays on the construction of the poetic line—"On Measure—Statement for Cid Corman" and the " 'Author's Introduction' to *The Wedge*" (1944)—he claims that a resemblance exists between the poet's task and that of the American inventor or tinkering mechanic working on a machine made out of movable parts. The emphasis in these essays is on poetic technique and on the abstract design of the poem as an instrument, a type of man-made machine, useful to produce the appearance in representation of common things that would remain trivial if considered outside the formal pattern of the poem. In the " 'Author's Introduction' to *The Wedge*," for instance, Williams defines the poem in a way that stresses its materiality while holding on to a conception of it as an organic part of the natural world. The poet's relationship to the work is technical, although the language of the garden is also noted by Williams in a way that Leo Marx would consider to be an example of how aspects of industrialism have often been made to appear in American literature as if they were natural embodiments of the pastoral ideal: "A poem is a small (or large) machine made of words . . . pruned to a perfect economy."[9] Rivers, by contrast, validates the local idiom exclusively from within; the town's faith in him reflects its faith that it possesses the linguistic and spiritual resources to heal itself without help imported from outside its borders.

In the story Rivers may not, like the mature Doc, come across as a paradigmatic exemplar of the rise in professionalism, but unlike most other members of either the "heroic" or the "kitchen" school from the nineteenth century, Rivers is described as being a somewhat responsible practitioner of the modern clinical examination. "In sum," Doc informs any reader who might wish to discount Rivers as being only another dangerous quack, "his ability lay first in an uncanny sense of diagnosis" (*FD*, 82). The practice of collecting experiential data to develop reasonable clinical statistics, which allowed diagnosis to become a finer art, was developed in

9. See Leo Marx, *The Machine in the Garden: Technology and the Pastoral Ideal in America*; Williams, "'Author's Introduction' to *The Wedge*," in *Selected Essays*, 256.

Paris by Pierre C. A. Louis (1787–1872). His moderate and patient practice was exported to the United States by an elite group of American physicians who began to study his work in France between 1820 and 1860. Medical historian John Duffy notes, however, that although skepticism about such treatments as bloodletting became widespread as 1900 approached,

> the art of diagnosis was limited to the better physicians, and most practition-
> ers relied largely upon quizzing and observing the patient before prescribing.
> In fact, the ability to prescribe was considered the real art of medicine. The
> thermometer, stethoscope, and other diagnostic instruments were slowly
> making their way into the better medical practices, but physical diagnosis
> remained handicapped by the reluctance of patients, particularly females, to
> bare their skin to the probing, palpation, or percussion of the physician.[10]

Opium, quinine, and alcohol continued to be used as tools for the treat-
ment of most illnesses well into the period in which Rivers, and then
Williams and his fictional persona, Doc, practiced, particularly in treat-
ments among the poor in the United States. Rivers's concern for diagnosis
is, then, a sign that Williams is stressing the legitimacy of Rivers's training
from a contemporaneous point of view. The description of his type of di-
agnosis as "uncanny," an adjective that suggests a paradoxically unreliable
form of reliability because based on an inability to classify the illness, sug-
gests that Doc wishes to both accept and call into question the precursor's
method of taking precautions before engaging in medical action.

Rivers's willingness to use anesthetics on a male of the working class
for reasons other than restraint would have by itself separated him from
mainstream university regulars such as his nemesis, Dr. Grimley. At the
time the story takes place, most physicians felt that working men of this
class were insensitive to pain and so needed no anesthesia during surgery.
Pain was understood by medical regulars such as Grimley to be a punish-
ment for moral failure.[11] In treating a rowdy, hulking man named Millikin
for acute appendicitis, however, Doc in the role of the young intern helps
to anesthetize the unsettled patient with ether. Doc observes that the
patient was "scrubbed up, the sheet in place, just waiting" (*FD*, 84). What
separates Rivers's practice from that performed by well-trained surgeons

---

10. *The Healers,* 232–33.
11. See Martin Pernick, *A Calculus of Suffering: Pain, Professionalism, and Anes-
thesia in Nineteenth-Century America.*

of the Paris school such as Grimley, who are oblivious to the psychology of distrust for professional medicine among the poor and uneducated in the United States, is his ability to modify in an immediate and improvisational way the standard European practices of sanitary clinical procedure in order to respond to the fears of people wary of doctors in possession of formal medical skills. Because of Millikin's heavy drinking, the anesthetic in this case fails to take effect. Rivers responds quickly by enlisting his intern to hold the man down as he applies chloroform. Proper hygiene is abandoned in order to keep the patient from refusing treatment altogether, which Rivers, in this case correctly, considers a lesser option: "I wanted to scrub. He said, No, put on the gloves. I obeyed. There was nothing else to do. Asepsis had gone to the winds long since in our efforts to keep the man from walking out of the room" (*FD*, 84). Millikin recovers from the surgery, and Doc learns a lesson about how to administer aid with the spirit of improvisation to those skeptical about surgeons who claim legitimacy only through a traditional, European training. Doc has learned how to administer care from the liminal position between members of the lower-class culture in need of service and the European type of hygienic practice. Rivers knows the rules of careful medical hygiene, but he also knows (or thinks he knows) how and when it is appropriate to break them. Rivers, however, has no standard measure for judging his performance or for knowing when he has transgressed upon an established ethics of service. He follows no procedure, relying instead on his own intuition and his passion to serve. Doc's criticism of Rivers's recklessness shows one of the ways in which the younger physician will differ from his erratic teacher.

Although the narrator's description of another performance by Rivers is energetic, it also questions Rivers's self-possession at taking "particular delight" in making quick decisions that will influence the rest of the life of his patient:

> When a street laborer was clipped once by a trolley car, his arm almost severed near the shoulder, Rivers was the first to get there. Such cases were always his particular delight. With one look he took in the situation as usual, made up his mind, and remarking that the arm could be of no possible further use to the man, amputated it there and then—with a pair of bandage scissors.
> Such deeds took the popular fancy and the rumor of them spread like magic. (*FD*, 102–3)

This patient is not consulted after Rivers makes his diagnosis or before he decides, with supreme confidence and no ambivalence, to operate.

Rivers, here, "as usual," is not careful; he needs to take only "one look" before rather nonchalantly using the bandage scissors.

Rivers's ability to practice is challenged by one of the university-trained physicians, Dr. Grimley. Grimley is furious over Rivers's risky treatments. In the case that particularly upsets him, a Hungarian woman dies after Rivers performs a hernia operation on her that Grimley had warned against. In spite of the legitimacy of Grimley's strong reservations about the ethics of Rivers's practice, Grimley does not understand, or understands and is too envious to accept ("he was fairly foaming at the mouth" [*FD*, 104]), the community faith in the mystical nature of Rivers's power. Grimley's concern for the safety of the patients in the town is motivated by an acute self-interest, and he wishes to use his position to undermine Rivers's hold on the townspeople. Grimley's charge against Rivers is never brought to court, however, because of the community's faith that Rivers would "see them through."

In terms of professional alliances, Williams wants to distance his medical reputation from Rivers's to the extent that Doc is portrayed in this story (and in the medical fictions of his practice to follow) as a sober, cautious doctor who tends to maintain boundaries between physician and client through the language of professionalism. Doc is consistent in his rounds, thorough in his hygienic practice, and less interested than Rivers in performing risky, but spectacular, maneuvers that are really egoistical performances. Not addicted to drugs and not presented as psychically disturbed, Doc will be making his rounds for a long time to come. Unlike Rivers, he has made an alliance to an institutional style of medical practice. (Doc tells this story by obtaining facts from research in the hospital records.) By recalling a "powerful fetish," a figure who claimed authority for his actions through his mythic strength and who was successful because he spoke the language of the community and shared problems with them, Williams is also asserting a connection to a working-class American source of medical cure. He is creating what Michel Foucault defined as a genealogy, that is, "the union of erudite knowledge and local memories which allows us to establish a historical knowledge of struggles and to make use of this knowledge tactically today."[12] This genealogy, which legitimates a

12. See Michel Foucault, "Two Lectures," in *Power/Knowledge: Selected Interviews and Other Writings,* 82. Foucault argues for the "insurrection of subjugated [popular] knowledges," the discovery of which, he claims, "has made it possible to produce

"disqualified" or neglected source of "subaltern" power, turns Doc in such stories as "Old Doc Rivers" and "A Night in June" back toward an older style of healing that rests its claim beyond rational science or commercialized medicine.

Williams and Whitman

As was the case in Williams's criticism of Whitman's signature line of poetry, Rivers's break from the practices of the "medical regulars" trained in Europe is only in part admired by the younger Doc as a step in the right direction. "Whitman was right in breaking our bounds," Williams remarks in the 1954 essay "On Measure—Statement for Cid Corman." "But, having no valid restraints to hold him, [he] went wild." Similarly, in other essays Williams supported Whitman's recognition that the American ground was viable for poetic representation. In 1955, Williams praised the first edition of Whitman's *Leaves of Grass* as a "new book of American poems" because it contained the "shocking truth" that poetic material might be found on this "common ground."[13] As with Doc's criticism of Rivers, however, Williams also claimed that because Whitman's poetry lacked a measure of restraint derived from rules found outside the intuition of the author or the nature of the material, the words in Whitman's poems eventually fell into chaos in subsequent editions of *Leaves of Grass.* Williams wrote that Whitman allowed the words to "run all over the map" with "no discipline at all." The result of this lack of discipline, according to Williams, was "a sort of looseness that was not freedom but lack of measure. Selection, structural selection was lacking." Because Whitman did not know how to bring the warring elements of freedom and discipline together, he was a "magnificent failure."[14]

In contrast to Whitman, Williams claimed that in his own poetry the additional "discipline" of liminal types of prosodic restraint (for example,

---

an effective criticism of the asylum and likewise of the prison" (81), in other words, a disqualified content that ruptured, or struggled against, the erudite discourse of power/right/truth/knowledge that Foucault calls "a theoretical, unitary, formal, and scientific discourse" (85).

13. *Selected Essays,* 339; "An Essay on *Leaves of Grass,*" 903.

14. Williams, "Against the Weather: A Study of the Artist," in *Selected Essays,* 212. The "magnificent failure" remark appears in a 1932 letter from Williams to Kay Boyle (*Selected Letters of William Carlos Williams,* 135).

his use of enjambment, which literally means to straddle or to sit astride) allowed him to maintain the distinction between poetry and reality while pulling the poetic line away from what he considered to be the resonances of feudalism in the measure of ten. Through claims to scientific and technological expertise, Williams asserted that he had developed a method to reconstitute the revolutionary gesture of the Whitmanic line of free sense by balancing the necessity of some form of governance with the desire to obtain individual rights: "The English of Shakespeare is medieval in the structure of its poetic periods. It is magnificent but outmoded. Were we to submit to the implications of its structure we should, in our way of thinking, be pushed back to the 16th century . . . [we need] some sort of measure, some sort of discipline to free us from the vagaries of mere chance and to teach us to rule ourselves again."[15]

The focus on discipline is essential to Williams's self-characterization as a literary professional. In the short fiction, Doc relied on "discipline" and "expert" management of disease. Rivers, on the other hand, relied upon "magic"—shamanic access to sublime force—or "uncanny" diagnosis without associating himself with a scientific discipline with procedures to help bind or frame the space of healing to reduce the dangers of practicing to both physician and client. Through his medical education Williams is claiming that he has obtained *a* discipline, which is to say, the command of an established discourse of the authority to heal. In a second sense of the word *discipline,* Williams is also claiming for himself *the* discipline or, to use a phrase from Williams's criticism of Whitman's "headlong composition," the aesthetic discipline to "take out what is useful and reject what is misleading." Although one might question what attention to the formation of poetic lines has to do with social governance outside the text, Williams, following contemporary physicists' lead in concentrating on the *least* visible particles of matter as containing energies of a world-threatening magnitude, held on to the principle that general importance and visibility existed in inverse proportion: "It is no matter that we are dealing with a comparatively unnoticed part of the field of our experience, the field of poetics, the result to our minds will be drastic. You cannot break through old customs, in verse or social organization,

15. Letter to John C. Thirlwall, June 13, 1955, *Selected Letters,* 335.

without drastically changing the whole concept and also the structure of our lives all along the line."[16]

Williams's restraining device of enjambment created the distinctive visual features of his poems. Enjambment also acted as a means for him to establish a relationship to traditional English prosody by marking lines of varying length as "rhythm units" and placing them into a variety of formal patterns. The additional restraint or technical "discipline" of enjambment enabled Williams to create, through the line, a guide to meaning that often, in its structure, also suggests the objective content of the material, as in such poems as "Rain," "The Banner Bearer," "The Yellow Chimney," and "Poem" ("As the cat / climbed over"). Enjambment restrains the "free" flow of the poet's feeling in a way that draws attention to a technical means Williams found to create an identification between his poetry and an English tradition of poetry in which value and meaning are placed at the end of the poetic line. In Williams's case, however, meaning is enhanced at the end of the line through the ambivalent visual statement of enjambment rather than through the semantically arbitrary repetition of sound in rhyme. Williams enhances the formal or designed quality of his poems through the sequencing of line breaks into patterns that can be predicted by the relative "violence" (the transgression away from an end-stopped line) that he admits into the isomorphic relationship between line and full sentence. Stephen Cushman has argued convincingly that by juxtaposing end-stopped lines consisting of complete sentences with those in which the sentence is broken through a linear enjambment that to varying degrees violates the completion of the end-stopped line as complete sentence, Williams creates a dialectical equation between freedom and conventional restraint in his poems.[17] Williams's acceptance of the impersonal structure of the poem as a form of limitation to the unchecked flow of the poet's words as they aspire to the page through the restraint only of the poet's physiological form stands in mimetic relationship to Williams's sense of the kind of freedom that was embodied in his view of Whitman and of Rivers as the "local shrine" whose excesses embody "a measure of the poverty which surrounded them."

16. Letter to John C. Thirlwall, January 13, 1955, *Selected Letters*, 332.
17. *Williams and the Meanings of Measure*, 45.

Whitman described the power of words and the capacity of the po-
etic line in spiritual terms, rather than in the scientific/mechanical ones
Williams used to describe his prosody. "Names are magic," Whitman wrote.
"The pleasure of poems is not in them that take the handsomest measure
and similes and sound." Like Rivers's form of therapy, which was depen-
dent on the vitality of his personal magnetism, the development of "the
greatest poem," for Whitman, was an informal matter dependent on the
quality of the poet's soulful presence and not on his studied mastery of
empirically derived techniques: "All beauty comes from beautiful blood
and a beautiful brain. . . . The greatest poet has less a marked style and is
more the channel of thoughts and things without increase or diminution,
and is the free channel of himself."[18] As was the case with the mature
Doc's assessment of Rivers's practice, Williams finds error in Whitman's
view of poetry as a "free channel of himself."

Rivers's ability to adapt traditional medical practices to the actual condi-
tions in which the care is administered (recall his intuitive and immediate
response to Millikin) becomes his contribution to Doc's restrained and
technically advanced medical program and his privileging of the represen-
tation of acts over the acts themselves. The criticism of Rivers's methods,
and the criticism of Whitman's lines that "shed the perfume impalpable
to form," was that the precursor had transgressed too far from established
systems of restraint.[19] Williams wrote in "On Measure—Statement for
Cid Corman":

> The thing is that "free verse" since Whitman's time has led us astray. He was
> taken up, as were the leaders of the French Revolution before him with the
> abstract idea of freedom. It slopped over into all their thinking. But it was
> an idea lethal to all order, particularly to that order which has to do with
> the poem. . . . At the last [Whitman] resorted to a loose sort of language
> with no discipline about it of any sort and we have copied its worst feature,
> just that.[20]

As his beautiful statements of empathy with the Union dead show, Walt
Whitman was a nurse who cared for others during the American Civil War.
In his representations of himself as nurse, he honors the body as sacred. He

18. Whitman, preface to *Leaves of Grass* (1855), ed. Cowley, 12, 10, 13.
19. Ibid., 10.
20. *Selected Essays*, 339.

is, however, unable to preserve life except in elegiac form: "Dead, dead, dead" ("The City Dead House"). Death becomes in Whitman's poems, as it does for Stevens in "Sunday Morning," the limit that enables pleasure and the meaning of having lived to appear. Whitman could attend to the fallen Union soldiers, "dead and dying," as he presents himself doing in *Specimen Days* and in "The Wound Dresser" from *Drum Taps,* but he could not prolong a life because he did not know how. Whitman possessed the sympathetic or maternal code of healing associated with homeopathy, with Samuel Thomson, and with Old Doc Rivers. His celebration of American plants such as the chokecherry and the pokeweed, his seeing of the live oak growing in Louisiana as a fact of essential importance, bears a kinship to Thomson's claim that the cures to native disease are available in humble things found growing in the soil of provincial regions of the United States. Unlike Williams or Doc, however, we could not say of Whitman that he possessed the knowledge to prolong the life that was authorized by death.

II. "The Girl with a Pimply Face": Williams, *Time,* and the Magic System

From the start of his career as a poet who published his work at his own expense in 1909, William Carlos Williams was interested in how to encode his poetry with value by associating it with the meaning of his name. In *The Autobiography* he recalls how he decided upon his "literary signature": "I had a great time making up my mind what my literary signature should be—something of profound importance, obviously. An advertising friend of my father's spoke up strongly for plain W. Williams. 'It's a common name,' he said, 'but think of the advantage of being *the* W. Williams.' To me the full name seemed most revealing and therefore better" (*A,* 108). Like few full names in modern American poetry, *William Carlos Williams* is uncommon in that it carries a common meaning and definition in the popular imagination. We think of the pediatrician and poet who for forty-two years composed imagist lyrics on the pop-up typewriter in between meetings with patients at his crowded home office at Nine Ridge Road. However reductive this image is of the complex man, it is interesting to examine how Williams shaped in his fiction this meaning for a name that is not the "common" one suggested by the advertising executive in 1909. Further, it is interesting to trace how the image of the doctor-poet became associated with what Jean Baudrillard would refer to as the "sign value" of Williams's contribution to American letters.

I will now turn away from Williams's use of his narratives to situate himself in relationship to his literary inheritance, as he did with "Old Doc Rivers." Instead, I return to the focus of my first chapter, Williams's interest in the appearance of high cultural figures in popular American periodicals. As I do with my reading of *In the Money* in the following chapter, I will consider how Williams's relationship to the material culture in which he lived influenced how he treated characters in his fiction. In "The Girl with a Pimply Face" Doc plays the role of social agent for a girl with skin disease whose appearance is normalized when he initializes her into the uses of medical products and consumer goods. Williams's representation of himself as Doc is mirrored by Doc's sensitivity to the public appearance of the girl in the story. Doc is involved in representing her image by enabling her to consume products that promise wonderful transformations in the lives of those who use them. That Williams's image as Doc became assimilated after 1938 into popular American culture through *Time* suggests that a parallel relationship exists between doctor and patient and poet and ordinary reader. Both Williams and Doc possess uncommon knowledge. This knowledge is mysterious and rare, and because mysterious and rare, considered especially valuable to ordinary citizens untutored in the languages of modernism or the medical arts. Williams's persona as the American poet who refused, in the words of one *Time* reviewer, to be "barricaded behind private mutterings or elaborate mythical references" and who instead insisted on seeing with "clinical honesty" what another *Time* writer called "the hard images of industrial New Jersey and the harder images of brutality the poet found there" was designed by Williams in the fiction and, later, by the *Time* reviewers to introduce modern poetry to a nonelite audience and to situate Williams as the poet most suitable to perform this representation of and for the majority of Americans.[21] His lack of complete success at being understood by members of his intended audience (the line "Geeze, Doc, what does it mean?" from *Paterson* is attributed to a patient in the cutline to a photograph that accompanies one of the reviews) reflects the difficulty Williams faced in trying to gain popular acceptance for his avant-garde poetry (the noniambic, three-stepped lines of *Paterson,* for instance) and for his narrative prose.

21. "Poetry Between Patients"; "He's Dead."

In the first years of his relationship as a professional author with New Directions, Williams published a collection of short fiction (*Life along the Passaic River*) and two parts of his autobiographical Stecher Trilogy of novels (*White Mule* and *In the Money*). In the stories, Williams reanimated himself as a new kind of public writer on the American scene. Just as Williams was without fellow among poets in his application of modernist literary techniques to the representation of the marginal persons of New Jersey—in poems such as "Proletarian Portrait" and "To a Poor Old Woman"—Doc is without fellow among the physicians affiliated with Rutherford General in his willingness to apply the techniques of the professionally trained physician to those who dwell in the tenements of Rutherford and who cannot afford, or are unwilling to trust, the doctors in residence at Rutherford General.

Williams decided in midlife to tell stories about his work as a doctor rather than to concentrate exclusively on further experimentation with designing the poetic "thing itself." This generic decision suggests his sensitivity to the emergent consumer or semiurgic culture developing in the United States as he shaped his image in his New Directions prose. In a consumer culture, as Raymond Williams, among others, has theorized, images of celebrated persons as cultural models become associated with the sign value of products that are advertised as able to bring recognition and social legitimacy to the consumer. "Publicity has been developed to sell persons. . . . The material object being sold is never enough . . . [the objects] must be validated, if only in fantasy, by association with social and personal meanings which in a different cultural pattern might be more directly available." Although some form of advertising has always been with us, if by advertising we mean "the processes of taking or giving notice of something," Raymond Williams argues that "an institutionalized system of commercial information and persuasion" did not gain cultural dominance until the revolution in communications associated with the Industrial Revolution changed the nature of advertising. And it was not until this century that selling moved beyond what we now refer to as the "classified ad" as well as beyond the sensational catchphrase that dominated American advertising for medical products (or snake oil) in the 1880s. It is only when production capabilities outstripped consumer demand in the first decades of the twentieth century that advertising began to engage in what Raymond Williams called "new methods of psychological warfare." In order to create consumer demand, advertisers attempted to sell a magical satisfaction only connotatively related to the material object being sold. What was being sold was the meaning of personal imagery. As Raymond Williams points out, such selling often appears in contexts that are not overtly promotional:

> Enough stories get through, and are even boasted about, to indicate that the paid practice is extensive, though payment, except to the agent, is usually in hospitality (if that word can be used) or in kind. Certainly, readers of newspapers should be aware that the "personality" items, presented as ordinary news stories or gossip, will often have been paid for, in one way or another, in a system that makes straightforward advertising, by comparison, look respectable.[22]

In the "camouflaged" advertising that was fashionable in slick magazines in the 1920s and especially in the 1930s, when the Great Depression led businesses to promote with great intensity the consumption of products in a shrinking economy that also encouraged the purchasing of items on credit, it was often unclear what was "news" and what was "hype." The Fisher Body Girl, for instance, appeared simultaneously as the cover girl on many issues of the *Saturday Evening Post* and as a figure who embodied the prestigious values of sleekness and luxurious appeal in the ads for General Motors cars within the same issue.

Although his intention was to reverse the direction of the consumer ideology while, simultaneously, using it for his own purposes of authorial legitimation, Williams, in his prose fiction and especially in the "Doctor Stories," presented a similar semiotic encoding of his value of an American poet. His desire to mount what he called a "selling campaign" on behalf of his poetry at the time he landed his first sustained publication contract with Laughlin's fledgling New Directions Press, coupled with his perception that his innovations in poetic forms from the 1910s and 1920s were being slighted or forgotten by both critics and readers of modern poetry after his investment of three decades on literary experiment, animated his shift toward the discursive practice that relayed the news of his insertion into a space of renown.

In *All Consuming Images,* Stuart Ewen points out that styles of dress and personal appearance were crucial for the integration of eastern

22. "Advertising: The Magic System," 183, 185, 170, 180, 184.

European immigrants into American cities in the first decades of this century: "The city was a place where surfaces took on a new power of expression. The very terms of everyday experience required, as part of the rules of survival and exchange, a sense of *self as alien,* as an object of scrutiny and judgment. From this vantage point, immigrants learned that matters of dress and personal appearance were essential for success in the public world." Warren Susman has described this shift in the experience of immigrants as one from an emphasis on "character," or an internal dimension of the self best displayed within a small community, to an emphasis on "personality," which is, in Ewen's terms, a "moldable, extrinsic self." Through their manipulation in the images of advertising copy, consumer goods became the instruments that enabled the construction of a self that would appear normal in the public sphere. According to Baudrillard in his essay "Sign Function and Class Logic," in a late capitalist culture in which "sign" value replaces both "use" and "exchange" values, consumer goods acquire a conservative political function in that they are taken as "indices of *social* membership." "Class conflict," Douglas Kellner writes, "is displaced as exploited classes succumb to the allures of consumption." According to Baudrillard, the consumer ethic fosters a new "slave morality" among the socially dispossessed. Frantic consumption by members of the lower classes is itself "a sign of their social relegation" that "marks the limit of their social chances."[23]

In the case of the "Doctor Stories," Baudrillard's monstrous vision of the consumer society does not adequately account for the possibilities for expression of the individual will to resist or else to integrate in independent ways the symbolic meaning of the tenets and restrictions of such an economy. Baudrillard's basic thesis that a shift has taken place in Western society perhaps as profound as that from feudalism to industrial capitalism, however, is a suggestive way to approach a writer such as Williams, whose attention to social characterization in his fiction crossed the boundary between product orientation and consumer orientation. While there are good reasons Williams is often remembered as a champion of the dispossessed, we can also critique the actions of his fictional

23. Ewen, *All Consuming Images: The Politics of Style in Contemporary Culture,* 72, 74; Susman, "'Personality' and the Making of Twentieth Century Culture"; Kellner, *Jean Baudrillard: From Marxism to Postmodernism and Beyond,* 26; Baudrillard, *For a Critique of the Political Economy of the Sign,* 35, 61.

surrogate, Doc, by using Baudrillard's understanding of consumerism as an exclusionary indexing of social prestige and a means for diffusing class consciousness and radical social critiques. Williams's "Doctor Stories" can be understood as part of his narrative campaign to saturate his objectivist literary product with the meaning of his image as a public figure. His attention to an encoding of this image in his fiction reflects—and, by reflecting, perhaps helped to further—a more general shift in American culture from making things to creating systems of value to attract consumers to things already made. In "The Girl with a Pimply Face," Williams champions an iconoclastic physician who, like the poet who honored the world "between" and "behind" the facades of social power and caring in "Between Walls," is able to cure patients through a compassionate understanding of their "broken" or nonidiomatic dialect. He also cures patients through an understanding of the mechanisms of the consumer society described by Raymond Williams, Ewen, and Baudrillard. That is to say, Doc fosters a respect in his patients for the tenets of a culture in which products are promoted as able to transform and to normalize the appearances of those persons who feel themselves to be outside mainstream American culture.

Doc's public function in "The Girl with a Pimply Face" is to act as a social agent for a fifteen-year-old Russian immigrant girl whom he meets on a house call initially made to cure her baby sister of a heart defect. He shuttles between the medical practitioners who can access the medical goods that can transform appearances and those dispossessed persons who reside in poverty in the tenements of Rutherford behind "one of those street doors between plate glass show windows" with "a narrow entry with smashed mail boxes on one side and a dark stair leading straight up" (*FD,* 117). Without Doc's signature on a slip from his prescription pad they would have no way to access these socially valuable medical goods. Doc works in a transitional phase of a culture that has since the 1920s shifted attention to the "moldable, extrinsic self" and away from the space internal to the person. As the title of the story indicates, Doc turns his attention away from internal medicine (the baby with a heart defect) and toward the treatment of a benign skin disease that makes a difference only to the public presentation of another member of the family of the very sick baby. Doc's emphasis on the external appearance of the teenage girl is indicative of Williams's overall concern for the fashioning of his public image in these stories and, more generally, in his personal and familial description through the didactic fiction he published with New Directions.

In "The Girl with a Pimply Face," Doc's therapy is linguistic in the sense that it arises from his ability to define the girl's malady in terms of a commercial form of medical knowledge, and then to present consumer goods to her (soap, cold cream, lotion) as the answer to this disease that has been named by the medical community and, once named, made available to cure through commercial goods and medicines. In the following passage, Doc translates medical jargon so that it makes plain sense to the girl:

> You have what they call acne, I told her. All those blackheads and pimples you see there, well, let's see, the first thing you ought to do, I suppose is to get some good soap.
>
> What kind of soap? Lifebuoy?
>
> No. I'd suggest one of those cakes of Lux. Not the flakes but the cake.
>
> Yeah, I know, she said. Three for seventeen.
>
> Use it. Use it every morning. . . . There's a lotion I could give you to use along with that. Remind me of it when I come back later. (*FD*, 120–21)

On the return visit, Doc arranges for the girl to obtain from a pharmacy the lotion that she would be unable to buy without his signature:

> How about that stuff for my face you were gonna give me.
>
> That's right. Wait a minute. And I sat down on the edge of the bed to write out a prescription for some lotio alba comp. such as we use in acne. . . . Sop it on your face at bedtime, I said, and let it dry on. Don't get it into your eyes. (*FD*, 125)

Unlike the girl, who identifies Lux soap by its sale price or "exchange" value, and not by its unique significance as a branded version of a familiar product, Doc is, as the first passage shows, sensitive to the different meanings of branded goods and is able, by virtue of the unspoken but already assumed prestige of his medical authority, to "suggest" (albeit in a rather folksy manner) that she purchase one brand over the other without his having to discuss with her why he has made his choice. The second passage shows him communicating meaningfully to two classes of speakers, the immigrant girl and the officers of the medical establishment. He identifies himself with the medical establishment through his use of the first-person-plural form ("such as we use"), and he uses his access to the medical establishment by agreeing "to write out a prescription," which implies that his signature is, indeed, an "uncommon" one, a legitimate part of the code that carries meaning to other medical officers.

Doc differs from the other doctors of Rutherford in that he uses the value of this signature to benefit someone considered by them to be unworthy of entrance into the exclusive system of acknowledgment, that is to say, unworthy of the face-making goods of a consumer culture that the girl could not access without Doc's advice and, more important, without the inscription of his name. In his willingness to demystify the language of the "medical regulars" at Rutherford General, Doc's style is in keeping with the alternative healing tradition described by historians of nineteenth-century homeopathy. Regina Markell Morantz has shown that part of the work of alternative medicine was to warn consumers against being overwhelmed by the sophisticated rhetoric of university-trained doctors. Writing about health reform from a perspective that associates "home" cure with the idea of "woman's moral power" and "female energies" that enhanced women's status "at a time when cultural and economic changes had obscured her role and narrowed her usefulness," Morantz describes the "subaltern" rhetoric of the home tradition:

> Health reformers deplored the complicated language of most medical journals. "Reader," warned the editor of the *Water-Cure Journal,* "if you cannot understand what an author is writing about, you may reasonably presume he does not know himself." "I would have the *highest science,* clothed in words, that the people can understand," wrote Aurelia Raymond, in her graduate thesis at the Female Medical College of Pennsylvania. "I have studied medicine because I am one of the people . . . to enter my protest against that exclusiveness, which sets itself up as something superior to the people."[24]

In addition to sharing his old-fashioned, homeopathic knowledge of hygiene and the use of plant extracts as cures for the girl's acne, Doc also becomes a consumer crusader for the immigrant family. He positions himself at the margin between the medical regulars' profitable business and the unfortunate consumers of their expensive style of care. "I pay ten dollar to hospital," says the mother of the baby with the heart defect. "They cheat me. I got no more money" (*FD,* 125). Doc's position is liberal and

24. "Nineteenth Century Health Reform and Women: A Program of Self-Help," 90, 77.

reformist, if not radical, in that he does not suspend his affiliation to the code of the medical establishment or to its relationship to the consumer culture. Rather than disabling the medical system altogether, he works in the intermediary space, admitting new members into the elite code and, by doing so, encouraging their re-presentation in a "normalized" form acceptable to other members of a culture that, in Ewen's terms, understands the self "as alien, as an object of scrutiny and judgment." Because of his professional training and position in mainstream culture, he is able to filter through the high, and therefore economically expensive, rhetoric of medical language in order to obtain on the girl's behalf the demystified or "use" value of products available only to those whose signatures are meaningful to the medical establishment.

In *In the Money,* Williams unmasked the relationship between economic domination and control of the means of representing value by implicitly linking the money order and the poem. In that novel he exposed the disguised aspects of the symbolic exchange using terms taken from the sphere of real value, economics. At the same time, in order to expose what was assumed to be the "good faith" economy of the literary market as an arena of economic exchange, Williams presented his argument through a fiction, a symbolic narrative. In his discussion of the relationship between symbolic capital, credit, and more direct forms of economic control in a capitalist culture, Pierre Bourdieu notes: "Once one realizes that symbolic capital is always *credit,* in the widest sense of the word, i.e. a sort of advance which the group alone can grant those who give it the best material and symbolic *guarantees,* it can be seen that the exhibition of symbolic capital (which is always very expensive in economic terms) is one of the mechanisms which (no doubt universally) makes capital go to capital."[25] In the following passage from "The Girl with a Pimply Face," Doc puts the girl at ease by using her "incorrect" grammar ("got" instead of "have") while giving her a message to take to the pharmacist:

> Tell them you only got half a dollar. Tell them I said that's all it's worth.
> Is that right, she said.
> Absolutely. Don't pay a cent more for it.
> Say, you're all right, she looked at me appreciatively. (*FD,* 125–26)

25. *Outline of a Theory of Practice,* 181.

This materialist relationship to an expensive consumer culture is ironic because Doc's obtaining for his client the "use" value of medical goods is a gift that he presents to the girl in a symbolic fiction that emphasizes the "sign" value of his medical style in terms of his literary value as an American writer sensitive to the representational needs of the dispossessed. "The Girl with a Pimply Face" encourages readers to think of Williams as the American writer acquainted both with the linguistic features and personalities found inside an exclusive system of acknowledgment as well as with the figures and linguistic resources found on the streets and in the tenements of urban New Jersey. He wins the trust of the girl by placing himself on her side in a scene in which the medical establishment is described as "them," in other words, as the corrupt outsiders: "Tell them you only got half a dollar." The comfort Doc provides for this girl (we know this through her amazed "Is that right") is registered in her bewilderment at finding one of "them" standing in her dank apartment speaking as one of "us." Doc's concern creates an enchanting moment for her, but it is also the moment when the encoding takes place in both the popular and the literary culture for Doc's position, and implicitly for Williams's position as a literary reformer situated at the crossing between high modernist, nativist, and radical social realist strains in American letters.

Doc's employment of the classic sales pitch "Don't pay a cent more for it" signifies the entrance of his signature and image into Raymond Williams's magic system of personal celebration. While the girl is excited that Doc has found an affordable way to clear her skin of acne, she has also accepted through him her entrance into the consumer ideology in which style, in Ewen's terms, becomes "the medium of encounter and exchange": "In a world where scrutiny by unknown others had become the norm, style provided people with an *attractive otherness,* a 'phantom objectivity' (to borrow a phrase from Georg Lukács), to publicly define oneself, to be weighed in the eye's mind."[26] To the degree that we as readers are seduced by his empathy for her, and to the degree that we are pleased that at the end of the story the girl has the courage to return to a public school that she had left because of her shame about her appearance, we may overlook the fact that the aura of magic that the girl believes Doc possesses remains a product of the mysterious discourse of medical

26. *All Consuming Images,* 77.

authority and of his ability to obtain for her as his special gift medical goods that she would have been unable to obtain without his signature.

In the sense that Doc turns his knowledge of consumer products and his professional medical affiliations inside out so that they will be of use to the immigrant girl who stands outside the dominant social class, it is possible to revise Baudrillard's rather grim notions of consumer culture, at least in the case of Williams's medical fictions. According to Baudrillard, the consumer ideology is a monolithic code of social evaluation. The code leaves those who participate in it no room to challenge or disrupt the social domination of the allures of consumption. That is, there is no place outside the dominant culture for persons to stand to display individual initiative in customizing or shaping purchased products to fit individual tastes and needs. In Baudrillard's scheme, consumer culture is strictly understood, according to Doug Kellner, as the way "capitalism establishes social domination through the imposition of a system of sign values whereby individuals are situated within the consumer society and submit to its domination through the activity of consumption."[27] Doc, we have seen, does engage in a semiotic revision of the girl's appearance through his position as a mediator of consumer products and as a purveyor of medical advice. Since the products he advises her to buy allow her to conform more closely in appearance to the women found in advertising displays, Doc is engaged in instilling the tastes and values of the dominant class in one from outside that culture. But it is also possible to think of Doc's act as a transgression upon and conversion of the exclusive and hierarchical nature of a commodity culture that establishes values by excluding some members of the society because they cannot afford to belong, or because they know no one whose signature will allow them entrance into its store of goods.

Williams's "Doctor Stories," like his autobiography and Stecher Trilogy, can be read as his development of a personal code onto a cultural narrative that inscribed extraneous but related values and meanings onto his poetry. Cumulatively, his prose constitutes an elaborate allegorical sign system that established his literary product as a social good and the poet as a cultural model. From this point of view, Williams's narrative simulations of his careers as author and medicine man reflected upon and helped

27. *Jean Baudrillard*, 27.

to authorize the shift from the culture of production to the culture of consumption through the creation of signs of value associated with the product. This entrance of the Williams persona into a system of sign values, however, did not necessarily endorse the world of expenditure and social prestige based on consumption that is endorsed by typical forms of product identification. Although Williams's self-fashionings reflect the imagination of a writer sensitive to a consumer society in which, as Baudrillard states, commodities "speak to us not so much of the user and of technical practices, as of social pretension and resignation, of social mobility and inertia, of acculturation and enculturation, of stratification and of social classification," the interests Williams valorizes and advocates in these stories call attention to the deficiencies of a political economy in which "have-nots" such as the girl with a pimply face are not adequately treated.[28] From this point of view, it is possible to think of Doc's access on behalf of the underprivileged girl to consumer and medical goods as an alternative practice, a subversive communication that reverses or challenges social relations based on access to consumer products. It would be fair to refer to Doc's practice in Edward Said's terms as part of a "culture of resistance."

In the story, Doc reverses the prestige of an establishment discourse so that it reflects the desires of a member of the group without political power. This act can be read as an encoding of Williams's identity as a poet in relationship to an exclusive literary establishment and as an introduction of his image to a new audience of readers of modern American literature. By attending to Doc's empathetic relationship to the girl, as well as to his concern for her appearance in the public sphere of impersonal judgment, Williams implicitly suggests his desire to form his own image in the minds of a general readership by representing himself as a physician sensitive to the needs of a marginalized community. *Time*'s reviewers picked up on the persona of Doc and distributed as the truth about Williams's relationship to his local community a biographical construction based on his own myth-making. The *Time* reviews are one outcome of Williams's desire to reach an audience of ordinary readers, as the poet's comments to Walter Sutton in a 1961 interview suggest:

28. *Critique of the Political Economy of the Sign,* 38.

The reception of poetry by the general public is very much better than it used to be. It used to be that when I attempted to read poetry they could not understand what I was talking about in the first place. And any man who dealt with poetry must be effeminate. And therefore he must compensate. But that's entirely in the past. I'm accepted by the ordinary people I know, my friends, in my town. They have come to accept me.[29]

Time's image of Williams mirrors the narrative inscription of him in the fiction, which must be a part of the compensation Williams said in the interview he needed to make in order to transform the image of himself and his work from being a part of an extraneous and exotic (Williams calls it "effeminate") modernist cultural avocation not recognizable to the quotidian experience of "ordinary people," to being appropriate to a male wage earner and grandfatherly figure of public trust who wants to be "understood" and "accepted" by friends in town. A reading of the *Time* reviews of Williams's books from 1938, when his medical fictions were first published by New Directions, until his death in 1963 reveals that this persona was absorbed in the popular weekly to the point that the unusual story of the man who delivered both poems and babies determined the value of the objective "things" themselves—the stories and poems under consideration. Because *Time* associates the Williams persona with the features of his literary work, it is fair to say that the doctor-poet competes with the literary work in terms of what *Time* is displaying and selling. The self-fashioned simulation of Williams as Doc has become a part of the object of consumption.

Time featured stories about Williams or reviews of his work eight times between 1938 and 1963. In each case the focus of the story or the review was on Williams as Doc. In addition to six book reviews, *Time* featured Williams in its people column in 1957 after he was awarded a $5,000 fellowship from the Academy of American Poets; in 1963, it offered, on the medicine page, a two-column obituary entitled "He's Dead," which noted, "He had mastered the knack of treating poems as patients and patients as poems, and both were the better for it." As in the obituary, the image Williams created in his short fiction was promulgated by *Time*'s reviewers in order to help readers assess his importance to American letters. The

29. Wagner, ed., *Interviews with Williams,* 50.

reviewer of the 1950 story collection *Make Light of It,* for example, wrote: "Delivering babies and wrestling with rashes in Rutherford, N.J. for the past 40 years has kept jumpy, impressionable Doc Williams close to the ordinary U.S. small towner and his day-to-day experience." A more detailed description of Williams appeared in a February 13, 1950, review of the first three books of *Paterson:* "Offhand, nobody would take Bill Williams for a poet, much less an avant-garde one. He looks like a doctor, talks like a doctor and slaps his knee like a doctor. Whenever there is a conflict between his medicine and poetry, medicine comes first. A man, says Bill Williams, has to respect his vocation."[30]

The description of Williams as a poet "nobody would take . . . for a poet" because he "slaps his knee like a doctor" suggests *Time*'s focus on the iconography of the maker rather than on the content of his work. It assumes a communal agreement about the stereotypical appearance of a poet and that what is refreshing about Williams's image is that it does not fit that romantic stereotype, but rather a conception of a literary man that would appeal to *Time*'s readers, a man who has a vocation, who "looks like a doctor," who is, like the painter Charles Sheeler, a grandfatherly figure of caring and public trust. Williams is praised for being sensible enough to put his medical "vocation" first, a testimony to his practicality and work ethic intended by the *Time* reviewer to appeal to "the average U.S. reader" who might have given up on modern letters as hopelessly opaque, if it were not for a poet such as Williams whose eye was trained on a clinical observation of everyday life: "The average U.S. reader will not bother to wait; he was bored or scared away from most modern poetry long ago. Nonetheless, there is more than a chance that some people who try *Paterson* for the first time will like it." This review, entitled "Poetry between Patients," features a two-column photograph of "William Carlos Williams and Friend" with the cutline "Geeze, Doc, what does it mean?" The picture shows Williams, in white coat and tie, pressing a stethoscope to the chest of a diapered baby boy. The connection between the physician trying to gauge the baby's heartbeat and the comment, made by a townsman, about the opacity of Williams's lyrics suggests a parallel between doctor and patient and poet and ordinary reader. In each case the Williams figure possesses extraordinary knowledge, and in each case

30. "He's Dead"; "Stories by the Doc," 106; "Poetry between Patients."

the Williams figure applies this knowledge in order to understand and to be understood by the ordinary people to whom his work, both as physician and as poet, is directed. Hearing the baby's heartbeat through his stethoscope is, metaphorically, related to the poet's attempt to capture the "heartbeat" of his townspeople through a type of esoteric knowledge—poetic knowledge—that he possesses but that members of his intended audience and the subjects of many of his poems do not.

Williams's lack of complete success at being understood by a member of his intended audience ("Geeze, Doc, what does it mean?") reflects the difficulty he faced in trying to gain popular acceptance for his non-traditional poetry. By calling attention to this difficulty, however, *Time* suggests that what is uncommon and strange about Williams's poetry is a part of its communal value. In a commercial culture in which a large part of waking life is spent in the workplace, Williams's decidedly non-commercial writing maintains an aura of the sublimity and autonomy of a quasi-religious literary movement applauded by inheritors of an Arnoldian liberalism for upholding values and meanings distinct from and opposed to the commodity culture in which it is, in this review, being assimilated.

Whether or not Williams's poetry was accessible to his patients, the unidentified author of "Poetry between Patients" tried to establish its significance by presenting Williams as a poet who created directly from materials familiar to most readers:

> Just off the main street of Rutherford, N.J. (pop. 16,000) stands the clapboard home and office of Dr. William Carlos Williams, M.D. 66, the best-known pediatrician in town. Doctoring is a busy life, but it is not enough for Williams: for over 40 years, on prescription blanks, old envelopes and other odd scraps of paper, he has been jotting down his impressions. A lot of the jottings turned out to be poetry.

There is a poignancy to this commentary in its awareness of the limited satisfactions of even the doctor's work. The "busy life" of the overworked professional is "not enough" to satisfy the practitioner. He must transform the objects of the work environment into objects of contemplation in order to find in them a surprising kind of beauty. He makes aesthetic objects of the imagination out of the waste of office life, the life of bills and correspondence (old envelopes), the "prescription blanks" on which Doc, in "The Girl with a Pimply Face," wrote out the prescriptions for the acne medicine. This description of the need to transform into poetry random thoughts on "odd" scraps of paper, the need to evaluate a world of things through a system other than economic use, is a sign of acceptance by the *Time* reviewer of the limits of the culture that *Time,* through its allegiance to its advertisers, and through the allegiance to the Republican party of its publisher, Henry Luce, was interested in maintaining. Williams's poetry, written, after all, on his break time and on the office's paper waste, was an acceptable addition to, as well as being an implied critique of, the world displayed on the pages of Time Incorporated's publications. Williams's working style was acceptable to *Time*'s readers, to its advertisers, and to its investors because no fundamental alteration of cultural, political, or economic conditions needed to take place to ground authentic American poetry. Williams's poetry is right here in front of us, at all times and everywhere, even in the doctor's office in suburban New Jersey, if only we are trained to look for it. We don't even have to leave work to look for the poem, or to look like a poet to look like a poet.

We are left with a question, perhaps inherent to the contradictions of capitalism, of whether the poet's shaping of a personal image that could meet with popular approval by readers unfamiliar with modern poetry provided an adequate response to the reader's question about his poems: "Geeze, Doc, what does it mean?" The answer is not clear. Through the inscription of his public image in the medical fictions upon which the *Time* reviews were based, Williams had entered his poetry into the sign system of a consumer society that designated the meanings of objects— and, by extension, the meanings of those who bought them—through the objects' association with images of another kind. By appropriating for his own purposes the logic of a consumer code, he also appropriated (as does Doc with the girl in the story) the tastes and social practices of a dominant class. This description of the story would be in keeping with the skeptical outlook of Baudrillard. On the other hand, if we do not perceive the consumer society as a totalizing monster that negates all alteration of its tenets for subversive or at least individualistic uses, we can also say that by turning the strategies of consumer marketing to the promotion of a writer and physician whose work was designed to empower dispossessed persons through their appearance in poetry, Williams challenged and opposed the exclusive economy of which his didactic fiction remained a part.

III. The Mature Doc, Commercial Medicine, and the Image of the Obstetrician in "A Night in June"

In "The Girl with a Pimply Face," Doc acts to save the baby with the heart defect in spite of his rational understanding that it will probably die. He is willing to act against his own training as a physician because he has learned to listen to an irrational plea for help spoken in a "broken" dialect and through the nonverbal language of sorrow—the tears shed by the baby's Russian mother:

> It had no temperature. There was no rash. The mouth was in reasonably good shape. Eyes, ears negative. The moment I put my stethescope to the little boney chest, however, the whole thing became clear. The infant had a severe congenital heart defect, a roar when you listened over the heart that meant, to put it crudely, that she was no good, never would be.
>
> The mother was watching me. I straightened up and looking at her told her plainly: She's got a bad heart.
>
> That was the sign for tears. The big woman cried while she spoke. Doctor, she pleaded in blubbering anguish, save my baby.
>
> I'll help her, I said, but she's got a bad heart. That will never be any better. But I knew perfectly well she wouldn't pay the least attention to what I was saying. (*FD*, 124)

Doc's response to the mother's language of tears signals a reversion in his medical style to an emphasis on the spiritually based kind of healing associated with the formation of communities of belief such as the one that surrounded Rivers. Rather than imposing his understanding about the nature and causes of life and death on the mother, Doc accepts the interpretive authority of an uneducated woman of the lower classes whose intuition here transcends his own medical understanding. Once authorized by her to become a medicine man who heals through a sacred trust between patient and doctor, he bypasses his initial diagnosis of the symptoms and agrees to treat the child. The fact that "The Girl with a Pimply Face" ends with the baby surviving through surgery ("she eats fine now"), in spite of what Doc initially believes about the child's inevitable fate, persuades us to believe in the authority of an illogical, perhaps theological or spiritually supported, power of healing based in faith in this "good doctor," as the Russian woman insists on calling him:

I started to explain things to the man who was standing back giving his wife precedence but as soon as she got the drift of what I was saying she was all over me again and the tears began to pour. There was no use my talking. Doctor, you good doctor. You do something fix my baby. And before I could move she took my left hand in both hers and kissed it though her tears. As she did so I realized finally that she had been drinking.

I turned toward the man, looking a good bit like the sun at noonday and as indifferent, then back to the woman and I felt deeply sorry for her.

Then, not knowing why I said it nor of whom, precisely I was speaking, I felt myself choking inwardly with the words: Hell! God damn it. The sons of bitches. Why do these things have to be? (*FD*, 128)

Now a split figure possessing ways of knowing associated with the masculine and the feminine, Doc can no longer distribute blame (to the individual parent, or to the economic and political system) because of his sensitivity to the desperate nature of the facts he witnesses. He sees that sound medical diagnosis, although necessary and useful, is an inadequate response to the trouble he must treat.

In "A Night in June," Doc appears anxious that he has lost touch with the "kitchen" style of practice exemplified by his empathetic relationship with the Russian mother at the end of "The Girl with a Pimply Face." He is concerned that he has, over the years, come to accept without sufficient discrimination the modern faith in commercial forms of medicine. He fears that this acceptance has damaged his relationship to his local place. In the story Doc attempts to reaffirm his commitment to the generative localism embodied in the figure of Rivers while accepting, with discrimination, the products of commercial medicine that were also displayed in his advice to the title character of "The Girl with a Pimply Face." "A Night in June" specifically addresses the complicated issue of fashioning an image of the word man and of the medicine man as an obstetrician, perhaps the most controversial form of medical specialization around the turn of the century. Williams presents Doc as able to avoid the negative associations between male surgery and violence to the female body while maintaining an association between his literary practice and aspects of medical training that had, by the early 1900s, come to be viewed as a discipline that inspired in patients (and his intended audience of readers) an almost sacred trust.

Criticism of surgery on the female body was directed in the second half of the nineteenth century in the United States primarily against those male doctors in the specialized fields of obstetrics and gynecology. This criticism was an act of resistance to the violent, needless treatment of women by such "lancet curers" as Dr. Rush. After 1900 patented home remedies such as Lydia Pinkham's Vegetable Cure-All grew out of this tradition of reform. Pinkham and other "home curers" like her developed their philosophy of sympathy toward the female patient at a time when medical specialization, particularly in gynecology, created a system of sanction for the dangerous overtreatment or mistreatment of women for the mysterious disease of "prolapsed uterus." Once presented with this faulty diagnosis, surgeons felt entitled, through the authority of their science and through their language skill, to "excise the uterus." A generation of formally educated female physicians, such as Elizabeth Blackwell and Mary Putnam Jacobi, opposed the practice of these surgeons, labeling them in public debate as mutilators and misogynists.[31]

Pinkham, a Quaker grandmother from Lynn, Massachusetts, converted women's skepticism and fear of gynecologists and male obstetricians into a strategy for promoting her "sure cure" for "female weaknesses." Her biographer, Sarah Stage, explains:

> Given the state of medical practice at the end of the nineteenth century, a woman suffering from female complaints might well have heeded Lydia Pinkham's advice and "let doctors alone." . . . The suspicion that men victimized women led logically to the conclusion that only women could be trusted. By 1883 Pinkham advertising openly expressed this new-found sense of sorority by proclaiming above each portrait of Lydia Pinkham, "Women Can Sympathize With Women—Health of Woman is the Hope of the Race.[32]

As would be the case in Williams's medical fictions from the 1930s, what Pinkham had to sell was largely a semiotic and iconographic system. This system was associated with the therapeutic powers possessed by a "heroic healer" who felt empathy with, rather than violence toward, women in pain. Stage describes the therapeutic message embodied in the image of Pinkham that appeared on the labels of her bottled cure-all, on billboards, in pamphlets, and in newspaper advertisements:

> At sixty Mrs. Pinkham was a dignified, handsome woman who possessed a benign motherly countenance. No better advertisement could be imagined.

31. Sarah Stage, *Female Complaints,* 77–79, 81–82.
32. Ibid., 88, 108.

So, after a family council, Lydia Pinkham posed for the photograph, which
made advertising history. The picture conveyed the whole Pinkham mes-
sage. At a glance it inspired confidence. The attractive woman, sagacious
and composed in her best black silk and white lace fichu, appealed to her
audience as an idealized grandmother, sympathetic and compassionate.[33]

Pinkham's advertising program for better health made an indelible im-
pression on Williams when he attended medical school at the University of
Pennsylvania. In the "Ezra Pound" chapter of his *Autobiography*, he refers
to the 1905 jingle that promoted her product: "Those were strange spring
evenings when men would sit in groups on the grass in the Triangle and
sing of Lydia Pinkham's Vegetable Compound, reputed to cure all the ills of
the female race!" (*A*, 57). Despite the tone of his remembrance, this jingle
made enough of an impression for him to recall it in the late 1940s, over
forty years after he heard it sung by a group of fraternity boys on the Penn
green. As we have seen in his essays on prosody, Williams wished to claim
access to scientific knowledge in order to separate his identity as a techni-
cally advanced literary professional from his image of Whitman as a poet
who, "having no valid restraints to hold him, went wild." Considering the
associations of violence and insensitivity to the female body that were part
of the medical identity of a male obstetrician that Williams was about to
adopt in his fictions in the 1930s, it is understandable that Williams chose
to negotiate with special care his image as a male obstetrician and surgeon.

In "Old Doc Rivers" Williams identified the "irregular" tradition of heal-
ing that Doc wanted to introduce to readers as part of his inheritance
of an American medical tradition. "A Night in June," published with New
Directions six years later, shows Williams reaffirming his ties to what is
referred to at the end of the story as an "older school." Although he finally
resists the allure of commercialization in medicine, Doc feels as if this
resistance is a self-conscious simulation of his old practice. As will be the
case with Williams's relationship to his gigantic personal construction
in poetry, Paterson, Williams is here concerned that his entrance into
representation has blocked his ability to participate in the lives of ordinary
citizens in the world outside the text. Doc is presented as aware of being
in a representation. When he dozes off, after hours of waiting for an Italian
woman to go into labor, he compares himself to a figure from a piece of

33. Ibid., 41.

art: "It was a pleasant position and as I lay there content, I thought as I often do of what painting it was in which I had seen men sleeping that way" (*FD*, 141).

Doc's awareness of being placed inside a work of art resembles Williams's situation in 1938 as a writer of stories about the self. By the late 1930s Williams's production of the "thing itself"—the imagistic poem—diminished in importance relative to his efforts to re-collect his poetry in uniform editions and to authorize his personal appearance through narrative fictions aimed at asserting his difference from other modernist contenders and establishing a greater market share. The spirit of experimentation that was evident in *Spring and All* had been replaced by a more systematic approach to literary dissemination in conventional narratives. Publicity for the maker of an act that was no longer new had been substituted for prolonged experimentation. Williams's feelings about what was gained and what was left behind by this transformation are evident in "A Night in June."

In the story Doc admits it has been at least two years since his last house call to deliver a baby. He also admits, ruefully, that "the hospital is the place for it. The equipment is far better" (*FD*, 137). Although his "kitchen style" practices are outdated, and his equipment bag is, in his word, a "relic," performing his role as if he were still Rivers's intern is presented as a pleasant challenge. I should pause here, as the narrator of the story does, over the significance of Doc picking up this "relic" equipment bag for the first time in years. It was given to him upon graduation from medical school by his uncle. If we combine fact (at least what Williams calls fact by telling it as autobiography) and fiction (which reflects back upon, and so in some sense creates, what we think of as "the real"), we can suggest that the uncle is a figure for Carlos Hoheb, Williams's maternal uncle, described in the autobiography as a "first-rate surgeon" who practiced first in Haiti and then, fleeing a revolution there in the early 1880s, in Panama; it was Hoheb in whose honor William Carlos Williams was given his middle name (*A*, 314). Doc's recovery of the uncle's bag in "A Night in June" is a sign that Williams is trying to reintegrate an earlier moment in his medical lineage into his acceptance of commercial medicine.

Whether or not we know the identity of the uncle as we read "A Night in June," Doc's dusting off of the contents of a bag that was still "where I had tossed it two or three years before under a table" suggests that it is an object laden with a symbolic charge. In the old black bag, Doc finds objects associated with both old and new aspects of the medical identity that he is searching to assert as uniquely his own. There are modern, branded goods: "I found a brand new hypodermic syringe with the manufacturer's name still shiny with black enamel on the barrel." But there is also a peculiar instrument from his early days as a physician that Doc has not expected to recover: "Also a pair of curved scissors I had been looking for for the last three years, thinking someone had stolen them" (FD, 137). The shape of the scissors connotes the craft of medical care performed by hand with few medical instruments; they appear to be a homemade item designed to exactly fit the physician's hand. Hidden or contained within the abandoned "relic," therefore, are emblems of both aspects of the medical identity that Doc has been searching for and that in his fictions Williams has been attempting to assert as his own. With his black bag, Doc links forms of caring that are associated with his Uncle Carlos with those that are "new," such as the quality control afforded by mass-produced, sterile objects. Doc employs these commercial goods in a setting that does not seem to be a part of modern times: "the kitchen where we stood was lighted by a somewhat damaged Welsbach mantel gaslight." His satchel is equipped with "one sterile umbilical tie," and "even the Argyrol was there, in tablet form, insuring the full potency of a fresh solution" (FD, 138). Doc can deliver to the patients on his house calls an ambulatory form of the advances offered by what in the *Autobiography* he will call "the big pharmaceutical houses," Argyrol being a trademark for a mild silver protein (A, 292).

The delivery of the baby girl in "A Night in June" takes all night. Doc's patience by itself connotes the slower pace of life implicit in the homeopathic credo of "letting nature take its course." During delivery, Williams stresses Doc's skill in making do with a minimum number of the tools available to the hospital physician, labeling with a human face and human hands a process that was becoming too reliant on mass-produced anesthetics. Even the most natural of human events, the giving of birth, now seemed to be a mechanical event devoid of the feeling of pain that is a sign of life. At the end of the successful delivery, Doc, as if responding to an afterthought, offers eyedrops to the baby to prevent gonorrhea. Although he believes the baby has "no chance" of having contracted gonorrhea because she is too clean, he agrees to follow to the letter the tenets of contemporary treatment: "Oh yes, the drops in the baby's eyes. No need. She's as clean as a beast. How do I know? Medical discipline says every case must have drops in the eyes. No chance of gonorrhea though here—but—Do it" (*FD*, 143).

Doc does not abandon "newness" or technological progress, and we wonder how Williams could refuse the use of new technologies, especially in medical science. He had invested his literary reputation with the idea that he had improved upon earlier models by tinkering with designs. How could he be fully in support of doing things the way they had always been done without succumbing to the conservative hegemony of fundamentalism associated with poets such as Eliot? The limit to the effectiveness of breaking with a conservation of the past, his criticism of "newness," in other words, is contained within his embrace of commercial medicine. Doc's ambivalent relationship to his administration of these goods is suggested by the cautious manner in which he applies them. He agrees to give the woman an injection of Pituitrin, another trademarked pharmaceutical product, but only after he has "asked her gently" if she wants this treatment: "I was cautious since the practice is not without danger." His willingness to consult the female patient before administering a vaccine is conjoined with knowledge of the properties of the drug and of their influence upon the body. We trust his relationship to modern science because we are told that he knew how to heal prior to the establishment of "normal" medical science. He is, therefore, in the rare position, perhaps one without fellow, of having a limited skepticism about medicine's claims while possessing the knowledge to understand these claims and to choose among them: "It is possible to get a ruptured uterus where the muscle has been stretched by many pregnancies if one does not know what one is doing" (*FD*, 141).

The pregnant Italian woman, who rarely speaks in sentences "more than three or four words long," is representative of the generation of neglected poor who immigrated to the eastern seaboard of the United States around the turn of the century. Doc wishes to enlist her as a patient, but she also represents a newly discovered constituency for Williams's poetry and fiction. We might say that she is a synecdoche for a neglected source of language, manners, and atmosphere for Williams's writings, as well as being part of a new audience to receive it. As was the case in *A Voyage to Pagany*, in which Evans's interest in the heroines of the expatriate culture such as Delise and Grace Black revealed that Williams's concern for the immigrant poor in the United States was not a part of his first instinct, Doc here admits that he has reversed his original judgment of the Italian woman: "This woman in her present condition would have seemed repulsive to me ten years ago—now, poor soul, I see her to be as clean as a cow that calves. The flesh of my arm lay against the flesh of her knee gratefully. It was I who was being comforted and soothed" (FD, 142).

Many years earlier Doc had failed to rescue her first baby from dying at birth. At that time he lacked the assistance or equipment now considered to be essential to making a difficult delivery: "without nurse, anesthetist, or even enough hot water in the place" (FD, 136). His unsuccessful effort to help her, however, gained for him a follower. Her allegiance to him is based on his perseverance and commitment to care, as well as on his tenderness toward—one could say love for and identification with—a neglected person, rather than on any spiritual power he might possess or on an egoistical show of his bravado. The woman remains loyal to his practice through seven other deliveries over two decades. In spite of the initial miscarriage, Doc recalls, "I won a friend and I found another—to admire, a sort of love for the woman" (FD, 136). This Italian woman "who could scarcely talk a word of English" is described as one empowered to value herself. Once a disenfranchised member of the European community, she has "recently come from the other side, a woman of great simplicity of character—docility, patience. . . . Devoted to her instincts and convictions and to me. Sometimes she'd cry out at her husband, as I got to know her later, with some high pitched animalistic sound when he would say something to her in Italian that I couldn't understand and I knew that she was holding out for me" (FD, 136). To Doc this woman is not "pure" and "clean" because she is a descendant of a genteel Victorian culture and so removed from the hardness of physical being in a body. She is "pure" and "clean" because she possesses an immediate relationship to the experience of pain. The experience of pain becomes an affirmation of presence, and a generator of a language of presence—tears. In the Italian woman Williams finds the connection between sound, sign, and human feeling.

To a degree, Doc ignores rational and progressive understandings of healing ("the exaggerated way") in favor of what he calls "the older school." This "older school" resembles the tradition of botanism, mid-wifery, self-healing, and folk remedies that self-made physicians such as Thomson employed in the nineteenth century to counteract the invasive practices of the heroic school. In the story, the debate between different medical sects is synthesized in a dream sequence in which Doc becomes converted to the method of Rivers. The "heroic school," now allied to commercial systems of medical administration, is the target of the first-person narrator's testimony and critique:

> Then I fell asleep and, in my half sleep began to argue with myself—or some imaginary power—of science and humanity. Our exaggerated ways will have to pull in their horns, I said. We've learned from one teacher and neglected another. Now that I'm older, I'm finding the older school.
>
> The pituitary extract and other simple devices represent science. Science, I dreamed, has crowded the stage more than is necessary. The process of selection will simplify the application. It touches us too crudely now, all newness is over-complex. I couldn't tell whether I was asleep or awake.
>
> But without science, without pituitrin, I'd be here till noon or maybe—what? Some others wouldn't wait so long but rush her now. A carefully guarded shot of pituitrin—ought to save her at least much exhaustion—if not more. But I don't want to have anything happen to her. (*FD*, 141)

After this scene of a partial conversion back to his humble origins as an American folk healer, Doc moves further away from his impulse to rely on anesthetics, rather than on the course of nature, to deliver a baby. He comes to embody an old-fashioned attitude toward his profession, an attitude in which the use of even hygienic gloves might disrupt the intimate, tactile concern for the body of the pregnant woman. Williams creates a beautiful scene of a rare form of health care that feels intimate without seeming to violate a woman's body:

> Maybe I'd better give you a still larger dose, I said. She made no demur. Well, let me see if I can help you first. I sat on the edge of the bed while the sister-in-law held the candle again glancing at the window where the daylight was growing. With my left hand steering the child's head, I used my ungloved right hand outside on her bare abdomen to press upon the fundus. The woman and I then got to work. Her two hands grabbed me at first a little timidly about the right wrist and forearm. Go ahead, I said. Pull hard. I welcomed the feel of her hands and the strong pull. It quieted me in the way the whole house had quieted me all night. (*FD*, 142)

Through his inner struggle, Doc redeems the "folk" tactics in opposition to the privileged system of commercial medicine. He achieves the balance he desires between freedom from the restraints of establishment practice and an acceptance of that practice—a balance that was beyond Rivers and beyond the young Doc. Intuition and tenderness now enhance, rather than oppose, a textbook kind of professional care. As was the case with Rivers and his long tenure in the community, Doc's authority to heal is now related to his record of persistent care without regard for lucrative gain. He has gained a form of emotional trust from his patients that is unrelated to their awareness of his medical background: "This one would make my eighth attendance on her, her ninth labor," Doc says; "We'd been through this many times before" (*FD*, 137, 141).

As Williams himself pointed out ("The imagination uses the phraseology of science" and medicine and poetry "amount for me to nearly the same thing"), and as many critics, among them Robert F. Gish and John Hildebidle, have said, Williams viewed as virtually synonymous his work as "word man" and as "medicine man."[34] I have taken their observations

34. In "The Doctor's Black Bag: William Carlos Williams' Passaic River Stories," George Monteiro sees Williams experiencing "conflicts between his learned professionalism and his effective impulse" (77). Monteiro associates the latter with a humanistic tradition that Williams, in "A Night in June," calls "the older school." The former is rational science. Monteiro shows that when Williams lets his emotional concern for his patients get the better of his professional discretion, the tension often leads to his violent treatment of his patients. The best example of this occurs in "The Use of Force."

In "Take Off Your Clothes: William Carlos Williams, Science, and the Diagnostic Encounter," Hildebidle recognizes that the technical or scientific ambience in which Williams wishes to bathe his literary productions is indicative of a modernist reaction to romanticism's view of art and science as antagonistic: "Williams is unique among Modernist writers in having something very like a professional training in science . . . it is hardly surprising to find him turning to science in his effort to define the nature of his own task as artist" (11). Hildebidle argues that what is "scientific" about Williams's poetry, and what links it to the diagnostic task of the physician making a house call, is the fidelity to the observation of empirical data, and that this observation occurs within a dynamic and processional human interchange between patient and doctor. Williams's viewing of bodies that he is never confident he will be able to cure as remarkable and as memorable provides a kind of artistic permanence. Diagnosis, Hildebidle adds, is the bringing of the particular event—the individual sick body—into a preestablished narrative design with the cure as outcome.

In "Word Man/Medicine Man: *In the American Grain*," Gish connects Williams's belief in the power of storytelling to native American and folk traditions: "For the tribe, the people, the folk story-telling serves not just to report events and occurrences but somehow, whether in an incantatory or reportorial way, to bring about healing and restoration, to reinstate health over illness, community over isolation, and the better life over the worse" (23).

to mean that when Williams is writing explicitly *about* medicine, readers are being invited to translate this overt subject back to his implicit subject matter, which is his claim to a therapeutic function for his poetry. This function of his poetry is conveyed to the readers of his short fiction through an image of the poet in possession of a priestly ability (because of the priestly position of access to the private accounts of others) to hear confessions (in the colloquial style in which these testimonial stories are written) and to absolve sins.[35] In the medical fictions, Williams is suggesting, covertly, that his sensitivity in capturing the language, stories, and everyday experiences of the working poor of urban New Jersey is a form of ennoblement that in its way could prevent death by enhancing the meaning of life. In *Paterson,* the poet will go so far as to say that because "The language is missing them," his townspeople "die also / incommunicado."[36]

In *Protocols of Reading,* Robert Scholes attempts to deconstruct the binary opposition between poetry as a transcendental object, which moves us toward contemplation, and other forms of rhetoric, particularly advertising, which move us toward consuming without considering what or why we are consuming. Scholes wants to undo the distinction between poetry and advertising. What brings his discussion to mind as I end this chapter is his description of reading a number of "seductive" poems by American poets, including Walt Whitman, Mary Oliver, Emily Dickinson, and William Carlos Williams. Scholes argues that when we accept the images of the world that the poet constructs, we are also accepting a point of view about how to value reality and how to organize knowledge. Borrowing the phrase *bewildering minute* from a letter written by T. S. Eliot to Stephen Spender, and also borrowing from the semiotician Charles Morris's understanding of poetry as "discourse which is primarily appraisive-valuative," Scholes describes the way in which "textual economy is marked, in particular, by exchanges of power and pleasure."[37]

---

35. Thomas Hugh Crawford argues that this role of the doctor-confessor is "an exertion of hegemonic power coercing proper moral behavior from patients" ("The Rhetoric of Medical Authority: The Early Writing of William Carlos Williams," 80). See also his *Modernism, Medicine, and William Carlos Williams.*

36. Williams, *Paterson,* 11.

37. Robert Scholes, *Protocols of Reading,* 108.

By "textual economy" Scholes means that when a reader "surrenders" to the pleasure of the images and the music of the poetic text, or, in my case, when a reader is won over to Doc's side by the beautiful description of a natural childbirth in a Williams story, the reader has entered into an exchange that entails for the gaining of pleasure a loss of some sovereignty. Scholes argues that this exchange must be critically examined, for if it is not an acceptance will take place, if not of a product for sale, as is obviously the case in the Budweiser beer ad that Scholes examines in *Protocols of Reading,* then of the ideological positions implicit within a poem, such as the high modernism or high Anglicanism of Eliot, or Whitman's connection of the human body to the body of religious beliefs, or the feminist perspective implicit within a poem by Adrienne Rich. Scholes's point is that we cannot consider poetry (or creative prose fiction) to be a discourse uninvolved in persuasion: "Poetry [does] not merely record what men have found significant, but plays a dynamic role in the development and integration of valuative attitudes and explicit evaluations."[38]

Scholes does not suggest that we refrain from taking pleasure in the textual/erotic experience of giving over our critical judgment for that "bewildering minute" of pleasure, or that we not accept Anglicanism, modernism, feminism, or Whitman's religion of physical sensation. He does suggest, however, that by analyzing critically the way a rhetoric of persuasion is employed through the cultural object we can return from the "bewildering minute" of aesthetic stimulation better able to "follow the exchange of pleasure and power in any textual situation"—that is, in a better position to make ethical judgments about the system of value being promoted. A function of criticism should be to enable us to step away from the seductive rhetoric of a literary work and allow us to at least admit that the text is a form of a discourse engaging in a show of power to fulfill the desire of its author. This rhetorical aspect of a story such as "A Night in June" not only suggests the point that Williams consistently made, which is that "medicine" and "literature," if directed to those who need the therapy each can provide, can serve the health of a community in similar ways, but also suggests that the language of these stories is part of a discourse/power relationship, although the terms employed tend to be those ignored in the usual hierarchical equations of power. Williams

38. Ibid., 111.

employed the previously identified discourse of high cultural status—the poem, or in this case the story that was promoted and distributed as a serious step in the direction of modern literature in its objectivist phase—to represent insufficiently regarded materials.

The outcome of this high cultural identification with common materials was the validation and renewal of dignity for the class of persons Williams represents. But such literary work also enforces the exclusive systems of discourse that might be said to maintain the very material and representational imbalances that the author claimed his project opposed.

Four

A Taste of Fortune

In the Money and the New Directions Phase

I.

In his *Autobiography,* Williams embraces a classic tenet of modernism by separating the literature of "contemplation" from the literature of "pulp" and claims he set his writing against the "calculated viciousness of a money grubbing society" (*A,* 158). As Herbert Leibowitz notes, Williams presents himself in that late text as a pure poet unaware of the intricacies of how reputations were constructed among the expatriates in Paris and uninterested in achieving commercial success in New York. In another recent study of *The Autobiography,* Ann W. Fisher-Wirth describes Williams's Franklinesque innocence as his "word for the source of his power."[1]

Leibowitz notes that in the chapters describing his 1924 visit to Paris, Williams presented himself "as Doc Williams from Rutherford, a suburban yokel cutting a sorry figure in the modish world of art and wealth." Leibowitz, however, shrewdly notices that this impersonation of "the artless provincial rogue" was a "ruse" that enabled Williams "to get literary business done." Leibowitz understands Williams's claim to innocence in psychological terms as a prop that allowed him, like a child, to take "the royal road to approval and reward." It was like a "second skin that shields a person from attack."[2] While allowing this psychological interpretation

---

1. Leibowitz, "'You Can't Beat Innocence': *The Autobiography of William Carlos Williams*"; Fisher-Wirth, *William Carlos Williams and Autobiography: The Woods of His Own Nature,* 33.
2. "'You Can't Beat Innocence,'" 36.

to stand, I will follow up on Leibowitz's suggestion and take literally the premise that "innocence" was a mask that enabled Williams "to get his literary business done." I will consider Williams's account of himself in the context of his complex, at times paradoxical, relationship to the literary marketplace(s)—both avant-garde and commercial—during the period in which his self-fashioning as a "literary innocent" took place through the fictional narrative he published with New Directions in 1940, *In the Money.*

In his readings of the Hemingway and Sheeler advertisements in *Life,* Williams accepted with equivocation that the criteria for literary value included the successful display among the general public of the iconography of the maker. He understood the development of a public self to be among his tasks as an American poet writing in a commercial age. In the 1930s and 1940s, Williams's creative interests tended toward that end. His concern for the spreading of the images of the artist in *Life* contradicted, and therefore caused me to question, commonplace assumptions about modern poetry and its disinterested relationship to popular culture and to advertising. The separation of "high" and "mass" art was a commonplace assumption of critics in the 1940s and 1950s, especially those associated with the *Partisan Review,* influenced as they were by the Frankfurt School of critics who had seen firsthand the dangerous connection between the "mass cult" and the totalitarian regimes then emerging in Europe. Remarks by art critic Clement Greenberg about the avant-garde poet's relationship to popular culture are paradigmatic: "Retiring from public altogether, the avant-garde poet or artist sought to maintain the high level of his art by both narrowing and raising it to the expression of an absolute in which all relativities and contradictions would be either resolved or beside the point: 'Art for art's sake' and 'pure poetry' appear, and subject matter or content becomes something to be avoided like a plague."[3]

In fact, as recent studies of Harriet Monroe by Claire Badaracco, of T. S. Eliot and Ezra Pound by Lawrence Rainey, and of James Joyce by Jennifer Wicke and Joseph Heininger have shown, modernism and hucksterism were often closely related forms of discourse.[4] Although avant-garde writing has been perceived as an institution that stood outside, or opposed

3. "Avant-Garde and Kitsch," 23.
4. Badaracco, "Writers and Their Public Appeal: Harriet Monroe's Publicity Techniques"; Rainey, "The Price of Modernism"; Wicke, *Advertising Fictions;* Heininger,

to, market conditions, the task of modernist impresarios such as Pound, when he sought to expose Eliot's long poem to a large audience in such popular magazines as *Vanity Fair* and *The Dial* was, according to Rainey, to transform modernism from a "minority culture" to "one supported by an important institutional and financial apparatus." Harriet Monroe, as well, understood her literary magazine, *Poetry Chicago,* to be the poetry industry's "house organ" or "trade publication."[5] Monroe's sense of her magazine as the organ of a publishing venture speaks to the fact that she did her editorial work during a moment in industrial capitalism when the production, rather than the consumption, of goods was emphasized. Williams looked at Sheeler and Hemingway in *Life,* and wrote his own narratives for New Directions, at a later moment in economic history when the cultural modeling of persons through the consumption of goods replaced the "use" value of the products themselves. His prose fictions reflect his affiliation with this postindustrial moment in American economic culture.

We have been taught to think of market pressures as somehow distracting writers from literary creativity. By reconsidering an overlooked but intriguing part of the Williams canon, the second installment of the Stecher Trilogy of novels, *In the Money,* I hope to adjust these commonplace assumptions. The tensions between the poet and James Laughlin, as well as the pressures Williams faced in resuscitating his career as a poet, generated authentic creativity at a time when Williams was unclear about his literary direction. *The Autobiography* was not the only narrative in which he presented an "innocent" main character in order to conceal his own professional ambitions. Williams's shift of emphasis during his first years with New Directions from impersonal lyrics toward didactic fiction, and his attention to telling stories that mirrored the way he wanted his literary reputation to be known by ordinary readers, occurred when he most acutely sensed his lack of renown in comparison to other modern poets. Laughlin could provide the funds to print his works but for ideological and personal reasons could not fully accept Williams as an author interested in reaching out to ordinary readers through commercial appeals. Williams

---

"Molly Bloom's Ad Language and Goods Behavior: Advertising as Social Communication in *Ulysses.*"

5. Rainey, "The Price of Modernism," 294; Badaracco, "Writers and Their Public Appeal," 39.

reacted to Laughlin's separation of the literature of "contemplation" and the literature of "pulp" by promoting his own image as a poet through covert depictions of himself and his literary competitors *within* his New Directions writings. The ruse of "innocence" described by Leibowitz and Fisher-Wirth that allowed Laughlin to think of Williams as a "literary saint" for whom commercial interest was a "sin" is mirrored in the smoke screen of innocence created by Joe Stecher in his quest to supplant the firm that holds a monopoly over the printing of money orders in *In the Money.*

The ruse of "innocence" in Williams's self-characterizations is also a structural feature of the novel insofar as Williams wrote ironic fictions for New Directions. He discusses one thing (printing money orders) while on another level he is addressing something else of greater personal importance to him (the question of printing literature for money). The novels that Williams wrote for New Directions were supposed to catapult him to a stronger market share. In content, they illustrated his conflicted relationship to what he calls in *White Mule* "the United States of America—money," and how the inscription of his literary identity as what Anne Janowitz has called "a thoroughly American, though not usually *poetic* type, the indigenous 'tinker,' or inventor" should take place.[6] Williams's ambivalence toward his new contract with Laughlin, his transition from obscurity to fame, his break with his friend and literary ally, Pound, his shame about making money from his allegedly anticommercial writing, and his doubts, at age fifty-five, about his own literary prowess, all influenced his decision to write *In the Money* and became the basis for the novel's deep structure.

In contrast to Laughlin's wish to ignore the "sinful" side of letters, Williams hoped the New Directions contract would be his springboard toward greater sales as well as an increased respect from other writers. If only Laughlin could think of his writing as merchandise. "You are young at the game of publishing," wrote Williams to Laughlin in January 1938. "[It] was distressing to me to have people asking as they still ask: Where can I get [*White Mule*]? Nobody seems to have heard of it" (*SL,* 27, 28). Over the course of their correspondence, Williams presented to Laughlin a tutorial in shrewd salesmanship. This education in the "publishing game" included advice about book design, information about why Laughlin should publish

---

6. Williams, *White Mule,* 13; Janowitz, "*Paterson:* An American Contraption," 301.

writers such as Louis Zukofsky in order to insure a distinct identity for the new firm, explanations of why the poet felt firms such as Random House and Harcourt Brace could better present his work than could New Directions, and instructions about which journals to place his lesser poems in to provide "good advertising" for the anticipated major effort, *Paterson.*[7]

In a typical letter, Williams acted as salesman for his poetry: "So, in the end, make your arrangements for distribution as complete as possible, especially make more detailed arrangements for advertising my stuff than you did with *White Mule.* I think inadequate management of sales cost us plenty that time" (*SL*, 28). At issue in this case was the production of *Complete Collected Poems (1906-1938).* After a flirtation with its publication at Oxford University Press that Williams said "would have meant a certain prestige for me which I have wanted, not too seriously, all my life," the work eventually appeared in 1938 from New Directions. *Complete Collected Poems* (1906-1938) was part of the publication strategy developed by Laughlin and the poet to bring all of Williams's work back into print as a set. Eight Williams titles appeared in the New Directions catalog from 1937, when Williams published *White Mule,* the first self-proclaimed "winner" with New Directions, until 1946. The New Directions collection marked by far the most concentrated attempt by any publisher to make Williams's work available to ordinary readers in a uniform edition. Williams, however, did not believe the books were marketed aggressively enough by Laughlin for him to reach a greater market share.

Laughlin said he published writers such as Williams and E. E. Cummings in order to enhance the public's taste for serious work. "I'll get a writers' press started that will be a force able to fight the New York bastards," Laughlin wrote to Williams, referring to the commercial publishing houses (*SL*, 22). Although Williams's poetry was set in opposition to commercial writing in that he wanted readers to perceive everyday objects from an

---

7. Williams advised Laughlin, "Zukofsky's *A* is another matter. It can't sell but may bring the press a certain distinction" (*SL*, 17-18). Besides repaying the debt he owed Zukofsky for publishing his first collected poems with Objectivist Press in 1934 and for providing advice and support throughout this period, Williams is also saying that all New Directions authors will profit through association with an author involved in high modern difficulty.

aesthetic, rather than a utilitarian, point of view, Laughlin's vision of a united group of experimental writers did not take into account divisions among the modern poets. It was about T. S. Eliot, and not about the New York publishing houses, that Williams wrote to Laughlin on March 26, 1939:

> Eliot is a cultured gentleman and cultured gentlemen are always likely to undersell the market. . . . I'm glad you like his verse but I'm warning you, the only reason it doesn't smell is that it's synthetic. Maybe I'm wrong but I distrust that bastard more than any writer I know in the world today. He can write. Granted. But—it's like walking into a church to me. I can't do it without a bad feeling at the pit of my stomach: nothing has been learned there since the simplicities were prevented from becoming multiform by arrest of growth—Birdseye Foods, suddenly frozen at 50 degrees below zero under pressure at perfect maturity, immediately after being picked from the canes. (*SL*, 40–41)

Williams elides the difference between poetry, religion, and commercial goods by comparing literary authors who "freeze" the development of poetic growth through their allegiance to prescribed forms of religious worship to those who market fresh produce through an innovative process that sacrifices further growth of the organic thing by converting it into a widely available packaged good distinguished by its logo and brand name.

Later in the same letter Williams directs Laughlin to "plan to print" a second impression of *In the American Grain* (1925) as the first in a series called the New Classics, which would make out-of-print modernist titles again available for a dollar apiece (*SL*, 43). Williams explains that he has chosen to repackage old work rather than to offer Laughlin the second installment of *White Mule* (*In the Money*) because he regrets that he is "not writing these days" (*SL*, 41). The bitter critique of Eliot for disrupting the organic growth of poetry by pressuring it into an easily consumed but now frozen or deadened form shows that Williams perceived with regret the direction in which his own creative energies had taken him: repackaging and selling old work as the result of his struggle for literary acknowledgment. Williams believed that the cultural war he waged against Eliot, presented as a struggle among competing brands of nationally marketed goods in an unconcealed market economy, had restricted his freedom to grow in "multiform" directions as a poet. Williams not only felt that his path toward literary creation—a path he described as originating "hot from the blood" as opposed to that stemming from "the tradition of literature purely"—was more difficult to follow than Eliot's and Pound's, but he also felt that their "camp" actively sought to sabotage his production:

> [The "hot from the blood" technique] is always under the great handicap of monumental invention for its contents and form. But the pimps of literature [Eliot and Pound] seize the position due great imagination and all its prerogatives and puff themselves up at [as?] the true artist.
>
> This wouldn't be so bad if they did not at the same time actively, very often, drive down the already sufficiently harassed man seeking to rescue and build up a present world in his creations. . . . By this they are actively the enemies of the highest reaches of the artist's imagination and will always be the ones to keep the artist down, seldom to help him up. (SL, 44)

Williams's version of international modernist literary culture is brutal and paranoid, a dramatization in the form of a gangster story of Harold Bloom's notion of poetic agon. Eliot and Pound are the primary conspirators in a plot to sabotage his bid for literary renown. This vision is reflected in the battle to secure a government printing contract that takes place in *In the Money*. The independent outsider, Stecher, must, like Williams against "the enemies of the highest reaches of the artist's imagination," struggle against an international firm of thugs that conspires against his professional success, Wynnewood and Crossman.[8]

The pressure Williams placed on Laughlin to advertise his work belies the poet's subscription to the publisher's view that modernism and huckstering were mutually exclusive practices. Williams, for instance, appreciated Laughlin's idea of reprinting what was advertised in the *New Directions in Poetry and Prose* annuals in the late 1930s as "his most famous prose work"—the neglected *In the American Grain*—as the first title in the New Classics series so that it would be available at the height of the 1939 Christmas buying season. As early as November 19, 1937, only five months after Williams described *White Mule* to Laughlin as the "splendid book, excellently presented" (*SL*, 7; May 31, 1937), he fired off

---

8. Williams, likewise, called the university the seat of the "worst scandal of our day" for refusing to accept poetry as an antitraditional "field of action" based in local language and local setting. See Mariani, *A New World Naked*, 290.

the first in a series of threats to leave New Directions for a larger and more established house that would persist until he did leave to publish prose works with Random House beginning with the collection of stories *Make Light of It* in 1950:[9]

> Many unusual advances are being made to me these days though most of them are sterile enough; *White Mule* did get my name around. . . . Tentatively I've been thinking that it might be wisest to approach a regular commercial publisher concerning it [his book on his mother] when it is ready. Harcourt, Brace once smiled at me and Simon and Schuster grinned broadly. . . . We know now that it comes out of the nose. I won't make a move without a talk with you. (*SL*, 12–13)

Laughlin's reply registers his fear over losing Williams:

> You are the cornerstone of New Directions and if you left me I think I wouldn't be able to go on with it. I have built my plans around you. You are my symbol of everything that is good in writing, and if you go over to the enemy I just won't know where the hell I'm at.
>
> Because they are the enemy. Look what they've done to our kind. Look what they've done to you yourself. Would they take the *Mule?*
>
> Now that you have made a success they want you, they think they can exploit you.
>
> It isn't a case of publishers. It is a case of life and death, or right and wrong, of good writers starving and lousy writers going to Palm Beach. . . . You are different from their trade. You are literature and not merchandise. (*SL*, 13–14)

The tone of Laughlin's reply reminds us that he was only twenty-three in 1937, a student on leave from Harvard. In 1937, Williams was fifty-four. In the letter, Williams is described by Laughlin in idealized terms as a "symbol" of all that is "good." Laughlin cannot accept that Williams might think of writing as "merchandise," or worse, that he might write out of jealousy over the success of other respected literary reformers such as Pound. It was Pound, after all, who had first suggested to Laughlin that he publish Williams's work.

---

9. In *Remembering William Carlos Williams,* Laughlin accuses his former sales and promotion manager, David McDowell, of courting Williams away from New Directions to Random House, where McDowell had been promised a job by Bennett Cerf if he "could come bearing a three-book contract with Bill" (32).

In order to hold on to his "cornerstone" author, Laughlin offered Williams practical reasons for staying with New Directions. Far from altruistic, these arguments were grounded in the specific marketing advantages the poet could gain by staying with New Directions for the long run. Laughlin mentioned that although Harcourt Brace had published a novel by Kay Boyle that sold twice as many copies as *White Mule*, Harcourt then refused to publish her poetry. "It's like that," Laughlin told Williams. "They want merchandise. They don't care about writing" (*SL*, 15). In contrast to this careless treatment of Boyle by a large trade firm, Laughlin told Williams he would always be "head man" at New Directions, even if his works did not sell immediately. Further, Laughlin assured Williams his works would remain in print because of the prestige they afforded to the entire operation: "With you, New Directions does stand for something and the people it prints will get a start and a break. . . . If you stick with me and Ezra perhaps comes in we'll be able to make a machine that can fight the New York Machine" (*SL*, 15). Beyond this flattery, and in spite of his persistent outrage at the way book selling had turned into a contest of escalating advertising budgets, Laughlin agreed to wage his version of a selling campaign on Williams's behalf. The promotional package involved printing or reprinting five volumes of Williams prose and "a good [critical] book about you"; the latter, eventually finished by Vivienne Koch in 1950, was the first full-length appraisal of Williams. The package also included "a steady barrage of Williams . . . backed by articles and reviews and word-of-mouth advertising. Also regular advertising where it is likely to do good. Thus, in the present N[ew] D[irections] you have a double page spread and we are sending along return cards with it" (*SL*, 16).[10]

This package, coupled with Laughlin's personal support ("You are the cornerstone"), convinced Williams to stay. In a letter of December 4 he backed down from his threat to leave New Directions by offering the transparent excuse that he thought it was Laughlin who was uninterested in his work, and not the other way around: "So be it. My chief reason for speaking of a publisher other than New Directions was that I didn't think you wanted to handle a book as bulky as the biography is likely to be. . . .

10. The double-page spread became a regular feature of the "advertisement" section of the New Directions annuals from 1937 to 1940. In 1937, 1938, and 1939 two-page spreads for Williams's work were featured, and in 1940 a one-page advertisement was offered.

I am convinced that my best chances now lie with you, looked at quite coldly. . . . It was impossible for me to know before this last letter what your plans could be" (*SL*, 17).

Williams decided in 1937 to stay with New Directions, although he remained a pushy and disgruntled author. He consistently scolded Laughlin for failing to treat his writing as merchandise. His New Directions fiction, especially *In the Money*, became a complicated fusion of his conflicted relationship to art and commerce, as Williams reflected in the novel on his professional concerns about the publishing contract, and on his ambivalence about yoking financial profit for the maker to the work of designing and printing a culture's signs of symbolic and economic value.

II.

Williams composed *In the Money* between August 1938 and the bleak winter of 1939–1940, as World War II escalated with Russian involvement and Japan's war on China. It was published by New Directions on October 29, 1940. Williams discussed its composition and initial publication with Laughlin in a number of letters, two of which I will quote at some length. These letters suggest Williams's ambivalence about commercial publishing, for even though he curses the big firms he still urges Laughlin to do business with them. The letters also reveal his hopes that the novel will be a moneymaker, as well as his growing disenchantment with the politics of Pound. This juxtaposition of discussions of *In the Money* with expressions of concern about Pound's emphasis on politics and economics rather than on poetry provides evidence that when Williams was composing his fictive "business battle," he was also planning his assault, in displaced form, against Pound's dominant status in letters by attacking his social views.

In the novel, paradoxically, Williams adopted his own version of Pound's Social Credit theory as his argument in favor of his receipt of a form of social credit (the Laughlin contract) for the work he had already done on behalf of modern letters. On June 7, 1939, Williams wrote to Laughlin that he "must get at the new *White Mule*":

> By the way, I've decided on the title for volume two: *A Taste of Fortune*.
> It has a somewhat musty flavor at that but it goes, I think, with the story. I
> did think of using, *In the Money*. Like that better? The second is snappier
> and more up to date. . . . Suppose you go into the plant? How about having
> somebody like Simon & Schuster or the other bastards buy up the sheets of

the original *White Mule* and bind the new volume up with them into one glorious whole. Just an idea. This time it's got to be pushed hard. (*SL,* 49–50)

In the same letter, Williams mentioned that Pound had spent the night of June 5 with the Williamses. He "spread himself on the divan all evening and discoursed to the family in his usual indistinct syllables," Williams wrote. While he grants in the letter that Pound's views are "important" and "inspiring," Williams also feels that Pound is "sunk . . . unless he can shake the fog of Fascism out of his brain during the next few years which I seriously doubt that he can do." Williams had supported the Loyalist rebellion against Franco's government in Spain, and it was in regard to this event that his split with Pound became permanent: "You can't argue away wanton slaughter of innocent women and children by the neo-scholasticism of a controlled economy program. Shit with a Hitler who lauds the work of his airmen in Spain and so shit with Pound too if he can't stand up and face his questioners on the point" (*SL,* 49).

In a letter written on December 14, 1940, less than two months after his novel's publication, Williams argued that Pound's political views proved he could not be trusted as a cultural worker in the United States. Williams reported to Laughlin the happiness of his wife, Flossie, "with her check," the initial royalty from *In the Money:* "[I]t will buy her a good coat with a fur collar! If there's to be more so much the better, good for you too." The rest of this letter shows that, even though Pound did not implicate Williams in his "fireside chats" over Rome Radio until July 30, 1941, Williams was becoming riled by Pound's letters to him from Rome during 1939 and 1940, the period in which he was composing the novel that spoke of a separation from an earlier professional allegiance. Pound's views, particularly in their unabashed anti-Semitism and in their support of Franco's crushing of the Loyalists, were abhorrent and worthy of censorship, even from old friends and supporters of his theories on monetary reform. Williams, however, capitalized on this political critique by suggesting that Pound's arguments on behalf of Mussolini were evidence that what Williams calls the original literary and intellectual "measuring" of Pound as the great teacher versus Williams as the naive pupil demanded the reversal supplied by the *In the Money* plot:

Ezra is an important poet, we must forgive him his stupidities. . . . But I prefer not to have to do with him in any way. He wants to patronize me. Don't tell me this isn't so for I know better. His letters are insults, the mewings of an 8th grade teacher. That's where he thinks I exist in relation to his catastrophic knowledge of affairs, his blinding judgements of contemporary values. . . . [M]y perceptions overtook him twenty years ago—not however my accomplishments. When I have finished, if I can go on to the finish, there'll be another measuring. (*SL,* 58-59)

Williams believed Pound's focus on economics diminished his concern for the craft of poetry. As early as 1934, however, Williams had turned his own attention to the relationship between economics and poetry. In a review of George Oppen's *Discrete Series* titled "The New Poetical Economy," Williams argued that a new social order could be implemented through attention to the details of crafts and industries, including the way poems were written:

> An imaginable new social order would require a skeleton of severe discipline for its realization and maintenance. Thus by a sharp restriction to essentials the seriousness of a new order is brought to realization. Poetry might turn this condition to its own ends. Only by being an object sharply defined and without redundancy will its form project whatever meaning is required of it. . . . [Oppen's] poems seek an irreducible minimum in the means for the achievement of the objective, no loose bolts or beams sticking out unattached at one end or put there to hold up a rococo cupid or a concrete saint, nor either to be a frame for a portrait of mother or a deceased wife.[11]

In *In the Money* Williams adopts the language of economics to discuss his relationship to literary forms. The *economic* aspect of the "irreducible minimum" of his imagist lyrics becomes the criteria through which Williams wants his own reputation as poet to be judged. In his description of *In the Money*'s Joe Stecher, Williams celebrates a pragmatic economic reformer whose philosophy of printing money orders resembles Williams's own theories about literary precision and his conception of the poem as a well-designed machine. Such a conception of the poem, according to Alec Marsh, reduces the usurious aspect of poetic language through its materialist focus.[12] Williams's objectivist style reduced language's ability to extend reality through the use of metaphor.

11. "The New Poetical Economy," 223-24.
12. Marsh, "Stevens and Williams: The Economics of Metaphor."

This limiting of metaphor allowed Williams's poetry to function as a relatively nonrhetorical object of interpersonal mediation. If properly designed, the poems could reflect the actual world without distorting its value in the process. Even when he employed the language of economic reform to discuss the best ways to produce and distribute wealth, Williams was addressing the question of how to write poems and how to distribute them. When Williams was asked to present an artist's point of view on Social Credit at a 1936 conference headed by Gorham Munson in Charlottesville, Virginia, he entitled his talk "The Attack on Credit Monopoly from a Cultural Viewpoint." Along with criticizing American communists and reiterating points Pound had made about Van Buren, Confucius, Hamilton, and Jefferson, Williams, as Wendy Flory reports, "spoke of his own difficulties in publishing his work under the present economic system."[13]

The poet's political function, Williams implicitly argued in places such as *In the Money,* was to focus on repairing the line and the idiom of the poem so that they reflected, rather than distorted, actual contemporary life in the United States. He abhorred the making of critiques of social systems extraneous to the poem, which was of course the practice of Pound, who in 1939 was lobbying the United States Congress and trying to meet with President Franklin Roosevelt and Secretary of Agriculture Henry Wallace to discuss money theory. Flory writes:

> Pound's role as a prophet of economic reform is clearly, in his view, merely a continuation of his role as reformer of poetry. . . . After World War I, it became clear that "cleansing [the] language" was not a stringent enough measure to protect the West from the recurrence of such a catastrophe. Once he heard Douglas's promise that his system of economic reform could cut to the very root of the causes of war, it was not just logical but even inevitable that Pound would give the Social Credit cause priority among his allegiances.
>
> Yet he overlooked the very real differences between being the focal point of the Imagist movement and being a central authority on the reform of the economic systems of America and Europe, which was, in fact, how he saw himself. . . . He chose to see no reason why he should not be able to have as much impact on the world of international finance as he had had in the London literary world before the war.[14]

13. Flory, *The American Ezra Pound,* 79–80.
14. Ibid., 83.

I have tried to establish that even when Williams was fashioning a professional identity for himself as a tinkering inventor, physicist, physician, printer, or business manager, these masks were situational tropes meant to affirm a specific role for him as a modern American poet. In contrast, Pound's career moved in the opposite direction, from a concern for literary development to economic and political crusading that was not a veil for literary placement.

III.

The model for Joe Stecher often has been identified as Paul Herman, a printer and the father of Williams's wife, Florence. Herman died, apparently accidentally, of a self-inflicted gunshot wound on March 26, 1930. According to Paul Mariani, Stecher's story constituted a "sympathetic living portrait of Paul." This is true enough, but it does not account for the nearly ten-year gap between Herman's death and Williams's composition of the novel in part based on his father-in-law's story. I find it interesting to ask why Herman's professional story was on Williams's mind around 1940. One possible answer involves Williams's identification with Herman as a betrayed member of a literary community that he believed he had once served faithfully. Herman's alienation from the literary community of Rutherford began in 1914, when he supported Germany against England as World War I began. Herman was ostracized for his pro-German stance by fellow members of a locally prestigious literary club known as the Fortnightly Reading Club. Herman, who had just been named president of the club, lost the respect of its members when in 1916 he cast the only vote against sending a letter to President Woodrow Wilson in support of the British cause. From that point on, Mariani writes, "many of his closest friends refused to have anything more to do with him . . . the Hermans were ostracized from the community for all practical purposes, and they soon left Rutherford for Monroe." Williams implicated himself in his father-in-law's problems by joining the Carlstadt Turnverein, a gymnastics club that was rumored to support the Kaiser. In a 1916 editorial in the *Rutherford American,* another doctor condemned "a certain young doctor in town who was openly supporting the Kaiser."[15] That Paul Herman's most important conflict occurred within the domain of letters, the Reading Club, allows us to link his ostracism to that felt by Williams in the 1920s

15. *A New World Naked,* 304, 22, 120.

and afterward, when he was refused admittance to the avant-garde literary circle in London and in Paris before fleeing back to Rutherford in 1924.

Mariani's indispensable biographical commentary aside, *In the Money* has not received sufficient critical attention. In his essay on the Stecher Trilogy, Neil Baldwin has come the closest to linking Williams's professional struggles with Stecher's. Baldwin correctly claims that the novel "moves closer to personal history and documentary [than] *White Mule*" and that it "is a record of Williams's encounter with his changing time." Instead of pursuing the idea of an "encounter with his changing time" by examining the relationship between Williams's attitudes toward his New Directions contract and what Baldwin describes as "Joe's preoccupations about the approaching competition for a contract he needs to gain," however, Baldwin links Stecher's attempt to start a printing firm to Williams's struggle in the first decade of the twentieth century to start a medical practice: "Joe is frustrated as he finds out just how difficult it is to be a small businessman with large expectations. It must have been equally difficult for a country doctor with two young sons to function at the outset of his career."[16]

Other critics have discussed the novel, but their interpretations do not come so close as Baldwin's to connecting Stecher's professional situation to Williams's. Linda Wagner and James E. B. Breslin have discussed the novel as symptomatic of the poet's general absorption in the late 1930s with issues of business and as an example of Williams's working in the 1930s and 1940s in a genre considered a lesser one than poetry. Working in prose, Breslin argued, allowed Williams to experiment with naturalistic techniques while waiting for liberation as a poet.[17] While these observations are reasonable, Breslin and Wagner, like Baldwin, neglect the market conditions under which Williams wrote the novel. They do not pay attention to the resonances of Williams's professional situation in Stecher's story. Wagner, however, is correct in her assessment of the manifest content of *In the Money:*

> In the daring of Joe's business venture lies the thread of plot. . . . Trying to win the government printing contract away from his present employer, Joe confronts black lists, sabotage, possible murder. . . . [H]eld down by

16. "The Stecher Trilogy: Williams as Novelist," 409, 406, 408.
17. *William Carlos Williams: An American Artist,* 126.

his present employers, disillusioned by the greediness of the unions, Joe feels he has no recourse but to go into business for himself. In becoming a capitalist, Joe seemingly denies the years he has worked actively in the printers' union.[18]

I speculate that Williams's construction of "the business battle" in the novel was in part shaped by his struggle to assert his identity as an author with an independent voice in a saturated market. Williams's description of the contest for printing a form of currency between Stecher and the firm owned by Wynnewood (the "Old Man" whose name resonates with T. S. Eliot's through his allegiance to the "Sacred Wood") and Crossman (whose name reminds us of Williams's accusations that Ezra Pound had engaged in double-crossing by abandoning America and placing his allegiance with Eliot) mirrors Williams's intermediate relationship to international and nativist literary cultures in the late 1930s.[19] In reading about Stecher's founding of a small but powerful printing house using a $50,000 loan made by someone named Lemon—"If it hadn't been for Lemon of course I couldn't have done anything, he lent me the money"—we cannot forget that Williams was in effect founding his own small printing company with someone else's cash by becoming the cornerstone and "head man" at New Directions.[20]

Lemon's willingness to loan Stecher the money to start his new firm echoes Laughlin's commitment to credit Williams's promise to produce the anticipated long poem, *Paterson;* the biography of his mother, later to be called *Yes, Mrs. Williams;* and his own life story. There is a direct relationship between Laughlin's New Directions and Gorham Munson's Social Credit journal, *New Democracy.* As Flory notes, "Pound had given James Laughlin an introduction to Munson, who put him in charge of the Social Credit and the Arts department which Laughlin chose to call New Directions."[21] Laughlin's commitment to Williams, based on the author's

18. *The Prose of Williams,* 124-26.

19. In an interview with Walter Sutton, Williams says he "went along with" Pound until Pound "switched to Eliot." Sutton later asks Williams if he thinks that poetry is compatible with the Eliotic "cult of the gentleman." Williams responds: "No, the cult of the gentleman will lead him to double-cross a man. The really cultured gentleman will do you dirt if he can get away with it, and not be found out" (Wagner, ed., *Interviews with William Carlos Williams,* 47, 49).

20. *In the Money,* 60; hereafter cited in the text as *IM.*

21. *The American Ezra Pound,* 78.

artistic accomplishments, stands as an example of Social Credit, the economic theory advocated by Pound, Munson, and Major C. H. Douglas. In the novel, Social Credit theory is used by Williams to justify his own benefits from his new relationship to the commercial literary marketplace.

The "business battle" between Stecher and the firm to which he once belonged begins in chapter 3, "Boss's Party." Stecher, the master printer who at the outset of the novel works for Wynnewood and Crossman, having presented himself to them as a simple craftsman "innocent" of any interest in owning his own firm, manages to underbid his old firm for a prestigious and lucrative contract to print United States money orders. Stecher's mask of professional innocence and commercial disinterest resembles the persona Williams constructed in order to accomplish what Leibowitz called his "literary business." In chapter 3, Stecher leaves for Washington, D.C., to make his bid without anyone else from the firm of Wynnewood and Crossman knowing about it. By having a pressman who lives in his neighborhood return his desk key to the office, Stecher gives other members of the firm the false impression that he has been in the building, rather than in Washington, on the day he delivers his bid. Wynnewood's lawyer, named Stevens, reports this news to Wynnewood and Crossman. (I will explain in a moment why it might be significant that this character is named Stevens.) News of this key becomes the first evidence that Wynnewood was mistaken not to lower his bid so that he could compete with Stecher for the Washington contract. In spite of his apparent lack of interest in owning his own firm, Stecher is, in fact, shown to be a cunning businessman. He is willing to use Lemon's funds to defeat the hold on the printing monopoly by "the organization." Stecher's apparent nonchalance ("Said he just found [the key] in his pocket," Stevens tells Wynnewood) veils his desire to win what the novel describes as "the final showdown" between the two sides that once were one.

Williams's decision to use the name Stevens for the lawyer who finds the key is significant in terms of the submerged criticism of other modern writers that informs many of the characterizations in the novel. Wallace Stevens wrote the important and controversial preface to the first edition of Williams's *Collected Poems,* printed in 1934 by Louis Zukofsky and the Objectivist Press. Williams knew he had taken a risk by asking Stevens to write on his behalf, but he said he needed a "name" author and allowed Stevens to go ahead. "It may sell the book yet—especially if the right

Sunday Supplement guy sees it and falls for it," Williams wrote.[22] To some extent the idea backfired because Stevens was the first critic to call Williams's poetry "anti-poetic," a description Williams abhorred. Stevens described Williams in the preface as "[h]e who insists that life would be intolerable except for the fact that one has, from the top, such an exceptional view of the public dump and the advertising signs of Snider's Catsup, Ivory Soap and Chevrolet Cars; he is the hermit who dwells alone with the sun and moon, but insists on taking a rotten newspaper."[23]

Stevens's claim that Williams was a romantic poet who gained insight from observing the "public dump" of the commercial world from his dwelling in the "ivory tower" was, ironically, the "key" to Williams's rhetorical strategy in *In the Money*. Stevens's observation that Williams's view of "advertising signs" fortified his imaginative writing accurately describes a structural principle that informs *In the Money*'s submerged plot. Indeed, Williams used the advertising method of hidden persuasion to wage a campaign against literary rivals, a publicity strategy valuable to Williams because it accommodated his publisher's sense of the decorum of the modernist project. In the "hidden dialogue" with his rival in *In the Money*, Williams presented Stevens as a "fool" working for the usurious side of the printing industry, parodying the image of Wallace Stevens as the capable actuarial in the gray flannel suit, the vice president in insurance from Hartford. Through Stecher's example, Williams also transferred the prestige of the capable money manager to himself (and away from Stevens, the insurance man; Eliot, the banker; and Pound, the Social Credit theorist).

A working draft of the opening section of "Guitar Blues," Williams's 1937 *Nation* review of Stevens's *The Man with the Blue Guitar and Other Poems,* presents further evidence that Stevens's recent commercial success as a poet was on Williams's mind as he composed *In the Money*. In the review, Williams recognizes the importance of the commercial investment in and the marketing of modern letters before turning to an evaluation of Stevens's poetry:

> Money is power, a power. Without capital investment, the market for poetry, like every other market regardless of its intrinsic worth, will slump. But

22. Mariani, *A New World Naked,* 339.
23. Doyle, ed., *The Critical Heritage,* 126.

Stevens has got himself published by a good firm. He is one of the few modern American poets to experience capital investment. Maybe there is money in it. Who knows? More power to him.

They've given him a small attractive volume in bright yellow boards costing them perhaps, I don't know, say four or five hundred dollars to print. The price is two dollars. If they sell a thousand copies they'll about clear expenses. How would you like to market an item entitled, The Man with the Blue Guitar? Counting colleges and libraries, maybe a fair bet.[24]

Williams projects Stevens's fortunes with Knopf on to his own hopes for success with New Directions through the depiction of Stecher receiving a "capital investment" from Lemon in order to print a form of what Williams calls "power, a power."

The focus of the submerged literary "business battle" in chapter 3 concerns Williams's desire to dethrone Eliot. As Wynnewood receives early signals from Washington that Stecher has, indeed, underbid his firm, he tries to gauge the scope of the damage to his international printing empire. Wynnewood is "pretty sure [Stecher] hasn't tied up with any of the big companies." When the news of Stecher's government contract becomes official, however, Wynnewood's response to Stecher's victory suggests a personal wounding, as well as the response of a spirited competitor: "Well, I'm a son of a bitch. Where the hell do you suppose—? How the hell . . . ? Where is he going to print them? How in hell did he . . . ?" The old man was speechless" (*IM*, 41). When he returns to speech, Wynnewood brushes aside his son's advice to accept defeat: "The sense of balance that I go by says, Don't get licked. And I don't get licked. Not by anybody. . . . Something tells me he's going to run into some pretty tough sledding before he gets through. Pretty tough going. If he's man enough, maybe he'll get by—maybe. If he's man enough" (*IM*, 42). Fearing that Stecher might be after "the whole God damn building," and unsure about "how far he's undermined my organization," Wynnewood vows to "kill that damned little bastard": "Who the hell owns this country? Him or me?" (*IM*, 43).

T. S. Eliot probably was not an equally engaged partner with Williams in their literary "business battle." Eliot, in fact, once said that Williams was only "of local interest, perhaps."[25] Williams, however, understood his

24. "Guitar Blues," unpaginated typescript to a review of *The Man with the Blue Guitar and Other Poems*.
25. Eliot quoted in Fisher-Wirth, *Williams and Autobiography*, 34.

position as a "nativist" poet after 1922 to be a maverick's response to Eliot's literary dominance. Leibowitz has noted that Williams needed institutionally sanctioned enemies to rebel against, and Eliot was the perfect foil to his transgressive art:

> Extremely competitive, when his insecurity was in the ascendancy he lashed out at his enemies with a nasty hysteria. He needed enemies, and the *Autobiography* contains many military images; he felt continually embattled. . . . His favorite villain or scapegoat was T. S. Eliot. . . . As though it were a personal attack, *The Waste Land* felled Williams like a "sardonic bullet." Derailed, he must pick himself up from the ditch and start over. . . . Williams relishes his malice towards Eliot: it made him vow to resume the struggle and uphold his "rebellious" experiments. He would count on final vindication.[26]

Wynnewood's reaction to Stecher's renegade activity can be interpreted as Williams's projection onto Eliot, who thought Williams "too small to feud with," of Williams's wish to have his rival respond to his publication contract, if not with "one of the big companies" such as Knopf, then with Laughlin's new press.[27]

Chapter 3 of *In the Money* ends with Wynnewood ready to mount his campaign of "dirty work," as his lawyer Stevens calls it, to undermine Stecher's new printing house. Here Williams sets up the contrast between "honest" attitudes toward the printing and distribution of signs of wealth (Stecher's) and "corrupt" ones (Wynnewood's). Williams casts Stecher as the "innocent" printer out on his own who faces a conspiracy to undermine his professional status. Any unsavory or, possibly, illegal action Stecher takes to implement his printing house, therefore, is viewed in this novel as an action driven by the ethical demand to put down a corrupt monopoly. Stecher's "inside trading" is justified because the outcome is monetary reform that will benefit the national economy. Even though both sides are implicated in dishonest practices, "honesty" becomes a Stecher virtue. Corruption in order to maintain a usurious regime becomes the definitive Wynnewood vice, as this comment from Wynnewood suggests: "How you gonna get any work done if somebody's always yelling honesty, honesty at you. Honesty is the best policy, huh? Christ, who the hell ever

26. "'You Can't Beat Innocence,'" 38.
27. Eliot quoted in Fisher-Wirth, *Williams and Autobiography,* 34.

cared about honesty but a lot of little craps that ain't in the money?" (*IM*, 44). In the contrast between the honest but insignificant "little craps" and those willing to put ethics aside to get "in the money," Williams is exploring the contradiction between business ethics and the work of creating a reputation in an economy of scarce resources that appears to award collusion.

Williams was interested in getting "in the money" by producing a popular novel about Stecher's unsavory relationship to commercial publishing. Williams, like Stecher, cast aside anonymity to put himself "in the money" by making a secret bid for renown through the critique of his former associates, Pound and Stevens, within his New Directions prose. Like Stecher, Williams had also gambled by entering into a publication agreement with Laughlin for books that he had planned and promised, but that he had not yet written. In order to separate himself from his former allies, Williams had practiced what Wynnewood correctly accuses Stecher of engaging in: "double crossing." The strategy that Stecher employs to win the government contract for the money orders resonates with a paradox that is at the heart of Williams's posture as an "innocent" writer who stands outside both the commercial literary market and the institution of modernism. In the novel, Stecher accuses Wynnewood and Crossman of graft. This accusation eventually leads to their indictment for grand larceny. Stecher himself, however, escapes legitimate accusations of inside trading (he knew the amount of the Wynnewood and Crossman bid before he cast his own) only through the technicality that he had quit the other firm days prior to traveling to Washington to cast a lower bid for his own new firm. Likewise, Williams directed a veiled critique against those poets who had led the literary movement to which he once belonged.

The drama in chapter 3 hinges on whether Stecher will be awarded the government contract. Once the contract is secured, the chapters that follow concern whether Stecher will receive the social credit that he believes he has earned through his years of expert printing. Other than the trust in his name as a printer, Stecher has no capital when he begins his quixotic mission to reform the trade. His reputation, however, brings him the support of most of the former laborers from Wynnewood and Crossman, as well as the crucial backing of Lemon, whose influence allows Stecher to get ink delivered from a "new firm beholden to nobody" named Faulheber and Schwartz—located, appropriately, in New Jersey.

Just as the struggle in chapter 3 for the printing contract includes hidden critiques of Stevens and Eliot, in the pivotal thirteenth chapter Williams turns his attention to his disagreements with Pound about the role the American poet should play in the economic and political governance of the country. In that chapter, Stecher is figured as deserving credit for his skill at printing the money orders on time and under budget, rather than manipulating bank funds in order to turn a profit through usurious practices, as is the practice of Wynnewood and Crossman. In order to make his pitch for the government account, Stecher visits Washington. He stands before no less a figure than President Teddy Roosevelt, who is described as a progressive, muckraking reformer who opposes the kind of public abuse of funds enacted in this fiction by Wynnewood and Crossman. The president comes to trust Stecher, but at first Roosevelt wonders why the public printer cannot handle the job. "Because they don't know how," Stecher tells Roosevelt (*IM,* 177).

Besides associating Stecher's activities in Washington with his own literary "know-how," Williams also used Stecher's successful bid to gain Teddy Roosevelt's support as a narrative reversal and critique of Pound's contemporaneous activities in Washington on behalf of the English economist Major C. H. Douglas's theory of Social Credit. In April 1939 Pound had returned from Italy to lobby on behalf of monetary reforms before members of Franklin Roosevelt's administration in Washington. As Mariani has noted,

> Whether or not Williams knew it, Pound had also headed south for Washington with his own inimitable cloak-and-dagger secrecy. Much of what Pound did there is shrouded in mystery, but he did attend a session of Congress and he did talk—as he reveals in the *Pisan Cantos*—with Senators Borah of Idaho (Pound's native state) and Bankhead. . . . He also talked with Secretary of Agriculture Henry A. Wallace. But he did not get to see Roosevelt and he did not avert World War II.[28]

In the novel, Stecher comments to his wife, Gurlie, that he had been speaking about his idea for monetary reform with "Senator Platt and Chauncey M. Depew, men like that," and that he had been gathering the support that led to his successful meeting with Teddy Roosevelt and

28. Mariani, *A New World Naked,* 427.

the four-year contract. There is an essential difference between Pound's arguments for money reform and Stecher's. Pound presented himself to Congress as an economist in 1939 on the eve of awesome and terrible shifts in world affairs, whereas Stecher presented himself as a professional printer in 1903 before a president associated with repairing an existing political institution. Pound was using *The Cantos* "to show how the misuse of money was at the root of all modern evils." Williams, through Stecher's story, created a plot literally about how to make money to suggest the value of his attention to the literary craft, rather than to abstract political or economic theory.[29]

In chapter 13, after the successful meeting with Roosevelt, Stecher enters into an interior monologue. Here, the tenets of his practice match Williams's ideas about literary nativism and precision:

> My policy! what else? My policy. Nothing works efficiently any more because of that idea. Church, government—the only thing that works is one man that pays attention to what he is doing and knows what to do about it. My brother plays the violin in Prague. My sister shows her legs on the stage—I'm a printer. I hope we do our jobs all right. Because if we don't—It's because it's to the advantage of someone or other, my policy!—or we'd plant as much as we want and need and we'd have a world worth living it.
>
> Waste, waste, waste. There's the solution to everything. Just cultivate that land, just that little bit of acreage of New Jersey, just as far as you can see on both sides of the train window, that is going to waste. That's all you have to do. But really use it. And there'd be no more poverty or misery in the entire world—Just put it to use. (*IM,* 180–81)

Stecher conceives of a pragmatic and objective approach to monetary reform, one that is disinterested in abstractions; praises efficiency in design; advocates a worker's expertise in one craft, be it music, acting, or painting; and focuses on reducing waste and poverty by gathering up local energy and materials. His theory of monetary reform, in other words, represents the classic Williams philosophy of political and social change, as well as his program for the right form of the poem, as he stated in

29. Ibid., 375. Mariani quotes a letter of March 25, 1935, from Williams to Pound: "If you can't tell the difference between yourself and a trained economist, if you don't know your function as a poet, incidentally dealing with a messy situation re. money, then go sell your papers on some other corner."

1951 in "Symposium on Writing": "We forget what a poem is: a poem is an organization of materials. As an automobile or kitchen stove is an organization of materials. You have to take words, as Gertrude Stein said we must, to make poems. Poems are mechanical objects made out of words to express a certain thing."[30]

From this point of view, Stecher's attention to details such as designing money orders that are difficult to counterfeit constitutes a reasonable political action for someone whose area of expertise is printing. Stecher's style resonates with Williams's use of what Anne Janowitz has called the "mechanical, manufacturing image for the 'creation' of a poem."[31] In contrast to Stecher, Wynnewood and Crossman are enemies of the pragmatic monetary reform represented by fidelity to the aesthetic details of the printing plates. From their point of view, reformation of the design of the money orders would only cut into profit margins. In chapter 5, Stecher explains to Gurlie that since Wynnewood has a monopoly on the contract he has refused to listen to Stecher's ideas about how to prevent counterfeit orders. The attention to the surface of the paper resonates with Williams's attention to the visual appearance of his poems:

> I wanted them to put in a new paper I found out about. But the old man wouldn't hear of it. It would stop the whole trouble with counterfeiting. If you change anything, it changes the surface of the paper. Well, that's where it started. I tried to sell it to him—for a year. I could see the advantages so when he wouldn't do it, I decided to see what I could do with it myself. I got a monopoly on it! (*IM*, 59)

Williams argued that the streamlining of the poem was an act of political reform appropriate to the poet's type of knowledge. Through Stecher's story Williams also argued in favor of his own ability to publish literature for profit by applying to his situation ideas found in Major Douglas's books on determining new criteria for the awarding of public credit. Douglas believed that Social Credit (examples of which would be in Williams's case the New Directions contract and in Stecher's case the government printing contract) should be offered only to individuals who performed communally useful tasks with technical expertise. Douglas wrote, "The

30. Wagner, ed., *Interviews with Williams*, 73.
31. "*Paterson:* An American Contraption," 301–2.

only claim which any individual or collection of individuals has to operate and administer the plant of society is that they are the fittest persons available for the purpose."[32] Stecher fulfills Douglas's characterization of an entrepreneur as someone who deserves "real credit" because of his accomplishments in his special field. His "honest" practice is performed without the graft of the "international organization" that includes Legal Talent, Wynnewood, Crossman, and "Ink" Nesbit. These insiders are usurers in the sense that they skim profits off every order book they produce, as Stecher explains later in the novel when telling Gurlie about how the graft worked at Wynnewood's Mohawk Press:

> We got paid outside the contract. The old man asked for 6 1/2 cents a book for delivery. Caldwell offered 4 cents. 4 1/2 cents was agreed on finally. Even that was far beyond the cost. The boys got the difference, about 1 1/6 cents a book. . . . We used to print books of 500 blanks but recently they never go out in any denomination higher than 200. That makes two and a half times as many books. Not a bad idea. (*IM,* 168–69)

The conflict between Stecher and the international firm is not between backers of "hard money" and those of "paper" currency, as might have been the case had Williams written *In the Money* about the Age of Jackson and the Bank Wars of the 1830s. At that time, "hard money" was supported by Andrew Jackson and by populists such as Senator Thomas Hart Benton, who framed the question of "whether people, or property, shall govern?"; in literature, it was supported by Ralph Waldo Emerson. "Cheap" or paper money was supported by the political descendants of Alexander Hamilton's centralized vision of American banking and, in literature, by Edgar Allen Poe.[33] The Bank War between "hard" and "paper" began when the charter of the Second Bank of the United States was about to expire in 1836. Jackson's 1836 "Specie Circular" provided that only gold and silver

32. *The Douglas Manual,* 89.

33. In "The Gold Bug" Marc Shell reads Poe's 1843 mystery story as a roman à clef that links the character Legrand's gold-seeking through his ability to decipher words (the map that leads him to gold) to Poe's ability as a professional author to generate wealth through his own "paper currency," the humbug story, a story about a thing which is not, that won a hundred-dollar prize from *Dollar Newspaper.* On the aesthetic and linguistic elements of the gold debate from the 1830s and 1840s, see Ian Bell's "The Hard Currency of Words: Emerson's Fiscal Metaphor in Nature." Arthur Schlesinger's chapter on "The Bank War" in *The Age of Jackson* is also useful.

were to be accepted by government agents in payment for the purchase of public lands. This nineteenth-century debate concerned questions about the power of the Second Bank, a private, elite, and centralized enterprise under no government jurisdiction to control the flow of money and credit to citizens and to the government. Paper money was distrusted by the anti-Bank movement because its circulation was understood to be more difficult to restrain than was that of specie-backed money.

Besides issues of class and federal power, the question about the gold standard, on a level of the philosophy of language, concerned the security of the connection between signifier and signified. The question was whether money was an unnatural abstraction, with no direct relationship to the thing it signified (a difference without a positive term) or itself a valuable "specie" (when backed by gold) that could be understood as a genuinely connected or natural medium of exchange. The question of whether one honored the stamp scripted onto the metal or the value of the metal itself was another problematic part of this debate. The distrust of making money out of money (the banker's work in lending credit at interest) was, from this point of view, the distrust of making something out of nothing. The distrust of usury, as understood by Aristotle, was also a distrust of a world made only of words on paper, or what was called by backers of the gold standard a "paper dynasty."[34]

Williams's political sympathies were on the side of Jackson in the sense that he figured himself in his fiction as opposed to monopoly capitalism and on the side of the working class. The debate about the printing of paper money is presented from a different angle in Williams's novel. Instead of "hard" versus "paper" currency, the conflict is between two attitudes toward the production of an abstract form of wealth, the money order blanks. This form of wealth is efficiently produced by Stecher, and so presented as deserving of the public trust, but made usurious through graft and monopoly by Wynnewood and Crossman, and so presented as not deserving credit. In the novel, Williams does not assume the natural

34. Pound's rage against usury suggests his uneasiness with purely linguistic exchanges that do not actually signify reality. Pound, as Richard Sieburth shows in "In Pound We Trust: The Economy of Poetry / The Poetry of Economics," was certainly interested in monetary reform, but he also held agrarian views of unmediated economic exchange that made issues of consumption of his product abhorrent. This anti-usury economic philosophy was also behind Pound's promotion of the Chinese ideogram in terms of poetic making.

authenticity of money as a medium for exchanging value. In the areas of both finance and poetry, his focus is on designing the artificial instrument of exchange (the poetic line, the money order). In both cases, he promotes forms of social mediation that reflect without distortion the actual conditions of life in the social world, whether through poems written in the "American idiom" with a reduced metaphorical content and a prosody based on the oral practices of native speakers, or through money orders produced in an inexpensive way that does not tend toward usury. In the novel, the boundary between the two cultures of art and commerce becomes elastic, perhaps to the point that it is impossible to distinguish between aesthetic and economic forms of symbolic exchange. Williams's mature iconography as a poetry technician and his theories about the value of poetry as a mediational instrument of social exchange are both found in Stecher's attitude toward the making of money orders. From Williams's point of view it is the poet's dedication to the object he or she creates—the poetic thing itself—that allows it to function as an accurate and usable form of exchange in the world outside the text.

Stecher's situation closely resembles Williams's situation as a writer in this period. Williams presented Social Credit theory in order to discuss the reordering of economics in the sphere of literature. He was calling for a decentralization of the control of publishing away from the Eliot-led "gang" that held international authority over literary judgments through control of the university and of influential journals such as *The Dial* and publishers such as Faber and Faber, and toward local control of publishing, represented by Laughlin's press.

In his letters to Laughlin, Williams described Eliot and Pound as "gang" leaders who were actively opposed to his advances in poetic technique. Williams's suspicion that other modernist writers were out "to keep the artist down" is reflected in the way Stecher must fight against efforts by Crossman and Wynnewood to sabotage his operation through the tactics of monopoly capitalism. In chapter 15, Stecher learns that Wynnewood and Crossman have paid the building inspector to claim that the warehouse Stecher rented is too weak to safely hold the presses. Then, in chapter 18, they warn ink sellers (and Nesbit, in particular) that if they trade with Stecher they will be boycotted by all Wynnewood accounts. When these attempts fail, they hire a group of thugs to bump Stecher off the Brooklyn Ferry. None of these schemes, however, keeps Stecher from filling the government order by the December deadline.

Wynnewood and Crossman's henchmen present an external challenge to Stecher's authority. The greatest challenge to his authority in the novel, however, stems from internal doubts about his own capabilities as a printer and fledgling entrepreneur. Although Stecher tells Gurlie that because his bid was lowest the contract has "been awarded to me," he still feels inferior to Wynnewood and Crossman. He wonders if the work he has done will meet with approval from other printers. Although Stecher's speech to Gurlie could describe Williams's fears that his New Directions writings would not meet with approval from literary critics whose judgment was sanctioned by university affiliations, he is talking to her about the government officials who must approve the quality of the money orders: "To make it official it will have to have the approval of the department and I suppose I'll have to appear and prove to them that I'm properly equipped and qualified in other ways to complete the order. That's business" (*IM*, 63). Stecher's paradoxical relationship to the establishment (his fear that the "insiders" are attacking his progress, as well as his concomitant need that the "insiders" validate his qualifications) reflects Williams's paradoxical attitude toward university-sanctioned literary professionals in the 1930s and 1940s.

After World War II, Williams attempted to consolidate his growing acceptance among influential critics such as Oscar Williams, Allen Tate, Robert Lowell, and Randall Jarrell through friendly letters and favorable reviews of their work. Of the glowing review of *Paterson* by Jarrell in 1946, for example, Williams wrote to Laughlin: "[He] sure gave me a boost, didn't he. He's turned out to be a firm friend. . . . Geezes, I must be getting somewhere" (*SL*, 132). It was not always that way. In 1942 a war was raging between what Phillip Rahv referred to as the "palefaces" and the "redskins." On January 23, 1942, Williams wrote to Laughlin about the Eliot followers who later became known as members of the "middle generation" of U.S. poets: "He [Eliot] has the habit of spawning the shoddiest of college professor and such drips as Randall Jarrell who certainly needs a radical operation on him somewhere to raise his voice a little. I don't think implants, though, would flourish in his meat" (*SL*, 67–68). Typically, Williams in this letter associates literary power with a masculine voice, which he claims Jarrell lacks. Later in the year, Williams wrote again to Laughlin about Jarrell, who had recently criticized the 1941 *New Directions Annual* in the *Partisan Review* as "a queer mediocre hodge podge":

> Jarrell is the worst. [The Eliot followers] all know the tricks. They all are
> conditioned by the same cerebral inadequacies. They, as a group and a
> reactionary trend, all pack the same dangerous illegal punch. Jarrell is the
> most unashamed. He goes out to maim and must be watched, he's dangerous.
> I don't know anyone I'm more determined to destroy. I confess he's tough
> and that I am still studying him, not able to handle him quite yet. . . . This is
> deep in my blood. These men are aimed at my guts and I at theirs. (*SL,* 76–77)

In the novel, Gurlie assumes that even if Stecher does not at the moment
have the ink and the presses to form his own company, he will have the
"best" press eventually. Stecher describes to Gurlie his worry about being
unable to "deliver": "This is government work. Suppose I break down in
the first six months and can't deliver the orders. It's happened before.
That's one thing about the old company. They have the equipment and
they can always deliver" (*IM,* 63). Stecher's fear, described in terms of
a fear of male sexual impotency, that he might "break down" before he
can produce the work he has promised Lemon resonates with Williams's
fear of a personal "breakdown" that would disable him from delivering
the literary work he had promised Laughlin for the 1940 New Directions
Christmas catalog. While he was writing *In the Money,* Williams was also
asked by Laughlin to put together a short pamphlet of his recent poetry.
It was to be published in an inexpensive "poet-of-the-month" series that
Laughlin proposed as another form of publicity for New Directions and
for the forthcoming installment of the novel trilogy. Williams, however,
had trouble coming up with even this modest quantity of new material.
He also had doubts about the quality of the work he finally did offer to
Laughlin. A November 24, 1940, letter to Laughlin about the pamphlet of
poems, which was published on January 2, 1941, as "The Broken Span,"
suggests some of Williams's fears, fears that were magnified when he tried
to write *Paterson* in the middle years of the 1940s:

> I suppose it's too late to make any changes in the pamphlet of my poems you
> are issuing in January? I've been looking the work over and find that there is
> more than one spot in which it is weak. . . .
>   Such situations as this are bound to occur when work is gathered quickly
> together. A verse maker should never be in a hurry. The mind is a queer
> mechanical machine that allows itself to be caught in traps. A rhythmical jig
> takes hold of us forcing us to follow it, slipping in the words quite against
> our better judgement sometimes. We grow enamored of our own put-put

and like to see the boat push ahead—even to its destruction sometimes: a
heavy figure for a stupid happening. (*SL*, 57)

In spite of her husband's self-doubt, Gurlie provides unyielding support
for his professional ambitions. Her description of his strengths in compar-
ison to those of the Wynnewood and Crossman "gang" is analogous to the
way in which Myra Thurber, the wife of another of Williams's surrogates,
describes the poetic skill of "Doc" Thurber in the 1949 play *A Dream
of Love:*

> They use you . . . the men, the great figures, the artistic paragons . . . not a
> kind face among them. I often wonder that you, who see so much, do not see
> them as they are—small, scheming little souls. More like mice than humans.
> They're watching you to see what you'll do for them. Look at the faces in
> the background of some of the snapshots you have of them—vermin startled
> when the light goes on, those who think they're not being observed.[35]

Similarly, Gurlie cannot understand her husband's lack of self-respect:
"You're a fool when you make yourself little, as if you didn't know more
than the whole pack of them rolled into one. . . . Haven't you learned
your lesson yet? Can't you ever learn anything? You're a great man, there's
nobody like you and you act as if you were a fruit peddler" (*IM*, 61).
Gurlie's description of her husband verges on Williams's final account of
the advantages afforded to his literary art by his career as a physician. In
The Autobiography Williams recalled feeling inferior to Pound when they
were both undergraduates at the University of Pennsylvania around 1905
because he took the pragmatic course of medical training while Pound
took the time to study the classics. Although Gurlie is referring to Stecher's
skill as a printer and not as a physician, she praises his professional training
as the reason behind his success: "They think because you had to earn
your living and because you had to work for it and learn a profession—a
trade, that you don't know anything. You don't see their faces but I do.
This will put them in their places" (*IM*, 71–72).

---

35. William Carlos Williams, *Many Loves and Other Plays,* 198. This structural
alignment is significant because *A Dream of Love* specifically describes Doc Thurber
as the author of such Williams poems as "Love Song" ("the stain of love / is upon
the world").

Perhaps Stecher's most acute self-doubt—one that resonates with Williams's fears about breaking out on his own with New Directions after 1937—concerns the ethically questionable business practices of both the printer and the poet. Events in chapter 15, "Final Offer," echo Williams's fears that his "hidden" selling strategy may not be deemed savory by other writers who do not appreciate his irony. Sure now that he is "licked," Wynnewood makes a futile attempt to buy Stecher back by allowing him to "name his price," so long as he returns to the firm and drops his public accusations that it is crooked. Stecher is concerned that the cost of winning a battle that was waged by his own underhanded dealings may backfire. Wynnewood says: "Why didn't you come out into the open and tell me you were going to put in a bid on the contract? Then it would have been a fair fight. You didn't have the guts to do it, that's why" (*IM,* 204, 205). Stecher answers that accusation by making the obvious point that Wynnewood would have simply underbid him and taken a loss on this single contract if Stecher had placed his bid in the open. Stecher becomes more agitated, however, when Wynnewood accuses him of stealing "all our training, all our methods, all our private knowledge." Stecher can defend himself against this accusation only by saying that he took "nothing out of your business that I didn't bring into it myself a hundred times over" (*IM,* 205). Stecher, however, cannot answer Wynnewood's complaint that "you didn't have to smear our personal reputations to win your dirty little contract away from us. You didn't have to do that and you won't get away with it without paying." Accused by Wynnewood of "blacken[ing] our names" and stealing letters from the firm in order "to establish your fifth-rate little print shop in New York," all that Stecher can say is "Take that back" (*IM,* 205). Wynnewood's accusation that Stecher had to destroy other reputations in order to promote his own career was the one Williams feared he could not answer about his own quest for literary renown through his "hidden critique" of Stevens, Eliot, and Pound.

In spite of the shaky moral ground upon which his new printing firm was built, Stecher remains, in the last third of the novel, proud of his accomplishments. As does *The Autobiography,* which Fisher-Wirth describes as "a paean of success," and as the text in which Williams "fulfills the plan conceived in the radical innocence of his young childhood: the plan to do it all," chapter 21, "Lunch at the Club," celebrates victories of battles Williams fought on many levels through the imaginative autobiographical vehicle of Stecher's ability to get out his first money order before the proposed December deadline.[36] "Lunch at the Club" registers Stecher's overcoming of his fear that forces, both internal and external to the self, would prevent his professional success. It is the last of the novel's important chapters regarding Stecher's professional struggle against corporate sabotage. The chapter leaves unresolved Stecher's response to Lemon's warning that conflicts between labor and management might eventually threaten his new success. Instead, it expresses Stecher's joy at success against great odds:

> "What do you really think of the whole business now that it's over? Was it worth it?" Mr. Lemon was speaking as if to the street in front of him.
> "Oh yes," said Joe.
> "Did you enjoy it? The fight, I mean."
> "Yes," said Joe.
> "I don't believe it," said Mr. Lemon laughing. "But you never can tell. And are *they* licked! You know I actually feel sorry for them sometimes."
> "Yah," said Joe. "So do I." (*IM*, 287)

Stecher's overcoming of personal and professional obstacles to "lick" the competition marks the final segment of the novel that Laughlin awaited for the New Directions Christmas catalog of 1940. By producing the story of Stecher's success under his own version of deadline pressure, Williams had, through the plot that refers back to the situation of its composition, overcome his own creative doubt and met his own deadline to produce a work that he hoped would bring him prestige or, perhaps, the riches that would compensate for a lack of prestige. Now that he had a publisher and the assurance of a steady audience, Williams, like Stecher, proved he could "deliver the goods" under the pressure of attention. For the first time in his career, Williams understood that his writing was destined to be read by an audience perhaps ten times as great as any that he had reached prior to *White Mule,* and he wanted badly to follow that work up with another "winner."

In spite of the spirited tone evident in "Lunch at the Club," we have also noticed a paradox at the heart of the book's moral critique of the corrupt practices of Wynnewood and Crossman. The paradoxes of Stecher's venture reflect the paradoxes of Williams's own situation as one of Laughlin's

---

36. Fisher-Wirth, *Williams and Autobiography,* 35–36.

"literary saints." Williams used Pound's friendship to gain a publishing contract that, covertly, enabled him to define his public image in opposition to his former associates, especially Pound. Just as we have seen that Stecher's position as an innocent outsider was constructed through his manipulation of his commercial position, the plot of *In the Money* promoted Williams's position as the innocent outsider looking to reform a publishing monopoly that he claimed refused to accept innovative ideas. The presentation of Williams as a literary "innocent," from this point of view, was an imaginative construction, a statement of Williams's literary strength enabled by his ambivalent relationship to literary markets. In the novel, Williams shows a nostalgia for producing a sign system in which the thing and the sign of value for the thing are aligned through Stecher's efficient (nonusurious) production of blank money orders. Williams's placement of this nostalgia within a narrative that has a secret alliance with another form of exchange (literary representation), however, reveals his version of the economy to be a cultural artifact. The money economy presented in *In The Money* is a cultural artifact to the same degree that the cultural artifacts that Williams hoped to promote in the novel (his poems) are revealed to be commodities available for exchange.

Five

The Costs of Beauty

A Return to the Self in *Paterson*

I. General Introduction

As we move toward *Paterson* as well as toward the conclusion of this book, let me recapitulate in slightly different terms my conception of the relationship between author and autobiographically based characters that I wrote about in the introduction. Although Williams's fictional heroes (Dev Evans from *A Voyage to Pagany*, Joe Stecher from *In the Money*, Doc from the short fiction) are not to be confused with Williams, these characters are still related to the author's life. They reflect strategies intentionally developed by the author to determine his place in a culture of renown that was not his to determine.

These strategies are called "authorial mechanisms" by the Hemingway biographer Jackson J. Benson and are defined by him as follows: "The author projects, transforms, exaggerates, and a drama emerges which is based on his life which has only a very tenuous relationship to the situation in its facts that might be observed from the outside. . . . He writes out of his life, not about his life."[1] Benson's model of authorship is attractive to me because it maintains intentionality while recognizing the "otherness" of the author in relationship to the reader, the "differentness" between biographical fact and fictional revision of "fact" understood as the recollection of events mediated through text, and, finally, the "separateness" between the living presence of the writer and the mask of the public person as it appears in the text.

---

1. "Ernest Hemingway: The Life as Fiction and the Fiction as Life," 350.

According to Paul de Man, textual figuration of the person dis-figures the authorial presence, as this presence becomes apparent to the reader through the autobiographical representation that de Man describes as a type of death mask.[2] I do not disagree with de Man or with Roland Barthes that what we know of an author such as Williams will be a matter of linguistic construction, but the point I want to stress is that these linguistic constructions were intentionally made by the author for purposes that are identifiable in the world that conditioned the work. The literary work is intended by an author such as Williams to make a difference in the world outside the text. Williams in the second half of his life presented his story in a variety of narrative forms to restrict and control the meaning of the poetry he had written primarily before 1925. He tried to claim its meaning in terms of its "Americanicity," its therapeutic function, its relationship to a Whitmanian linguistic inheritance, its intermediate relationship to elite cultural systems developed in Europe, and its similarity to efficient machines made out of movable parts. These fictions of self-creation function as acts of publicity on behalf of Williams's work as a poet who shuttled in the many ways I have described between elite and popular culture in the United States.

It is important to keep in mind that Williams as a poet turned toward many-layered narratives of the self in order to persuade the members of his intended audience of his legitimacy as an author interested in them. The major instance of Williams's self-construction in poetry is *Paterson,* a prosopopoeia or, literally, a making of a person. Into this long poem, originally published with New Directions in five volumes between 1946 and 1958, Williams incorporated the strategy of imaginative self-creation that we have seen in its preliminary forms in the prose narratives from 1928 to 1940. I will separate out the story of the self and its relationship to others as it appears in *Paterson* from the versions of the self that appeared in the prose narratives by pointing to Williams's own hesitation within the poem to seal his majority through an identification between man and city. Williams as a poet wrote within the (paradoxically) radical tradition of a poetics of process in the United States, the tradition that includes Emerson, Whitman, Stevens, Olson, Levertov, and Ashbery. Within this tradition, the fulfillment of the desire for a total literary construction of the

---

2. "Autobiography as De-facement," 67–81.

self is understood to be an unfortunate state of affairs. As a poet affiliated with this tradition, Williams can be compared to a figure in book 3 of *Paterson,* Harry Leslie, a nineteenth-century stuntman who, balanced on a tightrope, attempted to cross the Passaic Falls, complete with a stove on which he cooked an omelet. Harry Leslie's exploits are told in passages surrounding the description of the Danforth Public Library, which was consumed in a fire that devastated much of central Paterson on February 8, 1902:

> The place sweats of staleness and of rot
> a back-house stench . a
> library stench
>
> It is summer! stinking summer
>
> Escape from it—but not by running
> away. Not by "composition." Embrace the
> foulness
>
>   —the being taut, balanced between
> eternities[3]

Leslie's balancing act suggests Williams's dissatisfaction with associating literary accomplishment with the completion of another "stale" text that will "rot" and, finally, burn on a library shelf. Completion of the poem is understood to signify the disappearance of the self that has been unequivocally identified with textual representation. Williams instead wished to understand the self as a protean formation available to change through the writing of an endless text. The desire in *Paterson* is to defer majority, to balance his poetic speaker "between eternities," which signifies the division in Williams's mind between figuring himself as a culture hero and existing as a "lame" poet able to write poems meaningful to many individuals in Paterson, but unable to shape his culture's identity.

Williams's placement as a majority figure among the community of poets writing between the late 1930s and the middle years of the 1940s was insecure. Williams was sixty in 1943 when he mapped out the first two books of *Paterson,* which eventually appeared in 1946 and 1948. His

3. *Paterson,* 103–4. Hereafter cited in the text as *P.* On the Danforth Public Library, see *P,* 280n.

production and publication of poetry had fallen off markedly since the late 1910s and 1920s, when he helped develop an appreciation in the United States for experimental French poetry. However influential *Spring and All* and *Sour Grapes* would become in the late 1950s and 1960s to a younger generation of poets writing in the United States, these mixed-genre works, James Laughlin recalls, "failed to win [Williams] an audience." According to Laughlin, it was in an attempt to appeal to a wider readership that Williams "shifted to the 'straight' style and narrative technique of *A Voyage to Pagany,* the Stecher trilogy of novels, and his short stories, collected in *The Farmers' Daughters.*"[4]

In contrast to the period from 1917 to 1928, when Williams published four books of "improvisations" that contained many of his most recognizable individual lyrics, between 1935 and 1940 he published only one short book of poetry (*An Early Martyr and Other Poems*) and one pamphlet containing eleven new poems and a few Spanish translations (*Adam and Eve in the City*). Between 1939 and 1944, when Williams planned *Paterson* and published a collection of short fiction and a novel, he published no books of poetry. Although Williams worked at *Paterson,* he felt blocked when trying to complete it. In 1942, he felt he could salvage only "nine good pages" of the first hundred he had written. He still felt stalled in 1943, forcing Laughlin to schedule the printing of book 1 for 1944. In 1944, Williams did consider publishing a book of shorter poems that were originally intended as studies for *Paterson,* but, in part because of paper shortages due to World War II, Laughlin claimed he could not find the paper to publish the book that was eventually put out in 380 copies by Cummington Press and called *The Wedge.*

In addition to his writing block, Williams felt that he had been stymied by university poets and blocked by the New York crowd for being what Yvor Winters called a "wild man" whose poetry lacked "ideas." Winters was not alone in claiming that Williams lacked the authority of what Mariani calls "a sophisticated, urbane voice" such as Wallace Stevens displayed in his blank-verse lines in the acclaimed *Parts of a World,* published by Knopf in 1942. In *Paterson,* Williams blames "special interests" for limiting the distribution of both economic and cultural goods to immigrants and to other members of the lower middle classes in need of representation.

4. "William Carlos Williams and the Making of *Paterson:* A Memoir," 198.

In *Paterson* and *In the Money,* Williams applied this theory of "special interests" to his own situation as a poet. He claimed that the university poets had disrupted his relationship to his intended audience through negative reviews and by rejecting his poems and critical essays. Although poets such as Robert Lowell and, most important, Randall Jarrell, writing in the *Partisan Review,* praised *Paterson* on the evidence of the first two books, Mariani notes that in the period from 1936 to 1946 when Williams was approaching the poem "he'd been patronized by Blackmur, Winters, Jarrell, Tate, and the *Partisan Review* and dismissed by most of the other critics because he had not fit the acceptable university molds. And the more they ignored him, naturally, the more his own stridencies had increased."[5]

Williams was confronting another obstacle by writing a new version of the long American poem late in an already distinguished tradition. He said in the *Autobiography* that he was committed to discovering a "new dialect" that would be supplemented "by a new construction upon the syllables. . . . To *make* a poem, fulfilling the requirements of the art, and yet new, in the sense that in the very lay of the syllables Paterson as Paterson would be discovered, perfect, perfect, in the special sense of the poem, to have it—if it rose to flutter into life awhile—it would be as itself, locally, and so like every other place in the world" (*A,* 392). Williams wanted to found a cultural movement through the American long poem. Unfortunately, he was attempting to do something that was no longer new. Even apart from *Leaves of Grass,* Pound had already published over seventy of his *Cantos* by 1940; Hart Crane, who died in 1933, had written *The Bridge;* Stevens had just received acclaim for *Parts of a World;* and the archrival, Eliot, in 1943, had just published *Four Quartets.*[6] In "Notes toward a Definition of Culture" (1944), Eliot appeared to have aligned himself with a nativist agenda for poetry by describing the need for an "organic relationship" between "the capital, the country, and also the provincial towns." Although Eliot's statements should have spurred him

5. Mariani, *A New World Naked,* 499.
6. Many critics, including Sherman Paul in *The Music of Survival: A Biography of a Poem by William Carlos Williams,* have interpreted *Paterson* as another attack against the Eliotic emphasis on understanding the poetic accomplishment in relationship to a descent from great minds rather than on finding the resources of poetry through a contact with experience in the present moment.

on in his work, Williams told Horace Gregory that his poem, designed to register Paterson, New Jersey, as an appropriate location for a major poem, was not to be soon forthcoming. Believing that his earlier attempts to juxtapose prose and poetry in a single work had led to artistic failure, Williams, in 1945, told Gregory that he had to find a new way to construct a long poem. In a crucial letter to Gregory, Williams suggests reimagining the self as a literary artifact in order to construct *Paterson.* "I shall have to work like a fiend to make myself new again. Either I remake myself or I am done. I can't escape the dilemma longer. THAT is what has stopped me."[7] Williams's yoking of the search for a new poetic form ("unless there is / a new mind there cannot be a new / line," *P*, 50) with the quest for the establishment of a new identity in language marks a sea change in his philosophy about how poetry should be counted by readers as worthy of attention.

In Williams's most recognizable lyrics from his first six books of poetry, the reader's trust in him as speaker is not contingent upon the celebration of the poet as a figure of public renown. In fact, images of the poet rarely appear in Williams's most characteristic poems. He separated the poem as a work of art from the promotional work of constructing his identity through the poem. Published between 1909 and 1928 and often at his own expense, these books contain Williams's most intensive and influential work as an imagist poet. James E. Breslin describes the rise of imagism and its influence on Williams's style: "[The imagist poem] emphasized the solid, independent existence of the thing and the need to perceive its surface with care and precision. Modern poetry thus began as a radical repudiation of the romantic ego and the idealistic philosophy that supported it."[8] In Williams's "The Lonely Street," to present a typical lyric from *Sour Grapes,* the authorial speaker is conscious of his bodily presence in the poetic space ("It is too hot / to walk at ease"). By the caesural pause in line 2, however, the subjective presence of the lyric "I" is effaced and replaced by an externalization of lyric attention:

> School is over. It is too hot
> to walk at ease. At ease

7. For Williams's comments on Eliot's essay, see Mariani, *A New World Naked,* 489; Williams, *Selected Letters,* 235.

8. Breslin quoted in Margaret Glynne Lloyd, *William Carlos Williams' "Paterson": A Critical Reappraisal,* 31.

in light frocks they walk the streets
to while the time away.
They had grown tall. They hold
pink flames in their right hands.
In white from head to foot,
with sidelong, idle look—
in yellow, floating stuff,
black sash and stocking—
touching their avid mouths
with pink sugar on a stick—
like a carnation each holds in her hand—
they mount the lonely street.[9]

The poet's consciousness—his "living presence"—is suggested, but the reader's attention is drawn away from the experience of the author's hot body in the opening lines and directed outward toward the scene described. The poet gains the reader's confidence that his words are sufficiently related to place through the fidelity and precision with which he records speech rhythms (using enjambment), through his awareness of how the scene's characters have changed over time (the speaker has seen these girls grow up), and through the strangeness he is able to make out of this familiar scene of schoolgirls eating cotton candy. The poet's subjectivity is available to us, but not through his appearance in the poem, as is so often the case in *Paterson*. The poet appears through the trace of the maker's hand in the obvious craft of the poem; the formal lineation of the poem bears Williams's signature marks.

In a way that resembles Williams's attitude toward patients in his medical clinic, the poet maintains an appropriate distance from the scene of desire, the lonely street. His voyeuristic relationship to his subject matter is regulated through the poetic line. The line can be understood as a spatial device that allows the poet to negotiate an appropriate distance between maker and material. By only *suggesting* his presence through the craftsman's fidelity to the form of the poem, Williams presents the poet as curious, which is a form of caring, about a scene of intimacy in which his personal involvement is limited, but in which his involvement as a master of representational technique is evident. Because his attention is directed to the formal design of the literary work, the poet is able to represent this scene without having to possess or intimidate those involved in it. In

9. Williams, *Selected Poems* (1969 ed.), 20.

contrast to the restrained intimacy found in the carefully made artifact that is "The Lonely Street," Williams in *Paterson* books 1–4 turns from the objective treatment of material toward using the maker's quest to overcome personal and professional blockages as a primary thematic method of organization. In what follows I will suggest some reasons Williams shifted the terms of authorization when he did. I will also discuss the ethical dilemma he faced in representing other persons in his long poem. Finally, I will close this chapter by suggesting that Williams found a way out of the dilemma in the very late book 5 of *Paterson.*

In the first four books of *Paterson,* Williams identifies his gigantic personage both as terrain and city and as the incarnation of the poet as a point of collective awareness, as an Emersonian Major Man who has internalized his external environment. As Margaret Glynne Lloyd points out, "basic to the material theme is *the narrative of the poet Paterson's struggle* to establish a fertile contact with his environment and achieve a living language." The sequential movement of *Paterson,* as Jerome Mazzaro has also said, is the narrative of the ability of the genius loci to rescue meaning out of the lonely street. He attempts to find significance in the scenes of divorce, violence, and blocked communication by bringing the world into an order that mirrors the poet's own relationship to "real life" and to the textual traces of the history of the local scene as they relate to Paterson's experience.[10] The poet's desire is to overcome blockage in order to renew a tie between his subjectivity and what he describes as the "supplying female." Mazzaro has interpreted the "supplying female" to mean society or the immediate world, a connection to which becomes the desired outcome of a poem of communitarian interest figured in erotic terms.

The poem's movement might also be understood to consist of the various ways in which Williams, as the Whitmanic giant capable of arising from sleep in order to find a common language through which citizens could find beauty in their lives, might unlock his mind to discover beauty by witnessing the local scene without. The ways in which Paterson tries to unlock beauty include the recovery of meaning from "dead" history (the prose about Alexander Hamilton and the Society for Useful Manufacturers in book 1), a return to the location of cultural conservation in the library

10. Lloyd, *Williams' "Paterson,"* 44 (italics mine); Mazzaro, *William Carlos Williams: The Later Poems,* 24.

(book 3), self-indulgence (his erotic interest in Phyllis, in book 4), and, primarily in book 5, an affirmation of the power of art to preserve the imagination after the artist's death. Williams tries to fasten "real life" to his poetry and to make "real life" appear meaningful through the inclusion of "found" documentary materials, including newspaper clippings, letters from fellow poets such as Cress (Marcia Nardi) and "A. G." (Allen Ginsberg), advertisements, and charts offering geological data about Paterson. This "living newspaper" or documentary collage technique is related to literary, theatrical, artistic, and photojournalistic projects sponsored by Franklin Roosevelt's Works Progress Administration in the 1930s. These WPA projects were intended to create pride in place through the spreading of information about local history in such easily accessible venues as the public theater. Williams was certainly not averse to such projects. Although he rejected an offer to become director of the Writers' Project in New Jersey, he did, as Mike Weaver notes, "consent to be a member of the New Jersey Guild Associates, Inc., which in 1938 produced a guide to the state of New Jersey, compiled and written by members of the Writers' Project."[11] The government-funded projects attempted to define, and then to conserve, what was essentially American about a country faced with an economic and political system that was collapsing under the weight of unemployment, fiscal dilemmas, environmental disasters, and, until the Roosevelt administration, a loss of faith in the ability of the federal government to relieve the pain of victims of economic and environmental crisis. From this point of view, the inclusion of documentary material in *Paterson* may be construed as a recovery of a distinct sense of language and public culture in a depressed region of the United States.

Kathleen Matthews, however, has demonstrated that apparently unmediated newspaper and historical material in book 1 about the drunken tavern owner Tim Crane and the hapless Reverend Cumming was selected by Williams to represent subtle and not so subtle critiques of Hart Crane and E. E. Cummings. The Tim Crane episode illustrates how Williams's agonic relationships influenced the choices he made about which aspects of civic history were worthy of representation. Lightly veiled references can be found in the Tim Crane episode to Williams's younger and, at the time, better acknowledged literary competitor, Hart Crane, who was born in

11. *William Carlos Williams,* 102.

1899 and died in 1933. These references amount to negative stereotypes of Crane's project—and Crane's personality—probably gleaned from Philip Horton's 1937 biography. Many of the parallels between the romantic legend of Hart Crane and the description of Tim Crane as a tavern owner who falls into the Passaic involve Crane's relationship to alcohol and his suicide by drowning.[12]

Williams felt threatened by *The Bridge* because it was an attempt to make "living history" out of documents and legends regarding the foundation of the United States, including the diary of Christopher Columbus, which Williams accused Crane of stealing from a sample of the explorer's diaries that appeared in 1925 as a chapter of *In the American Grain.* In a letter to Ezra Pound dated August 11, 1928, Williams expressed his belief that Crane was "supposed to be the man that puts me on the shelf." Crane, of course, understood *The Bridge,* in his own words, as an attempt to capture "The Myth of America." Crane's project, as it was described in the dedicatory poem, "To Brooklyn Bridge," was to present the bridge as an artifact of words that could act as an instrument of harmony between the transcendental space, signified by the effortless movements of the seagull that flies above the Hudson Bay and that builds its own "inviolate curve" with extended wings, and the mechanical and commercial world of New York City. In a review of Crane's career published in *Contempo* in 1932, Williams said he admired the music of Crane's poetry, comparing it to "the sound of continual surf," but he criticized Crane for trying too hard to be "cosmic" and to please "someone in charge of a New York Sunday Book supplement."[13]

Crane, like Williams, believed the poem must make a difference in the actual world outside the poem, but he tended to disavow or not to see the inherent value or "radiant gist" in the nativist materials he represented. Although Crane wrote to Waldo Frank that "the artist must honestly anticipate the realization of his vision in 'action' (as an actively operating principle of communal works and faith)," he also told Frank

12. Crane, who wrote in the "Wine Menagerie" that "wine redeems the sight," believed in using liquor as a means for gaining extraordinary sensations. Crane's appearance in *Paterson* has also been discussed, with different emphasis, by Kathleen Matthews in "Competitive Giants: Satiric Bedrock in Book One of William Carlos Williams' *Paterson,*" and by Jay Grover-Rogoff in "Hart Crane's Presence in *Paterson.*"
13. Williams, *Selected Letters,* 104; "Hart Crane (1899–1932)," 1.

that the "forms, materials, dynamics," which were the "symbols of reality necessary to articulate the span . . . are simply non-existent in the world." Crane said that the poem rises out of "a past" and is not subservient to the present, as Williams claims it is in "The Library," but instead "overwhelms the present with its worth and vision [so] that I'm at a loss to explain my delusion that there exist any real links between that past and a future destiny worthy of it."[14] In spite of the differences between Crane and Williams in terms of their relationships to history and to a hope for transcendence through statements of access to the sublime, sections of Crane's long poem from 1930, most notably its part 2 ("Powhatan's Daughter"), used symbols for the ground of the United States that were dangerously close to the ones Williams used for his long poem, composed nearly twenty years after Crane's.[15]

The prose episode from book 1 of *Paterson,* gleaned by Williams primarily from Charles P. Longwell's *A Little Story of Old Paterson as Told by an Old Man,* concerns news of the erecting of a bridge across the Passaic Falls in 1829.[16]

> Crane was a hotel keeper and kept a tavern on the Manchester side of the Falls. His place was a great resort for circus men. . . . Crane built the bridge because his rival, Fyfield, who kept the tavern on the other side of the falls, was getting the benefit of the "Jacob's Ladder," as it was sometimes called— the "hundred steps," a long, rustic, winding stairs in the gorge leading to the opposite side of the river—it making his place more easy to get to. (*P,* 15–16)

The sponsors for the construction of the bridge did not have in mind exclusively the safety and pleasure of their community. They also were

14. Crane to Waldo Frank, June 20, 1926, *The Complete Poems and Selected Letters and Prose of Hart Crane,* 230, 231, 232.

15. Crane described the intention of "Powhatan's Daughter" to Otto Kahn in a letter, written from Patterson, New York, on September 12, 1927: "Powhatan's daughter, or Pocahontas, is the mythological nature-symbol chosen to represent the physical body of the continent, or the soil. . . . The five sub-sections of Part II are mainly concerned with a gradual exploration of this 'body' whose first possessor was the Indian. It seemed altogether ineffective from the poetic standpoint to approach this material from the purely chronological angle. . . . What I am after is an assimilation of this experience, a more organic panorama, showing the continuous and living evidence of the past in the inmost vital substance of the present" (*Complete Poems and Selected Letters and Prose,* 248).

16. See *P,* 259n.

motivated by a commercial interest, by a desire to promote themselves and to intimidate rivals. The main entrepreneur who supported construction of the bridge, the one who risked his life "to pull the clumsy bridge into position" in front of a large and enthusiastic crowd, was "the happiest man in the town that day . . . Timothy B. Crane, who had charge of the bridge" (P, 15).

Another figure of "large, rugged stature" "resembled" Crane: Sam Patch, a boss at the cotton mill. At first Patch is only an observer to Crane's unveiling of the bridge, which was designed to defeat *his* rival, Fyfield.[17] Eventually Patch steals the stage from Crane by saving the bridge from destruction through an act of heroism performed before everyone who had come to "watch the bridge placed in position" on "a great day for old Paterson":

> While all were expecting to see the big, clumsy bridge topple over and land in the chasm [one of the rolling pins had slid from the ropes into the water], as quick as a flash a form leaped out from the highest point and struck with a splash in the dark water below, swam to the wooden pin and brought it ashore. This was the starting point of Sam Patch's career as a famous jumper. . . . These were the words that Sam Patch said "Now, old Tim Crane thinks he has done something great; but I can beat him." As he spoke he jumped. (P, 16)

Patch gains recognition for his heroic deed of saving the bridge from tumbling into the Passaic River, but he loses his life through an act that privileges the celebration of the performer over the communitarian usefulness of his task. Patch "became a national hero in '28, '29 and toured the country / diving from cliffs and masts, rocks and bridges—to prove his / thesis: Some things can be done as well as others" (P, 15).

In another prose account that Williams includes in book 1 as part of his documentary of Paterson, New Jersey, Reverend Hooper Cumming is presented as falling into the Passaic Falls on June 20, 1812. Cumming also allows his wife, Sarah, to fall to her death in the falls because he mistakes the dangerous territory surrounding the water for "romantic scenery" (P, 14). Cumming is saved from drowning by a brave young passerby who,

---

17. The religious connotations of the ladder and the winding stair found in *Four Quartets* link Fyfield with Crane's and Williams's identical rival, Eliot.

like Sam Patch, dives into the water to perform a rescue mission. Cumming's need to be protected by a local man described in the prose account as a "guardian angel" can be compared to Williams's literary relationship to E. E. Cummings as it was expressed in the contemporaneous essay "Lower Case Cummings" (1946). In that essay, Williams presents Cummings as a "Deacon" who is "not robust, [who] is positively afraid of physical violence if he goes out of his rooms." Cummings's reputation must be rescued by Williams in the essay from a "species of Americans and certain other wild animals [who] are prone to attack a man going alone."[18]

Especially because it appears after the "Cumming" incident, Williams's recollection of Tim Crane's attempt to erect a bridge in Paterson comes to have the valence of a negative criticism of Hart Crane's design for an American long poem. The references to the Crane legend not only provide the community of Paterson with a "living history" such as was found in the WPA state guidebooks to which Williams contributed and are not only an instance of agonistic criticism directed at Hart Crane's "big, clumsy bridge." The Crane passage may also be read as Williams's criticism of the direction his own career had taken during the New Directions phase after he had turned his attention to the project of self-selling in the narrative fictions. Sam Patch originally helped Crane as an active participant in saving from disaster an event of local significance. He ended his life, however, by attempting to exploit, through a national tour, that participation for commercial reasons that called attention to the actor's daring. In telling Patch's story, Williams critiques a project that turns attention toward the celebration of the maker. He describes Patch's response to a dilemma: "as quick as a flash a form leaped out from the highest point and struck with a splash in the dark water below, swam to the wooden pin and brought it ashore" (*P*, 16). Patch's original intention was to provide his community with more direct access to a local landmark—metaphorically, to a source of linguistic origins (the falls); literally, to a source of economic strength. But Patch cannot recognize another maker's work as useful once his own commercial interests come to mind. He used the legend—the "news"—of his saving of Crane's bridge as "the starting point of Sam Patch's career as a famous jumper." The act is interpreted by the poem's speaker as a theatrical show of Patch's desire to dominate the local scene. The project

18. *Selected Essays*, 264.

becomes a deadly contest when Patch leaps into the falls to show the superiority of his skill and courage over that of Crane and to build his legend as a "famous jumper":

> Then he announced that before returning to the Jerseys he was going to show the West one final marvel. He would leap 125 feet from the falls of the Genesee River on November 13, 1829. Excursions came from great distances in the United States and even from Canada to see the wonder.
>
> A platform was built at the edge of the falls. He went to great trouble to ascertain the depth of the water below. He even successfully performed one practice leap.
>
> On the day the crowds were gathered on all sides. He appeared and made a short speech as he was wont to do. A speech! What could he say that he must leap so desperately to complete it? And plunged toward the stream below. But instead of descending with a plummet-like fall his body wavered in the air— Speech had failed him. He was confused. The word had been drained of its meaning. There's no mistake in Sam Patch. He struck the water on his side and disappeared.
>
> A great silence followed as the crowd stood spellbound.
>
> Not until the following spring was the body found frozen in an ice-cake. (P, 16)

Because the bridge is erased of its own value, the saving of it is turned toward the celebration of the hero. The performance imitates the original contribution. Patch becomes a spectacle, "a wonder," a disfigured sign of action now unrelated to place. The publicity for the culture hero is understood to be the "freezing" of the useful action. The moment when the useful act becomes a display of publicity is presented as annihilative of the hero and of his original desire to act on behalf of others.

The Patch-Crane incident in book 1 becomes charged with metaphorical significance when understood as representative of Williams's struggle to reach his audience in competition with designs such as *The Bridge.* The blocks of material coming into the poem from outside, as Ralph Nash argues, are relevant to the poet's quest for alignment of his personal struggle with the common past of his area of identification: "[A] letter (or anything else) written by someone other than the poet brings into the poem something of an air of documentation. Irrelevancies and private allusions emphasize that this is not exactly a piece of the poem, but a piece of the poet's world. No doubt Williams intends it partly as forceful marriage of his poem's world with that world of reality from which he is fearful of divorcing himself."[19] The emphasis in the readings by Lloyd, Mazzaro, Matthews, and Nash is on the poet's struggle to succeed in his quest to overcome a linguistic blockage rather than on his creation of "a living language" useful to the establishment of a community's sense of pride of place. While Lloyd has understood this yoking in *Paterson* of man and city to be an example of Williams's empathy with those persons and places he incorporates in his poem, the project, unlike a lyric such as "The Lonely Street," is often shown as preventing the experiences of other persons from appearing with autonomy. It is not strictly a project of "emphasiz[ing] the solid, independent existence of the thing and the need to perceive its surface with care and precision," as Breslin defined the imagist aesthetic that applied to Williams's poetry from 1921. It is one in which the environment, and the linguistic resources of the poem, including the desires of other persons, are presented as extensions of and publicity for the poet's mind and body.

II. The Damaged Pearl: Book 1

Book 1 contains many examples in addition to the Tim Crane incident that illustrate the ambivalent status of Williams's situation in *Paterson* as a public writer also concerned with establishing his literary identity within his major poetic work. The poet is portrayed as a mediator of local history, but also as a figure absorbed in his struggle for personal acknowledgment to the extent that his ability to value other voices is undermined. Throughout book 1, Williams shows how commercial ex-ploitation of local resources destroyed the natural beauty of the town of Paterson. The best example concerns an extraordinarily large pearl that was ruined by treasure hunters. A prose account included in book 1, part 1—which was probably taken from an article in the *Paterson Guardian* of May 1, 1857[20]—describes how treasure hunters boiled open the shell of the mussel that contained the pearl, damaging its rare beauty:

> In February 1857, David Hower, a poor shoemaker with a large family, out of work and money, collected a lot of mussels from Notch Brook near the City of Paterson. He found in eating them many hard substances. At first he

19. "The Use of Prose in Paterson."
20. See *P,* 256n.

threw them away but at last submitted some of them to a jeweler who gave him twenty-five to thirty dollars for the lot. Later he found others. One pearl of fine lustre was sold to Tiffany for $900 and later to the Empress Eugenie for $2,000 to be known thenceforth as the "Queen Pearl," the finest of its sort in the world today.

News of this sale created such excitement that a search for the pearls was started throughout the country. The Unios (mussels) at Notch Brook and elsewhere were gathered by the millions and destroyed often with little or no result. A large round pearl, weighing 400 grains which would have been the finest pearl of modern times, was ruined by boiling open the shell. (*P*, 9)

The passage speaks to a kind of perversion of the poet's own attention to finding "beauty in the commonplace" and to the idea of the "radiant gist," insofar as the rare beauty inside the mussel is destroyed in the act of discovering it. In the poem, Williams juxtaposes this account of commercial exploitation with an expression of his concern about his own textual exploitation of his region of identification in a way that mars, distorts, or calls attention from the object he is addressing.

In comic fashion, Williams follows the prose account of the pearl with an account of the poet as an aloof "majority" figure. In the following passage, Paterson appears to be more interested in his connections to religious and literary figures than in performing his public function of presenting a redeeming language:

> Twice a month Paterson receives
> communications from the Pope and Jacques
>   Barzun
> (Isocrates). His works
> have been done into French
> and Portuguese. And clerks in the post-
> office ungum rare stamps from
> his packages and steal them for their
> childrens' albums. (*P*, 9)

This mocking of Paterson's status as a celebrity who has, in a passage that follows, "gone away / to rest and write," is significant when we consider the shift I have described in Williams's understanding of the poem and other literary works as acts of self-creation for purposes of professional legitimation. While Paterson is receiving "communications" from leading figures in the traditional establishments of religion ("the Pope") and of secular culture (Columbia University Professor Barzun, who is identified with an orator and rhetorician of ancient Greece), the "people" of Paterson, New Jersey, "walk incommunicado" (*P,* 9). Williams's inclusion of information critical of the outcome to his project (the Cress letters, the narcissistic display of the publicized self evident in the preceding passage) is an act of demystification that by book 5, paradoxically, becomes one of Williams's strategies for enhancing trust in his authority as a writer concerned about the welfare of others. In the passage just quoted, and most prominently in descriptions of the poet in book 5, Williams acknowledges the limits to his authority over the lives of other persons who share space in his city. In book 5, Williams finally resists the desire to achieve a total identification of his personal construction with the meaning of his society, a will to power that was not resisted by other modern poets.

The related themes of Paterson's unwillingness to admit others to the privilege of representation and his fear of personal disfiguration once he enters into the language of the poem as a textual specter are presented in book 1 through two metaphors that employ natural imagery. Throughout book 1, Williams describes Paterson's imagination as being fortified by thoughts figured as trees: "They are trees / from whose leaves streaming with rain / his mind drinks of desire" (*P,* 30). In part 3, however, the poet finds his own representations of natural imagery to be in competition with "the rose," the source of mimesis. Paterson appears here, alone, in the thaw between late winter and early spring. The previous section ended with a letter from the poet Edward Dahlberg urging Paterson to avoid the conception of "the book [as] one thing, and the man who wrote it another" and, instead, "to submit to your own myths, and that any postponement in doing so is a lie for you" (*P,* 28). Then the speaker addresses himself in a voice of contempt:

> How strange you are, you idiot!
> So you think because the rose
> is red that you shall have the mastery?
> The rose is green and will bloom,
> overtopping you, green, livid
> green when you shall no more speak, or
> taste, or even be. My whole life
> has hung too long upon a partial victory. (*P,* 29)

Paterson understands that the rose, unmediated by representation, will exist through natural regeneration after the cessation of the construction of his poem and, by extension, after the disappearance of the poet's "real presence." In contrast to the regenerative possibilities inherent in the rose, the poem as object is conceived to be the "news," or dead trace, of the presence of a mind once entered by composition into what Charles Olson, in an essay that Williams included as chapter 50 of his autobiography, called the "field" (*A*, 330). Even when conceived as nothing more than the space of appearance available to the poet, the poem does not preserve natural presence as the poet desires. Instead, it is the trace of his failure to gain personal substantiation in language *or* appearance in the world outside the poem.[21] The poet has nowhere to go in this model of poetics, which holds that the life of the maker is extinguished with the cessation of the writing act: "you shall no more speak, or / taste, or even be."

In an interview with Edith Heal in 1958, Williams suggested the metaphoric aspect of his poetry about nature: "When I spoke of flowers, I was a flower, with all the prerogative of flowers, especially the right to come alive in the Spring."[22] In the next movement of book 1, Williams uses this strategy to make a humorous comparison with serious implications between his thoughts and the "thoughts" of a mature sycamore tree. This trope for the mature poet will then be presented as in competition with a younger figure. The competition is not between the world as text and the dominion of the world of natural things. Instead, through metaphor, Williams discusses his literary agony with a younger generation of successors such as Allen Ginsberg by using a term from nature as the vehicle:

> Who is younger than I?
>   The contemptible twig?
> that I was? stale in mind
>   whom the dirt
>
> recently gave up? Weak
>   to the wind.
> Gracile? Taking up no place,
> too narrow to be engraved
>   with the maps
>
> of a world it never knew,
>   the green and

21. This problem has been articulated most prominently by de Man in "Autobiography as De-facement."

22. Williams, *I Wanted to Write a Poem*, 21.

        dovegrey countries of
            the mind.

    A mere stick that has
            twenty leaves
    against my convolutions.
            What shall it become,

    Snot nose, that I have
            not been?
    I enclose it and
            persist, go on.

    Let it rot, at my center.
            Whose center?
    I stand and surpass
            youth's leanness.

    My surface is myself.
            Under which
    to witness, youth is
            buried. Roots?

    Everybody has roots. (*P,* 30-31)

The tree is a figure for Paterson as a cultural giant who is grounded in the natural world. It is an image of the poet as able to renew himself through replenishment from the local soil. The song is also in praise of maturity, but the praise is contingent on the singer's distancing himself from origins in "the dirt." Rootedness in the local soil was, paradoxically, supposed to have been Williams's call for a nativist poetics. The song reverses the order of the death of the father (or elder) before the son. The speaker claims to have "buried" the son within the convoluted—or, literally, rolled together—space of *Paterson.* The "mature" figure shows "contempt" for the younger version of itself. It is in a position of dominance that also suggests a desire to arrest change and a rage at eventually having to relinquish the superior position in this cyclical model of rejuvenation.

The narrative logic of the poem is that of a sequence prepared by a poet concerned with his cultural placement. The passages in book 1 following the Song of the Sycamore offer Paterson/Williams as the appropriate master for a nativist poetics. In what directly follows, the speaker criticizes "academic" poetry, as well as a university establishment that "blocks" the freedom of the poet to express parts of a world that had been considered by many other poets to be unworthy of representation. As will be the case throughout the rest of part 3, Williams is here less concerned with the production of poetry than with the way poetry is (or is not) disseminated to a new audience of readers:

> We go on living, we permit ourselves
> to continue—but certainly
> not for the university, what they publish
>
> severally or as a group: clerks
> got out of hand forgetting for the most part
> to whom they are beholden .
>
> spitted on fixed concepts like
> roasting hogs, sputtering, their drip sizzling
> in the fire (P, 31–32)

Williams is concerned with the distribution of materials to an audience wider than the cultural elite. He addresses this issue through a sequence of passages that form a dialogue between those who "hoard" (the university "clerks") and those who are interested in a more open way to distribute valuable material. After two ambiguous prose passages that describe Williams's work as an obstetrician—the first presents the overworked Doc obsessively concerned with removing the label from a mayonnaise jar that has been used by a patient as a specimen jar; the second describes a "young colored woman" who has asked someone (Doc?) to "give me a baby"—there follows an example of how not to manage scarce resources. Unlike Dr. Paterson, who, although irreverent and clearly overworked, has offered his medical expertise to a wide range of persons at the clinic, the economic managers in the following passage show no responsiveness to local needs:

> In time of general privation
> a private herd, 20 quarts of milk
> to the main house and 8 of cream,
>
> . . . .
>
> Grapes in April, orchids
> like weeds, uncut, at tropic
> heat while the snow flies, left
> to droop on the stem, not even
> exhibited at the city show. (P, 32–33)

The managers of an economic boom, through hoarding of resources, or through the improper distribution of wealth, block most citizens from access to material goods. Their hoarding induces waste and rot. Their failure to distribute needed goods is related, through juxtaposition in the poem, to the activity of the university clerks. The distribution of representation is placed into terms of economic privilege and economic scarcity.

The description of "Grapes in April, orchids / like weeds, uncut, at tropic / heat while the snow flies, left / to droop on the stem" suggests Williams had in mind the opening passage to the "Burial of the Dead" section of *The Waste Land* when he placed the scene of economic hoarding inside his poem.[23] If so, Eliot is condemned for his control of the literary and historical knowledge of the past and for limiting the clientele able to access the long poem as a document that sustains value. This version of Eliot is figured in Williams's parodic allusion to the opening of *The Waste Land,* where the pleasures of April and the renewal of the land are, paradoxically, a source of pain for the speaker. The possibilities for a comfortable relationship to love and sex—the possibilities, in other words, for the fulfillment of desire and for a healthy relationship to natural being—are called into question in Eliot's poem. We have seen that Williams was concerned with his own relationship to the natural world. He tried to assert his power over nature by transferring the grounds of the rooted natural thing, through metaphor, to the space of culture, the poem as organic object. But he was unable to accept a "natural" transference of power from father to son in the Song of the Sycamore. Through displacement, Williams projected his inability to transfer the grounds of nature into cultural work by presenting Eliot as disrupting his relationship to nature without benefiting from this disruption.

Traditionally, spring is the time of natural rejuvenation. It is a time associated with optimism about the survival and rebirth of the culture,

23. The poem abounds with veiled criticisms of Eliot's characteristic pose as Anglican, Royalist, and Classicist. Among them are a parody of "East Coker" from *Four Quartets* ("For the beginning is assuredly / the end—since we know nothing, pure / and simple, beyond / our own complexities," *P,* 3); the name of the failed initiator of the bridge over the Passaic, Fyfield (*P,* 16); the criticism of preacher Klaus Ehrens's emphasis on eternal life in the midst of cultural crisis (*P,* 66); and the mocking of Billy Sunday's "canonized feet": "He's on / the table now! Both feet, singing / (a foot song) his feet canonized / as paid for / by the United Factory Owners' Ass'n. / to 'break the strike'" (*P,* 171–72).

but this is not the case in Eliot's poem. Spring, in the opening passage to *The Waste Land,* is cruel; nature is rejuvenated, but the figures in Eliot's poem are disabled sexually, and so are refused the means of regeneration:

> April is the cruellest month, breeding
> Lilacs out of the dead land, mixing
> Memory and desire, stirring
> Dull roots with spring rain.
> Winter kept us warm, covering
> Earth in forgetful snow, feeding
> A little life with dried tubers.[24]

Characters in "The Burial of the Dead"—such as the Countess Marie Larisch, who was the confidant of Empress Elizabeth in the years before Austria's defeat in World War I lessened the nobility's wealth and influence—are presented, because of their wealth, as divorced from a relationship of likeness to the natural world, and even as unable to respond to changing economic and political states of affairs after World War I and the Russian Revolution. They are alienated from their natural and cultural surroundings. For these characters in Eliot's poem, snow is a means of forgetting. Cold is not a reminder of the hardness of experience when seen without illusion, as it is for the speaker in Robert Frost's "After Apple Picking" as he looks at the world through a pane of ice, or as it is for Wallace Stevens in "The Snow Man." In Eliot's poem, April is cruel; winter is warm. Winter is the season that enables the European elite to maintain their fiction of comfort and insulation from pain through their wealth. Although it may be unfair of Williams to attack Eliot through a critique of the desire for isolation found in such figures as Countess Marie Larisch, Williams is arguing against the values upheld by poems such as *The Waste Land.* Williams believes poems more sensitive to problems of class than Eliot's could, metaphorically, sustain the lives of those neglected from representation. Even in a time "of general privation"—both in terms of economic goods and in terms of access to cultural work—"orchids" would not be left to rot "like weeds" when they could have brought pleasure to a general population if "exhibited at the city show."

In book 1, part 3, Williams returns to the sequential dialogue between accessible and inaccessible forms of economic distribution by introducing

24. T. S. Eliot, *The Waste Land,* lines 1–7.

a notice about a farmer's bequest to his children: "Cornelius Doremus, who was baptized at Acquackonock in 1714, and died near Montville in 1803, was possessed of goods and chattels appraised at $419.58 ½. He was 89 years old when he died, and doubtless had turned his farm over to his children, so that he retained only what he needed for his personal comfort" (*P*, 33). The passage then details the items Doremus owned, and their cost, beginning with twenty-four shirts at eighty-two and a half cents. To Williams, Doremus is a model figure in terms of how he distributes his wealth. As a farmer, he is involved in cultural work that sustains life through a relationship to the natural world. He is able to transfer his wealth, and the means toward the continuity and sustenance of his family and community, by bequest. Doremus's relationship to his children is not blocked by his own fear of death, as is the case with Paterson in the first four books of the poem. Although Williams in the Song of the Sycamore was unable to imitate Doremus's relationship to his children in his own approach to a younger generation of poets, his presentation of Doremus's story contrasts with the display of cultural hoarding among the aristocratic classes in Eliot. In this sequence of images about the distribution of value, Doremus's story stands as the idealization of Williams's own relationship to a future generation of poets appearing on the American scene.

The first three movements of book 1, part 3, concern Williams's desire to place himself as the master of a sphere of representation. He refuses to relinquish this mastery either to nature or to a poetic successor. (We should note that even the name *Paterson* attempts to enclose the generative model all in one figure, consisting as it does of the Latin word for *father* and the English word *son*.) This obstruction to a positive evaluation of the voices of others, or to their claims to unique origins ("everybody has roots"), contradicts the objective of finding a common language that could introduce citizens of Paterson to their place, which is the stated goal of book 1. The speaker has presented himself as standing up against adversaries. He is proud to be able to "encompass" them. In order to stand up against them, he has chosen to understand his relationship to other cultural makers as one of possession, rather than the relationship of identification with the neglected other that was Williams's attitude toward his constituency when his poetry was working well.

The poet has chosen a nature metaphor as the basis for his work—the poem as organic process, rather than as superinduced form. He has raged against the "university" system of cultural authorization by arguing that this system privileges poets who are stuck in "fixed concepts" and, therefore, that it honors poets entombed within their texts. I will show in the next section that the logic of Williams's own conception of his mind in book 2 as a "red stone" similar to a grasshopper of stone discovered in Mexico City condemns his poetry to this status of representation, which is to say, inanimacy. The conception of a poetry of "fixed concepts" denies his contribution as a poet of "flow" or of "fire." These are the tropes for the work of the active mind engaged in transforming all things (found in both nature and culture) into a version of the mature self. The conception of "fixed concepts" is attached to the "university" poets in an act of displacement that is also an attempt to release Williams from the logic of his own representation as Paterson, a logic that he denies, until the reversal of book 5.

III. The Stone Grasshopper: Book 2

The general scheme of book 1 involves the quest to "unravel" the redeeming Ur-language found in the sound of the rushing water of the Passaic River that divides the poet from the "female" ground of the American countryside. The promise is for a renewal of what Stephen Tapscott has called "the verbal spirit in American 'soil.' "[25] Book 1 also examines the dangers to the poet who claims that his work embodies his presence. I have described the paradoxes of Williams's identifying the prestige of the self as constructed in the text with the independence of the local place in a political and literary sense. The problems with conceiving of Paterson in this way may be further shown by pointing to the image Williams chooses to symbolize a permanent artifact that conserves "some rumor / of the living presence that has preceded / it" (*P*, 47). This is the image of the statuette of a grasshopper found in Mexico City that appears at the beginning of book 2 ("Sunday in the Park").

As in book 1, Williams continues in book 2 to criticize the poor fit between the vulgarity of the industrial age and the metrical arrangements found in the aristocratic conception of poetry that cannot contain the speech rhythms of the lower-middle-class, largely immigrant, lovers in the park. The poet searches for a formal principle that will return to his place and time the mythic beauty of the falls and the permanence of art

---

25. *American Beauty: William Carlos Williams and the Modernist Whitman*, 186.

embodied in the carved grasshopper from Mexico. The book ends with the poet's failure to achieve his task on either a personal or a public scale. The poet leaves the park as a lonely wanderer, and the crowd is presented as an amnesiac giant beast. Wandering in the park, Paterson tries to discover a relationship between the artifact and the "world outside myself" without returning the poem to traditional metrical arrangements. Stumbling onto a cluster of grasshoppers, his mind is reminded of the artifacts:

> AND a grasshopper of red basalt, boot-long,
> tumbles from the core of his mind,
> a rubble-bank disintegrating beneath a
> tropic downpour
>
> Chapultepec! grasshopper hill!
>
> —a matt stone solicitously instructed
> to bear away some rumor
> of the living presence that has preceded
> it, out-precedented its breath .
> These wings do not unfold for flight—
> no need! (*P,* 47–48)

By remembering the discovery of this grasshopper, which appeared to archaeologists after a rainstorm destroyed "a rubble-bank," the poet suggests how the object transcends the lives of the ancient craftsmen of Mexico, who made it to preserve a trace, a "rumor," of their existence. The object is made to come alive through the "counter-weight" of the "mind's wings," or the wandering poet's own imagination of the previous maker's craftsmanship. This symbol of the stone grasshopper, however, is insufficient for suggesting a poetry of presence superior to "being" unmediated by representation. The inadequacy of this symbol is implicit in the poet's description of his own mind as "a red stone carved to be / endless flight" (*P,* 48). This symbol for the poet's mind suggests that in book 2 he cannot situate himself outside the representational space in which he has identified his presence with the movement of his imagination in the poem.

In book 2, the poet describes the inscription of his thoughts on the page as a kind of writing on stone that will endure "so long as stone shall last bearing / the chisel's stroke" (*P,* 49). In this conception, writing is less available to decay than is the writing that is preserved as text on paper in the library of book 3, but the presence of Paterson in this poem is not alive. Indeed, like the stone grasshopper that suggests the hands that carved the stone, only the "rumor" of presence is apparent. Like the "news" of a fire that is no longer new once reported, the space of the poem does not conserve the flesh of the poet ("the flesh dies").

IV. This Is Not a Text: The Library of Book 3

From the perspective of the medium chosen for representation, two forms are privileged in *Paterson:* those associated with a world prior to the Gutenberg Revolution (the world of the stone grasshopper in book 2) and those associated with a world posterior to book culture, the latter consisting of the array of electronic and mechanical means that have dominated the transmission of information in this century. *Paterson* of course is a printed text and not a radio broadcast, a filmic montage, a hieroglyph carved in stone, or an altogether unmediated performance. Although this is undeniably true, in book 3 the speaker attempts to repudiate his affiliation with print culture by attacking books written by other authors and by claiming that *Paterson* is not a text, but is instead a living embodiment of the presence of the poet. The library that gives the title to book 3 is presented as a place containing old books irrelevant to contemporary life in Paterson, New Jersey. Occupied by the tombs of poets that are themselves figures for bound texts, the library is set ablaze. The entombed poets are condemned because they had tried to escape the chaos of the "roar of the present" that the speaker of *Paterson* wants to "embrace."

"Embrace" turns out, however, to be an inappropriate metaphor for Williams to adopt when speaking about his attempt to introduce his constituents to their own "primary culture," or to a representational practice not alienated from local history, legend, speech practice, or soil. Over the course of the poem Williams tries without success to sustain a logic that will allow him to trust in Paterson as the substantiation of his real presence. Eventually, he releases his expectations for a representational embrace and final conservation of the human image as a replacement for the significance of lived experience. After this release takes place, the literary work can open up again to the world outside the poem as an object, rather than as the subject, of his lyrical meditations. In the fire scene at the library, however, Williams displaces his knowledge about the outcome of textual instantiation onto the authors of books discussed in *Paterson,* rather than onto *Paterson* itself. The books that go up in smoke at the Danforth Public Library are considered by the speaker to be objects of contempt.

The speaker tries to capture the language of his city by attempting to articulate the reveries of Noah Faitoute Paterson, Williams's major prosopopoeiac construction in poetry. Noah Paterson is the logical successor in poetic representation to the variety of heroic personages on the threshold between high and low culture that Williams developed in his conventional fictions beginning with *A Voyage to Pagany,* and including the medical fictions and *In the Money.* As well as being an extension of the desire he displayed in the fiction to present himself as a representative figure, *Paterson* is also a critique of, and, most intensively in book 5, a withdrawal from, the untenable identification of the poet with his instantiation in autobiographically based texts.

Noah Faitoute Paterson is a version of Williams as a majority figure, the one poet who survived the flood and "did it all." He is the giant made out of the stone from Garret Mountain who reclines beside the Passaic Falls before he awakens from a dream at the beginning of book 1 ("The Delineaments of the Giants"). Noah Paterson is, according to Williams, the "image large enough to embody the whole knowable world about me" (*A,* 391). Because he is made of stone, Paterson is a paradoxical inscription of Williams as a living presence able to embrace the primary culture of his city. Paterson is like a tombstone, or like a death mask. Although Paterson is a paradoxical figure made other than the poet through literary representation, the poem's speaker tries to argue in book 3 that what Charles Olson called the "high energy construct" of Paterson in the poem can be distinguished from other representations of authors found in "The Library." The Supreme Fiction of the first four books of *Paterson* is that representation in this poem embodies the speaker's "real presence" as it does not in any other poem. The metaphor is that of the writer creating a world that is literalized, or substantiated in Williams's case. The body of the world is said to enter the process of writing so that writing becomes a physical presence equivalent to reality.[26]

---

26. I have borrowed this formulation of Williams's myth of the bodily character of *écriture* from Eugene Goodheart's essay on Roland Barthes, "The Monster of Totality," 82.

The claim in book 3 is that *Paterson*—as the poetic speaker; as an account of the giant, physical dwelling space of the inhabitants of the poem; and as the poem itself in the form of a dynamic broadcast across the pages of five books plus fragments of a sixth—is distinguished from other poetry because of its performative, rather than constitutive, kind of meaning making. By performative I mean that the poem, according to Williams in the *Autobiography,* does not discuss "ideas" in a way that could be explained (or challenged) by another reader. In what I am calling the constitutive model of meaning making that Williams rejects, "ideas" are conceived of as available to the mind prior to the activity of writing. In this model, the meaning of *Paterson* is found in the spectacle of the poet, substantiated in language as a physical/textual presence. The poem is the embodiment of the poet's thinking through the unfolding of the material in a way that captures the performance of thinking without alienating it from textuality or from a reality associated with the act of writing: "The poet thinks with his poem, in that lies his thought, and that in itself is the profundity. The thought is *Paterson,* to be discovered there. Therefore the thinker tries to capture the poem for his purpose, using his 'thought' as the net to put his thoughts into. Absurd. They are not profound enough to discover that by this they commit a philosophic solecism" (*A,* 390-91).

In contrast to interpreting his own poem as the embodiment of a living knowledge, in book 3 Williams describes the work of other poets as enfeebling "the mind's intent" to contact the "attainable beauty" available in Paterson: "they cannot penetrate and cannot waken, to be again / active but remain—books / that is, men in hell, / their reign over the living ended" (*P,* 116). Juxtaposed to the criticism of the transference of the author's presence into bound texts as deadening, which is the general argument found within the twenty-page description of the mauling of the library in a fire that swept through Paterson, New Jersey, in 1902, *Paterson* is figured as a "living" embodiment of "real" materials from the local past. A figure of physical contact—"embrace"—is presented as superior to one of mediated contact—"composition." Paterson, however, can achieve satisfying relationships with others through neither figure of literary "contact." Paterson's imagination, containing traces of the New Jersey past, is compared to the fire that swept through the city in 1902. The poet's activity is considered to be both destructive and reconstructive of the materials it consumes. There is a coincidence between the identification of the substantiation of the poetic speaker and the temporal movement of the poem's language that consumes the world of appearances:

> Hottest
> lips lifted till no shape but a vast
> molt of the news flows. Drink
> of the news, fluid to the breath. (*P,* 118)

Without the attention to formal "composition" of the abstract design of the poem as an object other than the poet's living thought, the poet becomes identified with the exhausting action of the poem. The poem's movement is figured as a blaze of fire that eventually will become extinguished:

> Rising, with a whirling motion, the person
> passed into the flame, becomes the flame
> the flame taking over the person
>
> 　　—with a roar, an outcry
> which none can afford (*P,* 122)

I have described the paradoxes of the conflation of the poet's "living presence" with the "whirling motion" of the poem as a means for Williams to distinguish his project of self-construction from the work of other poets. I have also registered the poet's struggle to dismiss a relationship between his poem and the finished products of a print culture that can only produce self-portraiture through a textual restoration that, in de Man's terms, "deprives and disfigures" the sense of actual presence "to the precise extent that it restores."[27]

Let me examine the "fire" scene from another point of view. I want to establish the relationship Williams sets up with his intended audience by approaching this passage as Williams's confrontation with the outcome (no longer preliminary as it was in the narrative fictions) of assigning the value of his work to representing the author as a figure of cultural renown. In book 3, part 2, Williams approaches the problem of the literary establishment's refusal to release information to ordinary citizens. He presents himself as the only political and cultural reformer, the only poet

27. "Autobiography as De-facement," 81.

with knowledge of poetic technique, who is also willing to apply this technique to a neglected constituency:

> They have
>
> manoeuvered it so that to write
> is a fire and not only of the blood.
>
> The writing is nothing, the being
> in a position to write (that's
>
> where they get you) is nine tenths
> of the difficulty: seduction
>
> or strong arm stuff. The writing
> should be a relief,
>
> relief from the conditions
> which as we advance become—a fire,
>
> a destroying fire. For the writing
> is also an attack and means must be
>
> found to scotch it—at the root
> if possible. So that
>
> to write, nine tenths of the problem
> is to live. They see
>
> to it, not by intellection but
> by sub-intellection (to want to be
>
> blind as a pretext for
> saying, We're so proud of you!) (*P,* 113-14)

In *A Voyage to Pagany,* the "Doctor Stories," and *In the Money,* Williams's strategy for allowing readers to gain trust in the characters whose stories are surrogates for his own was to situate them in a position of liminality, or as messengers between codes of cultural affiliation. In *A Voyage to Pagany,* for example, he situated his description of Dev Evans's journey to Europe between a travel diary (suggesting an unmediated account of actual experience with no pretension to communitarian interest) and the narrative structure found in ritual rites of passage and "quest romance" tales. The codes of value found in the narrative fictions tend to break down into two categories. One is the tradition of imperial authority (the church and avant-garde culture in Europe in *Pagany,* the rhetoric and methods of science learned in Europe by the medical regulars in the Doctor Stories, and the "insider" knowledge of the corporate expert in *In the Money*). The other is the tradition of common or nativist discourse that Edward Said characterized as a class of language devoted to describing the land in a way that allows a decolonized people to ground themselves. These "low" forms are related to an affinity with the force of the native ground (Paterson as stone giant, the river and falls as an Ur-language, the soil as the female body Paterson must "marry"), as well as to an affirmation of the history of the place as it is told in popular culture. In the passage from book 3 that I have just presented, Williams straddles both sides of the equation of traditional (imperial) and radical (decolonial or nativist) legitimacy. He speaks to his "townspeople" from a knowledge of the practices of other poets who reside in Europe, referred to here as "they." But he is the one major poet, the one major "they," willing to share his knowledge of poetic structures with an audience of outsiders.

The equation of poetic force with the destructive/constructive elements of a fire that consumes and transforms is interpreted by the poem's speaker, in book 3, part 2, as a necessary defense against the literary "special interests." The speaker claims that the destructive activity of the poem as a consuming fire is necessary for Paterson's survival as a poet able to be in a position to write on behalf of others. The equation of the poem, the poet, and the transformational fire, however, has unanticipated consequences for the poet's relationship to his intended audience. His readers are now shown to confuse the construction of the persona with the overall contribution of the poem. In book 3, Williams admits that he has ignored the needs of his readers by focusing on displaying the image of the maker, rather than on the poem itself as an object of inclusion. He admits that he has misled his audience about what is of value in his poetry. His readers have, quite understandably, identified his personal fame and public image as his contribution to the cultural record:

> Clearly, they say. Oh clearly! Clearly?
> What more clear than that of all things
> nothing is so unclear, between man and
> his writing, as to which is the man and
> which the thing and of them both which
> is the more to be valued (*P,* 116)

Williams believes his intended audience fails to see that the "clear" thematic meaning to his work is, in fact, the author's confusion (and confession of his confusion) about the difference between an autonomous literary work and the poem as an act of self-creation. The speaker himself does not know if the creation of the poem and the creation of the identity of the poet through signs are the same act of general cultural value. He understands that the presence of the author as textual specter might be "the thing" that fetches a price. He does not know, however, if his "I" has become a "thing" that can be "valued," that is, has become a marketable "thing," an object even to the author, and so an object made other to the author.

The prose passage that follows the passage I have just quoted concerns the 1902 fire that "doomed" the city of Paterson. The juxtaposition of the "Clearly, they say" passage with the account of the actual fire underlines the poet's own fears that his poetic act has become so confused with the inscription of his image into the poem that the meaning of his project is no longer his to determine:

> When discovered it was a small blaze, though it was hot but it looked as tho' the firemen could handle it. But at dawn a wind came up and the flames (which they thought were subsiding) got suddenly out of control—sweeping the block and heading toward the business district. Before noon the whole city was doomed— (P, 116)

In this sequence, Williams is thinking of authorship as a form of self-sacrifice in the sense that the self is made other to itself. In a passage reminiscent of Williams's linking in *A Voyage to Pagany* of modern forms of creative initiation with "primitive" forms of sacred initiation, he presents an account of a ritual sacrifice that he adapted and rearranged from William Nelson's 1901 *History of the City of Paterson and the County of Passaic New Jersey*.[28]

> Whereupon as the smoke ascends on high, the sacrificer crying with a loud voice, *Kännakä, Kännakä!* or sometimes *Hoo, Hoo!* turns his face towards the east.
>
> While some are silent during the sacrifice, certain make a ridiculous speech, while others imitate the cock, the squirrel and other animals, and make all kinds of noises. (P, 115)

28. See P, 282n.

The ways in which the subjects of the sacrifice respond—for instance, whether or not they shout before the sacrifice—mirror the various responses of Sam Patch and others to their sensational falls into the Passaic in the nineteenth-century prose account of the "famous jumpers" in book 1, part 1. Patch, for example, "Made a short speech as he was wont to do. A speech! What could he say that he must leap so desperately to complete it? And he plunged toward the stream below" (*P,* 16). The leap into the falls was the metaphor Williams chose in book 1 to describe total contact with the local source of language.

The role of the public writer is understood in book 3 to be to sacrifice experience on behalf of access to a linguistic force that is devastating to the person exposed to it, but that is also understood to be the resource necessary for the community to appear in language. If the outcome of a leap into the falls is to become a character in a book, then the message contained about authorship in book 3 prefigures de Man in that this outcome for the poet is understood as an exchange of natural life for the disfiguring presence in the book. The fire that rips through the library, which is the metaphor for the poet who burns the books and changes the physical look of the place (fire being the thing that writing must become when recognition and survival are at stake), is the embodiment of the poet not only remaking the natural ground but also revising the meaning, "glazing" the meaning, of the objectivist poetry that was Williams's signature style and subject matter:

> An old bottle, mauled by the fire
> gets a new glaze, the glass warped
> to a new distinction, reclaiming the
> undefined. A hot stone, reached
> by the tide, crackled over by fine
> lines, the glaze unspoiled
> Annihilation ameliorated: Hottest
> lips lifted till no shape but a vast
> molt of the news flows. Drink
> of the news, fluid to the breath. (*P,* 118)

Paterson has become "a vast molt of the news." The active fire is a trope for the poet. The fire transforms all materials in its path into an announcement of its power to negate anything in its way. The fire replaces the objective artifact—the bottle—as the sign of imaginative value. The imagination of the poet is privileged over the material that he overwhelms. The record of the poet is even given a kind of headline slogan in the next stanza: "Poetry Beats Fire at Its Own Game!"

In book 1, part 3, the poet is described as being in competition with trees, with roses, with poets who wrote by superinduction, with younger poets. He is in book 3 described as being in competition with the natural force of transformation itself, fire. Here, the artificial or poetic means of transformation—speaking through metaphor—is described as being able to "outlast" fire and so "Beat you [fire] at your own game." Williams is working in the postmodern mode of re-creating (reflowering) a first thing. His work is that of the "second flame, surpassing heat." This "second flame" places Williams in the position of changing the meaning of a first act. To think of Williams's project in terms of self-revision, we can read the new glaze on the old bottle as a revision of an imagistic poem such as "Between Walls," with its final image of the shining and broken "pieces of a green / bottle." To think of Williams's project as a revision of public history in order to affirm his personal identity as a poet, we may read this "second flame" as his revision of the meaning of the "real" texts found in the Paterson Public Library by placing them in *Paterson*, where they reveal the force of the poet.

The confusion that Williams fears his audience feels is "clearly" something to be confused about. In "The Lonely Street" the reader can see that here is the thing that the poet made, even if the image of the hand of the poet does not appear in the poem. "The Lonely Street" is a communal object of reference; it has the feeling of a solid object. It is something that readers can experience as separate from themselves, and so discuss in a way that might create a community of interpretation. In this sense, the poem as object helps to create the presence of the reader who is authorized to make meaning out of it. In the first four books of *Paterson*, the poet is presented as a curious hero whose story illustrates an unsettling model for poetic construction. His poem, in fact, seems to consciously warn us against regarding his appearance as a tropological spectacle. Williams, as Paterson, calls attention to himself as an iconic figure, as what Eugene Goodheart would call a "monster of totality."[29] The figure of Paterson has become a curious aspect of the story of the City of Paterson. As a monumental personal construction of the author, Paterson is not

29. See Goodheart's "The Monster of Totality."

unlike the huge fish described in a prose passage from book 1 as "caught" and "captured a short distance below the falls basin" and then accounted for as a local wonder in "The *Bergen Express and Paterson Advertiser* of Wednesday September 3, 1918 . . . under the heading 'The Monster Taken' " (*P*, 11). Or, to point to another of the found pieces of documentary expression that Williams included in book 1 to create a sense of the mythic past of the region, Paterson has become like the "natural curiosity" or the "monster in human form," the man with the "remarkably large and prominent" eyes and nose who was once visited by General George Washington during the period of the American Revolution (*P*, 10). Williams realizes that his persona, by becoming another of Paterson's spectacular wonders, has become a textual artifact of the mythic past of the region, rather than the active speaker of the region's past that the poet hoped to revive through his poem's "living newspaper."

Williams, as Paterson, is an "I" witnessed as an imaginative object. Certainly he is no longer presented as a figure for the natural man. The poet, and not the poem separated from the poet, has become the point of collective awareness. The "man" has become news; the poem has become interpretation. A "glaze" has been applied to what was once an act that suggested, but did not reveal, the poet's hand. The means of displaying information—the printed text—has been understood as the tomb of the author. The alternative to thinking of the poem as a tomb has been, paradoxically, to see it as a fire that burns the books, but also burns itself, and burns out:

> The night was made day by the flames, flames
> on which he fed—grubbing the page
>   (the burning page)
> like a worm—for enlightenment
>
> Of which we drink and are drunk and in the end
> are destroyed (as we feed). (*P*, 117)

Williams claims in book 1 that he wants his poetry to be a "cure" to a general state of affairs in which "Divorce is / the sign of knowledge in our time" (*P*, 17) because "the language / is divorced from their minds" (*P*, 12). He says he wants his poetry to be a "relief for the conditions / which as we advance become—a fire." Williams means that he wants his poetry to be an antidote to a competitive model of literary and economic experience.

But Williams also says he is disabled from constructing his "antidote." He must employ his own competitive strategy because of the practices of those poets, university teachers, and critics who have attacked him. In order "to live" as a poet he must, ironically, construct his own majority through the prosopopoeia, or else become the slave to someone else's competitive designs. There is no room for two masters in this model of negotiation for human recognition through language.

V. The Return to Presence: Book 5

Williams published book 5 of *Paterson* in 1958, when he was, at age seventy-five, recovering from two severe strokes and from a concomitant depression that required hospitalization. This reopening of the poem suggests that Williams did not believe social redemption through the discovery of a common language had taken place, or that a project that aligned presence with écriture could ever achieve closure. In book 4, the poet is figured as a natural man with his dog returning from the sea, representing the death of the author as the poem is allowed to participate in the tyranny of the past. Ironically, book 5, which was designed to sustain authorial presence, celebrates the autotelic nature of art. Williams's insistence there on the poem as a work of art unrelated to his substantiation in the poem as a figure of renown or to his community's sense of its "living history" triggers an affirmation of, and a respect for, the possibility of fellowship with other citizens outside the poem. Relinquishing his identification of the poet with the poem, Williams diminishes his authority as a representative speaker. He is also released from the logic of self-creation as disfiguration, as this was described in the fire scene in the library in book 3. While Williams can no longer authorize his poem through the claims to heroism of the poet, he is enabled to play a less ambitious, but survivable, role in cultural affairs in the world outside the poem. This release allows Williams to accept the poem as an act of serious play that affirms his temporary presence through the act of making the work, and through the act of teaching others to make art, without his having to appear in the poem as a character such as Sam Patch, which is to say, as a subject made into a sacrificial object. By accepting the design of the poem as other than the self, Williams, in book 5, returns to positions about poetry he held, implicitly, in "The Lonely Street." In that poem, as I believe is the case in book 5, the poet's consciousness is suggested through attention to craft (the invention in *Paterson* of the three-stepped line, for example), but the reader's attention in terms of the poet's presence is directed outward, to the scene described, which is the appropriate site for the cultural work of the poet.

Paterson, as the king, is a dead hero in book 5. He is dead in the sense that his search for the unicorn, or the mythic beautiful thing, is a search for what is not to be found in the world of everyday experience. It is as if the inscription of the authorial self hovers between a realistic depiction of the aging natural man and the projection of a fantasy of the speaker's erotic life figured in terms of a medieval romance. The poet's sense of realism includes an accurate representation of the author as an aging married man who accepts fantasy and projection to be dimensions of the same creative imagination that has driven the poem through five volumes:

> —the aging body
> with the deformed great-toe nail
> makes itself known
> coming
> to search me out—with a
> rare smile
> among the thronging flowers of that field
> where the Unicorn
> is penned by a low
> wooden fence
> in April! (*P,* 229)

The erotic imagination of the poet as phallic hero (the wounded unicorn) is self-consciously presented in the poem as a representation. The image of the wounded unicorn appears as a "living fiction / a tapestry / silk and wool shot with silver threads" (*P,* 231). However perverse we consider the image to be, the poet as king-self interested in "the beloved and sacred image / of a virgin / whom he has whored" (*P,* 231) is not described at this point as overwhelming the poet's coming to terms with his life as a "married man" in an "aging body." The fiction is not of the monumental stone giant of book 1 who sees "Inside the bus . . . his thoughts sitting and standing" (*P,* 9). The primary self-description in book 5 is of the "married man" in the "aging body" who is more rather than less human because he admits to possessing a fantasy life that suggests an aggressive sexual instinct. The sexual fantasy on the tapestry of the "one-horned beast" is an example of how Williams links his sense of the erotic life with an imaginative action that is closely associated with writing *Paterson*. When Williams, after the "one-horned beast" passage, urges the fictional Paterson to "keep your pecker up" (*P,* 231), one senses the poet's awareness of the reality of his situation as living in a dying body. The slightly self-mocking imperative to "keep your pecker up" has about it the quality of self-acceptance; it is a nudge to continue to feel, to imagine, to fantasize, to create, to allow oneself to accept things as they are but also to allow oneself to indulge in fantasy that is not mistaken as a replacement for the real.

The giant is set in an explicitly imaginary space, on a tapestry, an interlaced textile identified as a narrative space unrelated to current states of affairs and, it appears, divorced from contact with the world represented in books 1–4:

> I, Paterson, the King-self
> saw the lady
> through the rough woods
> outside the palace walls
> among the stench of sweating horses
> and gored hounds
> yelping with pain
> the heavy breathing pack
> to see the dead beast
> brought in at last
> across the saddle bow
> among the oak trees. (*P,* 231)

In contrast to the tapestry scene of King Paterson, Williams presents a second version of Paterson. This one is figured on a human scale and contrasts with the prosopopoeiac figure we met in book 1:

> Paterson . . .
> . . . .
> has returned to the old scenes
> to witness
>
> What has happened
> since Soupault gave him the novel
> the Dadaist novel
> to translate—(*P,* 207)

The emphasis in book 5, as it has not been in the first four books, is on paying tribute to painters (Juan Gris, Picasso, da Vinci, Breughel, Toulouse-Lautrec, Jackson Pollock) and on honoring works of art in a variety of forms, including the Greek satyr play and the modern dance. However different these artists and forms of expression may be, each is honored for the seriousness of the "play" (playfulness and artifice) inherent in the work of imagination. Understanding the "work" as a form of "play" becomes an affirmation of the act of making art independent of the content of the work and how it may reflect on contemporary affairs. Of Toulouse-Lautrec's subject matter, for instance, Williams told Walter Sutton that the painter "was indifferent to it, and the poet is also indifferent to it. . . . He is a man that respected the truth of the design."[30] This indifference suggests a troubling disinterest in scenes of exploitation such as occurred in the Parisian brothels depicted by Toulouse-Lautrec, but I do not think it suggests that Williams was disinterested in the suffering experienced by those around him in Paterson, New Jersey. The constructive aspect of the attitude Williams suggests in his statement about Toulouse-Lautrec, and the aspect that he brings with him to book 5, is his perception of the poem as an object, a design, separate from the maker, rather than as the final destination for the imaginative person. The work of art is now to be measured by our experience of its form and not by our trust in the maker as an epic hero whose deeds are celebrated in the long poem.

In book 5, Williams registers a division between his conception of himself as a human author who speaks without raising his voice and his conception of himself as an oracular, representative figure. Although both are tropes in a poem, Williams registers the division between the stone giant (now a figure woven on a tapestry) and the author of the poem (now a man who receives guests, uses speech on the streets, appears on television, experiences sexual desire). As author of the poem, he tries to reach out to those he could only previously conceive of as the "thousand automatons" who were his "thoughts sitting and standing" on the bus.

> Paterson has grown older
>
> > the dog of his thoughts
> has shrunk
> to no more than "a passionate letter"

30. Lloyd, *Williams' "Paterson,"* 168.

to a woman, a woman he had neglected
to put to bed in the past .
                    And went on
living and writing
                    answering
letters
              and tending his flower
garden, cutting his grass and trying
to get the young
                    to foreshorten
their errors in the use of words which
he had found so difficult, the errors
he had made in the use of the
poetic line:
" . the unicorn against a millefleurs background, . " (*P,* 227)

The "dog of his thought," the poem, now contains a project of restricted scope reminiscent of the poems written by American poets of the middle generation such as John Berryman, Robert Lowell, and Sylvia Plath. It is split off from a second representation of the "hunt for the unicorn" under-taken on the tapestry by King Paterson. Williams's relinquishment of the relationship between the "living fiction" of Paterson and the presence of the mortal speaker is the alternative provided in Book 5 to the annihilative logic of self-representation suggested in the passages we have addressed from Book 3. Perhaps for the first time in the poem, we witness Williams as Paterson engaged in a productive relationship to a younger generation of poets; he is able to instruct, without possessing, new talent:

              and tending his flower
garden, cutting his grass and trying
to get the young
                    to foreshorten
their error in the use of words which
he had found so difficult, the errors
he had made in the use of the
poetic line:

Unlike the description of the mature sycamore, or the other images from the natural world in book 1 (the flowers, grass, and garden), the images of Paterson and his garden are not metaphors for the poet's clash with members of other poetic generations. The poem's speaker can identify Paterson in the third person "tending his garden," but in the progressive form of the verb. This suggests an enduring presence different from and outside the movement of the poem itself. The poet can focus on the craft of the poem as a made thing, rather than as a monumental representation of the poet's character—perhaps this is the error in the use of the poetic line referred to in the passage. The poet has finally produced a version of himself in *Paterson,* but he is situated outside the text, where the opportunity exists for him to meet others face-to-face.

Afterword

"A Visit"

Apart from the last book of *Paterson* (1958), in the lyrics Williams published in the last years of his life (*The Desert Music* [1952], *Journey to Love* [1955], and *Pictures from Brueghel* [1962]), the poet lifted off the mask of a literary giant (King Paterson) who, like Whitman, Crane, Pound, Eliot, and Charles Olson, had extended the reach of the self to include a plurality of selves and as much of American or international culture as each of these ambitious poets saw fit to include in his version of the long poem of epic sweep. What is most memorable about the poems in *Journey to Love* is their dedication, in the face of the death of the body, to the love of one woman, Williams's wife, Florence:

> Antony and Cleopatra
>   were right;
> they have shown
>   the way. I love you
>   or I do not live
> at all[1]

In lines such as these it is as if the massive attempt to define the poet's subject as well as the formal stage upon which the poet could situate himself to speak—Williams's lifelong struggle to name an American ground through a sound and form peculiar to it—has been fulfilled. Now he is able

1. "The Ivy Crown," in *Selected Poems,* rev. ed., 213.

to address the singular beloved in an open, honest, and direct way. The line is shaped as an adequate reflection of the human voice. "The Ivy Crown" is only one example of a late lyric spoken in a human voice, in contrast to the amplified version of the compound self found in much of *Paterson*'s historical collage. Except to say that he withdrew his commission to speak for a majority to choose instead a voice fragile enough to suggest relationships of intimacy that will perish with the death of the speaker, Williams's beautiful statements of love and his embrace of the natural world in the last books are beyond the scope of this examination of how the conflicts and literary negotiations between poet and publisher produced a major shift in the direction of his work in the 1930s and 1940s.

Instead of focusing on Williams's later lyrics, to close this study I will pay attention to how the same economic and cultural tensions that produced Williams's fictions also produced a moving testimony of friendship and love in a short fiction written by James Laughlin. Laughlin's short story "A Visit," which was not published until 1978 but was written after he visited Williams's home in Rutherford on April 8, 1960, reveals that the publisher had to his regret dismissed the significance of Williams's life as an ordinary citizen because of his own professional ambitions as a young man going into business for the first time as the founder of New Directions in 1936. "A Visit" is a thinly veiled autobiographical memoir concerning Laughlin's visit to the Hampton, New Jersey, home of a poet, which is filled with the artworks of John Marin and Charles Demuth. The Williams surrogate, named Homer C. Evans, can hardly form a sentence after suffering a massive stroke. The Laughlin figure, named Marshall MacDonald, has driven from New York City to talk with the poet about his feelings of loss and sadness over the disruption in their friendship due to professional disagreements. Their prior disagreements mirror the rift that caused Williams to leave New Directions for Random House in 1950, where he published the third part of the Stecher Trilogy, *The Build-Up*, before returning to New Directions to complete the publication of *Paterson* in 1958.

In "A Visit," Laughlin as MacDonald struggles to come to terms with a literary friendship. By "literary friendship" I mean that from the start of the story MacDonald must learn to understand and accept—as Williams did in book 5 of *Paterson*—the difference between what MacDonald calls the "halves" of Evans's life. MacDonald, who knew and admired the reputation of the modernist writer long before he met the man who made the work, continues to honor the textual trace of the poet, which is what will remain as a legacy to the literary artist through the works on paper and through the tradition of experimental American writing in large part modeled after Evans's own experiments. But MacDonald must also come to terms with the interpersonal relationships that formed the work and that shaped the perishable self of the maker that will not endure very long beyond the time and space of "A Visit." For MacDonald, there are and have always been two Evanses, and that paradox is what the publisher has decided to consider as the author. Through the story, Laughlin admits he had privileged early on in their relationship the impersonal and larger-than-life literary persona constructed by Williams in and through his literary designs, while ignoring the ordinary man whose trace I have shown appears as Dr. Paterson at the end of *Paterson*. Like Williams in book 5, MacDonald, facing the poet's dying body, turns his attention from the text-based imagination of the literary giant, which Williams described as the "image large enough to embody the whole knowable world about me" (*A*, 391). Instead, he privileges the natural life of the maker, whose identity, formed in fictions, has now been separated out and allowed to come through in moving ways in a dialogue with those in the world closest to him such as his old publisher and his great companion, here named Helen.

The story marks a fitting conclusion to my study because it is, essentially, the publisher's belated attempt at the end of Williams's life to respond in text to a rift caused by earlier textual disagreements between the two men concerning the founding of New Directions. "A Visit" is a testimony of respectful apology for the trauma suffered by both men due to the professional conflict and disparate understandings over the meaning and purpose of Laughlin's founding of New Directions with Williams as his lead author beginning with *White Mule*, the first full-length work by a single author brought out by the press. The story addresses from Laughlin's perspective many of the themes and issues I have discussed primarily from Williams's perspective. These are represented through descriptions of the impact Evans's appearance in *Life* magazine has had on his relationship to what he calls his "townsfolk clients" (the notoriety, ironically, has prompted the "townsfolk clients to pay their bills for his services"); of Evans's struggle to gain acceptance from the university establishment, which the publisher describes as the place of the "academic maggots";

and of MacDonald's sensitivity to the economic hardships he now realizes Evans had suffered as a small-town professional.[2] In the story the Williams figure is presented as a lawyer who works out of his home office. As a poet, he could not "take in from his writing in a year, or three years, what a writer of popular fiction will get from one story in the *Saturday Evening Post*" ("V," 266).

Of all the issues discussed in the story surrounding the early history of New Directions, however, none is more surprising than an ironic and startling confession disclosed by MacDonald under the urgent pressure of the poet's rapidly declining health. In the story Laughlin as MacDonald admits that the split between the two men was caused less by Williams's view of New Directions as a commercial house and Laughlin's view of it as opposed to the demands of the popular market than it was by Laughlin's exaggeration in his dealings with Williams of his conception of his press in order to cover his own professional ambitions. In the story Laughlin admits that he held fast to claims of commercial disinterest to deny his own ambitions as a young businessman and son of a powerful industrial capitalist. Laughlin admits that during World War II he chose to use his limited resources to promote those writers he thought held a greater sales potential than did Williams at that time. We recall that Williams had hoped to make money from the publication of *In the Money,* the second installment of the Stecher Trilogy, following the modest success of *White Mule.* The critical and commercial reception to *White Mule* pleased Williams but finally disappointed him. Although it sold out of an initial run of fifteen hundred copies, it could not be reprinted in time to take advantage of favorable reviews because, Williams complained in a letter to Laughlin, his publisher was away on a characteristic ski trip to New Zealand. As he set about to write the follow-up to *White Mule,* Williams was angry with Laughlin for failing to make "more detailed arrangements for advertising my stuff." He believed that Laughlin treated New Directions as a hobby, and not as a means for Williams to survive as an author: "Inadequate management of sales cost us plenty that time" (*SL,* 28).

The story's narrative surprise is presented in such a way that the narrative form resonates with its meaning. MacDonald, so moved at seeing

---

2. James Laughlin, "A Visit," 259, 260; hereafter cited in the text as "V."

the poet who once possessed a boundless energy now reduced to a state of paralysis in which he cannot write and is barely audible, and also perhaps so overtaken by the cost to their friendship of the literary enterprise, at first drives away from the Evans home after his thirty-minute visit forgetting to bring up the issue that he had made the trip to address: "MacDonald was well outside Hampton when it suddenly came to him that he had entirely forgotten the main purpose of his mission. It had completely slipped his mind—though he had thought about it long and seriously before coming. He had wanted to tell Evans that he was sorry" ("V," 268). The apology does not take place until MacDonald drives back to the Evans home, where he finds the poet upstairs in a darkened bedroom hovering between waking reality and a dreamy recollection of the trip he made to Italy and Switzerland in the 1920s. Williams of course took such a trip and then fictionalized it in his first conventional novel, *A Voyage to Pagany,* with a main character named Dev, rather than Homer, Evans. Laughlin overcomes his own block in accepting the reality of the market that separated author from publisher. As storyteller, Laughlin tries to remember and, through memory, to counteract on personal and human terms the force of the market that at once produced the shelf of important books that now dominates the Evans living room and also led to the separation of the two old friends. MacDonald enters the poet's bedroom at the moment when Evans, in imagination, revisits the site where he began to build the fictional persona that was sustained through the New Directions period. Laughlin reinstates the fraternity and affection between the two friends through the act of telling another story meant to cut through the fictional masks and to confront the dying man before it is too late.

The story occurs at an ironic moment from MacDonald's (Laughlin's) perspective. Evans (Williams), who MacDonald describes as an "electric little man who all his life had had command of words," now after his terrible strokes "had to fight to bring them from his brain to his tongue" ("V," 260–61). It is as if in this story Laughlin is carrying on in fictional form the other side of the dialogue between author and publisher that the poet had carried on in his fictions. The subject of the conversation, although cast in the terms of a commodity culture, is presented by Laughlin in interpersonal terms that contradict market demands. The conflict over the disparate meanings of the New Directions venture, cast by Williams in terms of commercial versus "pure" literary values, is approached by

Laughlin, quite correctly I believe, in terms of the issue Williams was struggling with in such places as *Paterson,* which was the impact his literary ambitions had on his personal identity and on his interpersonal relationships. As he lifted the veil on King Paterson and as he accepted his self-presentation, not as one or another masked personae (Dev Evans, "Doc," King Paterson, Joe Stecher), but as an old man in a body that was giving out, Williams at the end of *Paterson* was accepting the limitations of the natural body. He was in effect disavowing the modernist impulse found, for example, in Yeats's "Sailing to Byzantium," to cheat death by locating meaning in the permanent space of art.

Ironically, Evans's wish for such face-to-face meetings as Williams spoke about at the end of *Paterson* is in "A Visit" disabled by the same attitude of privilege toward the organic body as the final site of significance that he has come to accept in opposition to a deferred presence in the next world or the permanence of what is valued as stored in the museum space of artifice. Laughlin is interested in speculating about what endures beyond the body that has been accepted as the site of primary significance and value. Ironically, Evans's living room is now occupied by the shelf of books the poet wrote, and not by the poet himself. The books represent a legacy that will be carried on in the lively and immediate style of younger poets whose actual referents might be Denise Levertov and Robert Creeley. We realize along with the narrator that the four shelves of books were expensive to produce in interpersonal terms. The literary friendship produced the authorial presence apparent in the work on the shelf but also produced, in interpersonal terms, the discursive absence or virtual silence that developed between the two men:

> MacDonald imagined that Evans had betrayed him and wrote some bitter letters in which the word "knife" was prominent. Evans had replied with restraint but MacDonald's tone confirmed his decision and he went his way. MacDonald assumed a posture of injured benevolence, complaining very caustically to his intimates of the bad treatment he had received. His correspondence with Evans dropped off to a trickle of business letters. If they met at some gathering MacDonald was formally cordial; Evans was good-humored but at a loss for much to say to him. MacDonald could usually put up a good front of equanimity but inside he was a brooder. In certain moods his thoughts would focus, as if magnetized, on someone he supposed had wronged him and he would indulge himself in fantasies of revenge—nothing violent, but complicated stratagems for humiliating the offender. And he

> would snap at his wife if she happened, quite innocently, so much as to
> mention one of these occupants of his doghouse. ("V," 269-70)

MacDonald understands that he, perhaps more than Evans, allowed
the commercial possibilities of publishing a neglected but already distin-
guished modernist author to get in the way of understanding the human
implications of the younger man doing the work of expanding the repu-
tation of the older man by publishing him when he was on the verge of
being forgotten. MacDonald realizes that the poet understood publicity
to be a gesture of friendship and care while the same act was perceived
by the young man to be an impersonal professional transaction of mutual
benefit to both participants. When he sees the crumbled shell of the poet
who once possessed a boundless energy and an intense gaze, MacDonald
enters into an empathetic relationship to the personal hardships the poet
endured as a middle-class professional with a family in a small town, trying
to make ends meet while also attempting to find the time and energy to
write experimental poetry and prose. MacDonald notes that "even on
weekends he seldom had time to sit down to write with an open space
of a whole morning before him" ("V," 259). The privileging of the literary
accomplishment over the struggle of the man who produced the work is
evident from the moment he enters Evans's living room:

> [There] was a tier of shelves built across the corner that always attracted
> MacDonald. There, filling nearly four shelves, were all of Evans' books, from
> the first little green pamphlet that had been printed at his mother's expense
> by the local newspaper printer to the collected volumes of his poems and
> essays. And the three books about him, and runs of the magazines that he
> helped to edit, and the translations into foreign languages. MacDonald had
> read most of them and had copies of many of them at home. Five of them
> had been published by his firm. ("V," 256-57)

Juxtaposed to his attraction to the trace of the life on paper, MacDonald
hears coming from upstairs a noise "that he couldn't at first identify.
It was a series of regular, repeated sounds—first a kind of soft scrape
and then a little thump . . . then another scrape and thump. Suddenly it
struck him; Evans must be dragging himself downstairs, holding onto the
bannister and dragging one leg that had lost its mobility. It had gotten
to that, the poor man could hardly walk anymore!" ("V," 257). Although
the relationship between the two men had been built on a shared sense

of responsibility for an American literary revolution, it is the sight of the stroke victim that creates in MacDonald the wish not to defer his disclosure any longer. He knows it is time to reach out toward the older man, to embrace him, and to apologize for the time lost between them. "MacDonald had an impulse to embrace him, to throw his arms around him, but he checked it. He did take Evans' hand in both of his and held it as he greeted him" ("V," 257). MacDonald experiences remorse over the way he had treated Evans in the early years of their professional alliance. He realizes that from the start of their relationship his attraction to Evans's work (the four shelves of his books) overwhelmed his ability to identify the sounds of the natural man struggling to live his life in physical hardship.

The story helps us to realize that a primary source of conflict through-out the Williams–Laughlin relationship was the publisher's inability "to identify" the author's struggle to live while remaining dedicated to the construction of a secure literary identity, a text-based persona that the young publisher mistook for the actual fact of the author's experience. We recall that in their correspondence from the 1930s and 1940s and in his prefaces to the New Directions annuals in that same period, Laughlin presented himself as hesitant to engage in commercial practices in order to promote the reputation and increase the profile of his press through agreeing to Williams's demands for extensive advertising:

> It is hard to conceive of a new social order except by revision of verbal orien-tation. And it is the writer alone who can accomplish that reorientation. But it will not be the slick paper writers who cater to inferiority complexes, or the editor who will print nothing "unfamiliar to his reader" or the commercial publisher's hair-oil boys. It will be men like Cummings or Carlos Williams who know their business well enough to realize the pass to which language has come and are willing to endure obscurity and poverty to carry on their experiments.[3]

During the early years of New Directions, anything Williams said to Laughlin that had the whiff of the business of literature would bring about a vitriolic response from the young publisher: "The hell with reputations, making money, poets' jealousies, ambitions, wars, struggles of all kinds, and mostly anything that impinges on the effect in life of a good art form"

---

3. Laughlin, preface to *New Directions in Prose and Poetry* (1936).

(*SL*, 89). Laughlin neglected to disclose in his letters to Williams or in his introductions to the 1930s and the 1940s New Directions annuals the commercial intentions he held out for his press. "A Visit" suggests that Laughlin, like MacDonald, thought about the business of literature even in his decision to publish a "name" (Evans/Williams) author "well known in highbrow literary circles." Throughout MacDonald's discussion of the period when he was "a young man starting in business for himself," Evans's hardships are perceived less as difficulties for Evans in an economic sense than as the background that provided MacDonald with "the opportunity to start his list with a writer who could give it literary prestige" ("V," 268):

> There had been trouble in their relationship of author and publisher, rather bad trouble. MacDonald, as a young man starting in business for himself, had taken on Evans at a time when the poet's career, or at least his acceptance by the public, was in the doldrums. It was soon after the Depression and no one of Evans' early publishers wanted to continue with him. His name was well known in highbrow literary circles but poetry was not selling. For three or four years Evans had published no new books and most of his older ones had gone out of print. MacDonald had seen the opportunity to start his list with a writer who could give it literary prestige, who could set a standard for what he hoped would follow. He brought out Evans' backed-up books and re-issued some of the best that were out of print. He put Evans back into active circulation, for which the poet had been very grateful, the gratitude taking the forms of a kindly and generous friendship. They grew very close, with Evans assuming for MacDonald the role of a literary father.
>
> This was at first a wonderfully exciting experience for MacDonald, but as time went along, without being aware of it, he began to take Evans too much for granted. As his business grew he became interested in other writers and, perhaps only because they were demanding, while Evans never made any demands—it just wasn't his way—he had worked harder at promoting these other writers' books than ever he had done for Evans. He went on publishing Evans, but, without intending to, and always thinking of him as a dear friend whose work he venerated, he neglected him. It came to the point, during the war, when paper for books was rationed along with most other commodities, that he put Evans off when a new book was ready, pleading the paper shortage, although it was obvious that he had paper enough for books by S. and B. (whose work happened to be easier to sell). ("V," 268–69)

"A Visit" provides the mechanism through which Laughlin, with a compelling sincerity, can abandon his earlier position of service to the strict demands of modernist formalism, which failed to take into account the material conditions in which the work was produced. Laughlin as Mac-Donald appreciates Evans's reasons for eventually leaving New Directions. He admits he had perceived Evans as a literary commodity—an impersonal piece of literary property that he possessed—and not as a sensitive person with complex needs from the professional alliance:

> At the time MacDonald had had no understanding of what he was doing to Evans, so it came to him as a brutal shock when Evans, as tactfully as he could, suggested that he might best accept an offer that came to him "out of the blue" (he had not gone to look for it) from another firm. MacDonald took it hard. He had come to feel that Evans was almost a personal possession, something to which his merit in publishing him when others were not eager had given him title. MacDonald was a great believer in his own virtue and fully expected his just rewards for it. He had illusions about gratitude and had always expected that Evans' gratitude would go on forever. ("V," 269)

The son of a prominent steel manufacturer who reaped the rewards of power and wealth by harnessing the raw materials of the northeastern United States, Laughlin faults himself for not recognizing the value of the human resource, William Carlos Williams, who had been producing the literary material—the modernist poems—that Laughlin for a long time could not see was the work of an individual who produced under conditions that were anything but tranquil:

> In fact, the busy mixture of two full careers had been the taut spring that kept the mechanism turning. A vintage portable Corona had always sat at one side on the desk in his law office and phrases for a poem or ideas for a "Letter from Nowhere" would be pecked out on it between calls when they drifted into his head. And some of his best poems had had their birth in the county courthouse in pencil scrawlings on the margins of a brief. ("V," 259)

Laughlin as MacDonald admits that he saw the poet less as a person than as a thing that produced other things of commercial value. In the passage quoted above the poet is still described in the language of industrial capitalism. The poetic imagination is thought of as a "mechanism" set in motion by the interaction between the careers of the man who made his living as a small-town lawyer and the poet who on his breaks from serving clients fit in a random moment of creative activity. MacDonald admits that from the very start of their relationship he perceived Evans as an impersonal piece of literary property. MacDonald felt he could claim ownership to Evans and his work because he had the business savvy to rescue the reputation of the author at a time when no one else thought the writing valuable enough to keep it in print. "A Visit" gives Laughlin the chance to experience the hardships Williams endured and, through the kind of empathy to the suffering of others that characterized Williams's relationship as physician and as poet to the immigrant poor of northeast New Jersey, to mend through text the texture of the relationship.

The story is a testimony to the elements in Williams's literary practice that will survive in the work of younger writers who have since come to embrace the American idiom. In the story Evans, now accepting his own limitations due to the inevitable limitations of the body, takes pleasure as his wife, Helen, reads aloud to him poetry by "the kids [who] all send me their books" ("V," 262). The role that Helen Evans now plays in the poet's literary life also suggests, by necessity perhaps, that the elevated place to which the poet had aspired as a unique literary genius whose ordinary needs were met by a wife is no longer his model for literary authority. Williams as Evans has now entered into a dialogic literary relationship with Flossie as Helen, whose confidence has increased, although she still is perceived as valuable in relationship to her husband's accomplishment: "Now that his illness had made him so dependent on her in his writing she was growing more self-confident, more sure of her right to be the wife of a man in whom she had always seen so much more greatness than the world had at first recognized. . . . [S]he seemed to MacDonald to have blossomed under this pressure. A happy woman was talking to him [MacDonald] and the thing that made her beautiful, as she now was, was the radiance of her fulfillment" ("V," 266-67). MacDonald is aware that Evans's ability to perceive the ordinary American ground in lively and immediate ways will be carried on by the movement that the poet helped to promote; in this sense, and in this sense only, will Evans cheat death:

> "She reads to me, too. The kids all send me their books and she reads them aloud to me. Some of them are good, too. That girl that you published, what's her name . . ."
>
> "Campbell . . . Daphne Campbell."
>
> "That's the one. She's all right. I think she's got it. A lot of them have got it. They've figured it out. It's taken thirty years but they've caught on. It's American now. It really sounds the way we sound. It isn't just warmed over England anymore." ("V," 262)

Evans's description of his difficulty with using his right hand to type, as well as his description of the mental "fog" that keeps him from finding the cherished right word at one point during the visit, proves nearly too much for MacDonald to bear. MacDonald fears he will weep at seeing a figure he has held as an idol in such a fallen state. Evans, so long the empathetic respondent to the immigrant poor who lacked the ability to communicate with him except (as in the poignant emotional exchange between Doc and the Italian woman in "A Night in June") through tears, becomes himself the source of the fundamental and very physical sign of human empathy. The relationship between Evans and MacDonald, built on conflict over the meaning of words and how to publicize them, is narrowed and intensified into the silent language of tears, a language that signifies an emotional response to the suffering of a beloved, to the difference between the present sight of the beloved and the possibilities for their life that have now become exhausted.

Laughlin's "A Visit," like Williams's *In the Money,* is a creative act enabled, ironically, by tensions related to the sparse market for literary modernism. The substance of the story is initiated by the paradoxes inherent in the separation of the literature of pulp from the literature of contemplation. The purpose of the story is to heal through a linguistic gesture the painful interpersonal split precipitated by the literary context that brought Williams and Laughlin together in the 1930s and that also pulled them apart virtually from the beginning of their relationship. In Williams's late lyrics and in much of book 5 of *Paterson,* written language is put in the service of healing old wounds caused by the necessary distancing of literary ambitions that, in the case of *Paterson,* caused Williams to perceive ordinary townspeople as "automatons" rather than as unique subjectivities. In "A Visit," written language serves to repair a relationship that was broken when Laughlin failed to see Williams as an author who had constructed the persona of the dedicated modernist and not as the struggling family man with worries of his own. In the story the Laughlin figure realizes that the professional issues involved in Williams's sense of himself as a public author—the poet's desire to reach a popular audience and to gain recognition by his peers—were Williams's expression in displaced form of his desire for a personal embrace. Publicity for the authorial self, Laughlin realizes, was Williams's metaphor for a sign of trust and friendship from those around him, especially from the younger man who perceived, in Laughlin's own words in the story, Williams to be "a literary father." MacDonald realizes, twenty or more years later, that his failure to promote Evans's writing in the late 1930s was taken by the poet not as a professional decision but as a personal wound, a sign of a breach in friendship—a breach that Laughlin's story attempts to mend with a heartfelt apology.

Bibliography

Agee, James. *Let Us Now Praise Famous Men.* New York: Ballantine Books, 1939.

Badaracco, Claire. "Writers and Their Public Appeal: Harriet Monroe's Publicity Techniques." *American Literary Realism* 23 (winter 1991): 35–51.

Baldwin, Neil. "The Stecher Trilogy: Williams as Novelist." In *William Carlos Williams: Man and Poet,* edited by Carroll F. Terrell. Orono, Maine: National Poetry Foundation, 1983.

Baudrillard, Jean. *For a Critique of the Political Economy of the Sign.* St. Louis: Telos, 1981.

Bell, Ian. "The Hard Currency of Words: Emerson's Fiscal Metaphor in Nature." *ELH* 52 (fall 1985): 733–53.

Benson, Jackson J. "Ernest Hemingway: The Life as Fiction and the Fiction as Life." *American Literature* 61 (October 1989): 345–58.

Berlant, Lauren. *The Anatomy of National Fantasy: Hawthorne, Utopia, and Everyday Life.* Chicago: University of Chicago Press, 1991.

Berry, Ellen E. "Modernism/Mass Culture/Postmodernism: The Case of Gertrude Stein." In *Rereading the New: A Backward Glance at Modernism,* edited by Kevin Dettmar. Ann Arbor: University of Michigan Press, 1992.

"A Birthday for 'Poetry.'" *Life,* November 24, 1952, 103–4.

Blake, John B. "From Buchan to Fishbein: The Literature of Domestic Medicine." In *Medicine without Doctors: Home Health Care in American History,* edited by Guenther B. Risse, Ronald L. Numbers, and Judith Walzer Leavitt. New York: Science History Publications, 1977.

Bloom, Harold. *Agon: Towards a Theory of Revisionism.* New York: Oxford University Press, 1982.

———. "The Internalization of the Quest-Romance." In *Romanticism and Consciousness,* edited by M. H. Abrams and Harold Bloom. New York: Norton, 1970.

———. "Poetry, Revisionism, Repression." In *Poetry and Repression.* New Haven: Yale University Press, 1976.

Bourdieu, Pierre. *Outline of a Theory of Practice.* Translated by Richard Nice. Cambridge: Cambridge University Press, 1977.

Bowers, Anne. "Williams' *A Voyage to Pagany:* The Impossible Search for It." *William Carlos Williams Review* 17 (fall 1991): 39-51.

Bremen, Brian. *William Carlos Williams and the Diagnostics of Culture.* New York: Oxford University Press, 1993.

Breslin, James E. B. *William Carlos Williams: An American Artist.* Chicago: University of Chicago Press, 1985.

Burke, Kenneth. "Heaven's First Law." In *William Carlos Williams: A Collection of Critical Essays,* edited by J. Hillis Miller. Englewood Cliffs, N.J.: Prentice Hall, 1966.

———. "Subjective History." *New York Herald Tribune,* March 14, 1926.

Conrad, Bryce. *Refiguring America: A Study of William Carlos Williams' "In the American Grain."* Urbana: University of Illinois Press, 1990.

———. "William Carlos Williams and Europe: The Trans-Atlantic Construction of America." *William Carlos Williams Review* 18 (spring 1992): 1-9.

Crane, Hart. *The Complete Poems and Selected Letters and Prose of Hart Crane.* Edited by Brom Weber. New York: Anchor Books, 1966.

Crawford, Thomas Hugh. *Modernism, Medicine, and William Carlos Williams.* Norman: University of Oklahoma Press, 1993.

———. "The Rhetoric of Medical Authority: The Early Writing of William Carlos Williams." Ph.D. diss., Duke University, 1988.

Cushman, Stephen. *William Carlos Williams and the Meanings of Measure.* New Haven: Yale University Press, 1985.

Diggory, Terence. *William Carlos Williams and the Ethics of Painting.* Princeton, N.J.: Princeton University Press, 1991.

De Lauretis, Teresa. *Alice Doesn't: Feminism, Semiotics, Cinema.* Bloomington: Indiana University Press, 1984.

de Man, Paul. "Autobiography as De-facement." In *The Rhetoric of Romanticism.* New York: Columbia University Press, 1984.

Dettmar, Kevin J. H., ed. *Rereading the New: A Backward Glance at Modernism.* Ann Arbor: University of Michigan Press, 1992.

Douglas, Major C. H. *The Douglas Manual.* Compiled by Philip Mairet. New York: Coward McCann, [1935?].

Doyle, Charles, ed. *William Carlos Williams: The Critical Heritage.* London: Routledge and Kegan Paul, 1980.

Duffy, John. *The Healers.* Urbana: University of Illinois Press, 1980.

"Edible Slice-of-Life." A review of *In the Money. Time,* December 2, 1940, 83.

Eliot, T. S. *The Waste Land.* In *The Norton Anthology of Modern Poetry,* edited by Richard Ellman and Robert O'Clair. New York: Norton, 1973.

Emerson, Ralph Waldo. *Essays.* Boston: Phillips, Sampson, and Company, 1855.

Ewen, Stuart. *All Consuming Images: The Politics of Style in Contemporary Culture.* New York: Basic Books, 1988.

———. *Captains of Consciousness: Advertising and the Social Roots of the Consumer Culture.* New York: McGraw Hill, 1977.

Fiedler, Leslie. "Some Uses and Failures of Feeling." *Partisan Review* 15 (August 1948): 924–31.

Fisher-Wirth, Ann W. *William Carlos Williams and Autobiography: The Woods of His Own Nature.* University Park and London: Pennsylvania State University Press, 1989.

Flory, Wendy Stallard. *The American Ezra Pound.* New Haven: Yale University Press, 1989.

Foucault, Michel. *Foucault Reader.* Edited by Paul Rabinow. New York: Random House, 1984.

———. *Power/Knowledge: Selected Interviews and Other Writings, 1972-1977.* Edited by Colin Gordon. New York: Random House, 1977.

Fox, Stephen. *Mirror Makers: A History of American Advertising and Its Creators.* New York: Morrow Press, 1984.

Gish, Robert F. "Word Man/Medicine Man: *In the American Grain.*" In *William Carlos Williams: A Study of the Short Fiction.* Boston: Twayne, 1989.

Goodheart, Eugene. "The Monster of Totality." In *The Skeptic Disposition in Contemporary Criticism.* Princeton: Princeton University Press, 1984.

Gray, Rockwell. "Relentlessly Clever: Ezra Pound's Correspondence with Publisher James Laughlin." *Chicago Tribune,* Sunday, August 14, 1994, sec. 14, p. 5.

Greenberg, Clement. "Avant-Garde and Kitsch." In *Pollock and After: The*

Critical Debate, edited by Francis Frascina. New York: Harper and Row, 1985.

Grossman, Allen. "On Management of Absolute Empowerment: Nuclear Violence, the Institutions of Holiness, and the Structures of Poetry." *Agni* 29–30 (1990): 268–78.

———. "Why Is Death in Arcadia?: Poetic Process, Literary Humanism, and the Example of Pastoral." *Western Humanities Review* 41 (summer 1987): 152–88.

Grover-Rogoff, Jay. "Hart Crane's Presence in *Paterson.*" *William Carlos Williams Review* 11 (spring 1985): 20–29.

Guillory, John. "The Ideology of Canon-Formation: T. S. Eliot and Cleanth Brooks." *Critical Inquiry* 10 (September 1983): 173–98.

Gunn, Thom. "William Carlos Williams." *Encounter* (July 1965): 67–74.

Hahn, Stephen. "Williams' Homage to Keats in *A Voyage to Pagany.*" *William Carlos Williams Review* 11 (spring 1985): 6–12.

Hartman, Geoffrey H. "The Romance of Nature and the Negative Way." In *Romanticism and Consciousness,* edited by M. H. Abrams and Harold Bloom. New York: Norton, 1970.

"He's Dead." Obituary. *Time,* March 15, 1963, 47.

Heininger, Joseph. "Molly Bloom's Ad Language and Goods Behavior: Advertising as Social Communication in *Ulysses.*" In *Molly Blooms,* edited by Richard Pearce. Madison: University of Wisconsin Press, 1994.

"The Hemingways in Sun Valley: The Novelist Takes a Wife." *Life,* January 6, 1941, 42–52.

Hildebidle, John. "Take Off Your Clothes: William Carlos Williams, Science, and the Diagnostic Encounter." *Modern Language Studies* 17 (summer 1987): 10–30.

Historic Totowa Falls. Paterson, 1942.

Howe, Susan, and Charles Ruas, eds. *The Art of Literary Publishing: Editors on Their Craft.* New York: Pushcart Press, 1980.

Hughes, Robert. "The Rise of Andy Warhol." In *Art after Modernism: Rethinking Representation,* edited by Brian Wallis. Boston: David Godine, 1984.

Huyssen, Andreas. *After the Great Divide: Modernism, Mass Culture, Postmodernism.* Bloomington: Indiana University Press, 1986.

Ingham, John. *The Iron Barons: A Social Analysis of an American Urban Elite, 1874–1965.* Westport, Conn.: Greenwood Press, 1978.

Jameson, Fredric. "Postmodernism, or the Cultural Logic of Late Capital-
ism." *New Left Review* 146 (July–August 1984): 59–92.

Janowitz, Anne. "*Paterson:* An American Contraption." In *William Carlos
Williams: Man and Poet,* edited by Carroll F. Terrell. Orono, Maine:
National Poetry Foundation, 1983.

Janson, H. W. *History of Art.* Englewood Cliffs, N.J.: Prentice Hall, 1977.

Kellner, Douglas. *Jean Baudrillard: From Marxism to Postmodernism
and Beyond.* Cambridge, Mass.: Polity Press, 1989.

Koch, Vivienne. *William Carlos Williams.* Norfolk: New Directions, 1950.

Laughlin, James. Preface to *New Directions in Prose and Poetry.* Norfolk:
New Directions, 1936.

———. *Remembering William Carlos Williams.* New York: New Direc-
tions, 1994.

———. "A Visit." In *William Carlos Williams and James Laughlin: Se-
lected Letters,* edited by Hugh Witemeyer. New York: Norton, 1989.

———. "William Carlos Williams and the Making of *Paterson:* A Memoir."
Yale Review 17 (winter 1982): 185–98.

Lears, T. J. Jackson. "Sherwood Anderson: Looking for the White Spot." In
The Power of Culture: Critical Essays in American History, edited by
Richard Wightman Fox and T. J. Jackson Lears. Chicago: University of
Chicago Press, 1993.

Leibowitz, Herbert. " 'You Can't Beat Innocence': *The Autobiography of
William Carlos Williams.*" *American Poetry Review* 10 (March/April
1981): 35–47.

Leiss, William. *Social Communication in Advertising: Persons, Products,
and Images of Well-being.* Toronto: Methuen, 1986.

Levine, Lawrence. *Highbrow/Lowbrow: The Emergence of Cultural Hi-
erarchy in America.* Cambridge: Harvard University Press, 1988.

Lloyd, Margaret Glynne. *William Carlos Williams' "Paterson": A Criti-
cal Reappraisal.* Rutherford, N.J.: Fairleigh Dickinson University Press,
1979.

Longwell, Charles Pitman. *A Little Story of Old Paterson as Told by an
Old Man.* Paterson, 1901.

Lowell, Robert. "William Carlos Williams." In *William Carlos Williams: A
Collection of Critical Essays,* edited by J. Hillis Miller. Englewood Cliffs,
N.J.: Prentice Hall, 1966.

Lynn, Kenneth. *Hemingway.* New York: Simon and Schuster, 1987.

Marchand, Roland. *Advertising the American Dream: Making Way for Modernity, 1920-1940.* Berkeley: University of California Press, 1985.

Mariani, Paul. *William Carlos Williams: A New World Naked.* New York: McGraw-Hill, 1981.

Marsh, Alec. "Stevens and Williams: The Economics of Metaphor." *William Carlos Williams Review* 18 (fall 1992): 37-49.

Martz, Louis. "The Unicorn in *Paterson.*" In *William Carlos Williams: A Collection of Critical Essays,* edited by J. Hillis Miller. Englewood Cliffs, N.J.: Prentice Hall, 1966.

Marx, Leo. *The Machine in the Garden: Technology and the Pastoral Ideal in America.* New York: Oxford University Press, 1964.

Matthews, Kathleen. "Competitive Giants: Satiric Bedrock in Book One of William Carlos Williams' *Paterson.*" *Journal of Modern Literature* 12 (July 1985): 237-60.

Mauss, Marcel, and Henri Hubert. *Sacrifice: Its Nature and Function.* 1898. Reprint, Chicago: University of Chicago Press, 1964.

Mazzaro, Jerome. *William Carlos Williams: The Later Poems.* Ithaca: Cornell University Press, 1973.

Miller, J. Hillis. *Poets of Reality: Six Twentieth-Century Writers.* New York: Atheneum, 1969.

———. "Williams' *Spring and All* and the Progress of Poetry." *Daedalus* 99 (spring 1970): 405-34.

Monteiro, George. "The Doctor's Black Bag: William Carlos Williams' Passaic River Stories." *Modern Language Studies* 13 (winter 1983): 77-84.

Moore, Marianne. "A Poet of the Quattrocento." In *William Carlos Williams: A Collection of Critical Essays,* edited by J. Hillis Miller. Englewood Cliffs, N.J.: Prentice Hall, 1966.

Moore, Robert L. "Ritual, Sacred Space, and Healing: The Psychoanalyst as Ritual Elder." In *Liminality and Transitional Phenomena,* edited by Nathan Schwartz-Salant and Murray Stein. Wilmette, Ill.: Chiron Publications, 1991.

Morantz, Regina Markell. "Nineteenth Century Health Reform and Women: A Program of Self-Help." In *Medicine without Doctors: Home Health Care in American History,* edited by Guenter B. Risse, Ronald L. Numbers, and Judith Walzer Leavitt. New York: Science History Publications, 1977.

Morris, Daniel. "Ernest Hemingway and *Life:* Consuming Revolutions." *American Periodicals* 3 (1993): 62-74.

Nash, Ralph. "The Use of Prose in *Paterson.*" *Perspective* 6 (1953): 191–99.

Nin, Anaïs. "The Personal Life Deeply Lived." In *The American Autobiography,* edited by Albert E. Stone. Englewood Cliffs, N.J.: Prentice Hall, 1981.

"Nine and Two." A review of *Complete Collected Poems. Time,* December 26, 1938, 41–44.

Numbers, Ronald L. "Do-It-Yourself the Sectarian Way." In *Medicine without Doctors: Home Health Care in American History,* edited by Guenter B. Risse, Ronald L. Numbers, and Judith Walzer Leavitt. New York: Science History Publications, 1977.

Paglia, Camille. *Sexual Personae: Art and Decadence from Nefertiti to Emily Dickinson.* New York: Vintage Books, 1991.

"Part-Time Poet." A review of *The Autobiography of William Carlos Williams. Time,* October 8, 1951, 118–22.

Paul, Sherman. *The Music of Survival: A Biography of a Poem by William Carlos Williams.* Urbana: University of Illinois Press, 1968.

Pearce, Roy Harvey. "Williams and the 'New Mode'." In *William Carlos Williams: A Collection of Critical Essays,* edited by J. Hillis Miller. Englewood Cliffs, N.J.: Prentice Hall, 1966.

People column. News of Williams's award by the Academy of American Poets. *Time,* January 7, 1957.

Pernick, Martin. *A Calculus of Suffering: Pain, Professionalism, and Anesthesia in Nineteenth-Century America.* New York: Columbia University Press, 1985.

"A Poem of America." A review of *Paterson, Book IV. Time,* July 16, 1951, 94–96.

"Poetry between Patients." A review of *Paterson Books I & II, and Book III. Time,* February 13, 1950, 94.

Pound, Ezra. "Dr. Williams' Position." In *William Carlos Williams: A Collection of Critical Essays.* Edited by J. Hillis Miller. Englewood Cliffs, N.J.: Prentice Hall, 1966.

Raeburn, John. *Fame Became of Him: Hemingway as Public Writer.* Bloomington: Indiana University Press, 1984.

Rainey, Lawrence S. "The Price of Modernism: Reconsidering the Publication of *The Waste Land.*" *Yale Review* 78 (winter 1989): 279–300.

Rourke, Constance. *Charles Sheeler, Artist in the American Tradition.* 1938. New York: Kennedy Galleries, 1969.

————. *Roots of American Culture, and Other Essays.* Edited by Van Wyck Brooks. New York: Harcourt Brace, 1942.

Said, Edward. "Yeats and Decolonization." In *Nationalism, Colonialism, and Literature,* edited by Seamus Deane. Minneapolis: University of Minnesota Press, 1990.

Sayre, Henry. *The Visual Text of William Carlos Williams.* Urbana: University of Illinois Press, 1983.

Sayre, Robert E. "The Proper Study: Autobiographies in American Studies." In *The American Autobiography,* edited by Albert E. Stone. Englewood Cliffs, N.J.: Prentice Hall, 1981.

Schlesinger, Arthur. *The Age of Jackson.* Boston: Little Brown, 1945.

Schmidt, Dorothy. "Magazines, Technology, and American Culture." *Journal of American Culture* 3, no. 1 (1980): 3–16.

Schmidt, Peter. *William Carlos Williams, the Arts, and Literary Tradition.* Baton Rouge: LSU Press, 1988.

Scholes, Robert. *Protocols of Reading.* New Haven: Yale University Press, 1989.

Schott, Webster. "A Gigantic Poet Who Wrote American." *Life,* November 18, 1966, 8–9.

Schroeder, Gertrude G. *The Growth of Major Steel Companies, 1900–1950.* Baltimore: Johns Hopkins University Press, 1953.

Schwarz, Daniel R. *The Case for a Humanistic Poetics.* London: Macmillan, 1990.

"Sheeler Finds Beauty in the Commonplace." *Life,* August 8, 1938, 42–45.

Shell, Marc. "The Gold Bug." *Genre* 13 (spring 1980): 11–30.

Sieburth, Richard. "In Pound We Trust: The Economy of Poetry/The Poetry of Economics." *Critical Inquiry* 14 (autumn 1987): 142–72.

Simpson, Louis. *Three on the Tower: The Lives and Works of Ezra Pound, T. S. Eliot, and William Carlos Williams.* New York: Morrow, 1975.

Spivak, Gayatri Chakravorty. "Subaltern Studies: Deconstructing Historiography." In *Selected Subaltern Studies,* edited by Gayatri Chakravorty Spivak and Ranajit Guha. New York: Oxford University Press, 1988.

Stage, Sarah. *Female Complaints.* New York: Norton, 1979.

Steinman, Lisa. *Made in America: Science, Technology, and American Modernist Poets.* New Haven: Yale University Press, 1987.

Stevens, Wallace. "Art as Establisher of Value." In *The Modern Tradition,* edited by Richard Ellmann and Charles Feidelson, Jr. New York: Oxford, 1965.

————. *The Collected Poems of Wallace Stevens.* New York: Knopf, 1954.

"Stories by the Doc." A review of *Make Light of It. Time,* December 4, 1950, 106–10.

Stott, William. *Documentary Expression and Thirties America.* Chicago: University of Chicago Press, 1986, reprint of a 1973 release.

Susman, Warren. " 'Personality' and Making of Twentieth Century Culture." In *Culture and History.* New York: Pantheon Books, 1984.

Swanberg, W. A. *Luce and His Empire.* New York: Scribner's, 1972.

Tapscott, Stephen. *American Beauty: William Carlos Williams and the Modernist Whitman.* New York: Columbia University Press, 1984.

Thomson, Samuel. *A Narrative, Of The Life And Medical Discoveries Of Samuel Thomson; Containing An Account Of His System Of Practice . . .* 1822. Reprint, New York: Arno Press, 1972.

Thoreau, Henry David. *The Portable Thoreau.* Edited by Carl Bode. New York: Viking, 1944.

Tichi, Cecelia. *Shifting Gears: Technology, Literature, Culture in Modernist America.* Chapel Hill: University of North Carolina Press, 1987.

Tompkins, Jane. "The Other American Renaissance." In *The American Renaissance Reconsidered,* edited by Walter Benn Michaels and Donald E. Pease. Baltimore: Johns Hopkins University Press, 1985.

Torgovnick, Marianna. *Gone Primitive: Savage Intellects, Modern Lives.* Chicago: University of Chicago Press, 1990.

Turner, Victor. "Social Dramas and Stories about Them." In *On Narrative,* edited by W. J. T. Mitchell. Chicago: University of Chicago Press, 1981.

van Gennep, Arnold. *The Rites of Passage.* Translated by Monika B. Vizedom and Gabrielle L. Caffee. Chicago: University of Chicago Press, 1960.

von Hallberg, Robert. *American Poetry and Culture, 1945–1980.* Cambridge: Harvard University Press, 1985.

Wagner, Linda. *The Poems of William Carlos Williams: A Critical Study.* Middletown, Conn.: Wesleyan University Press, 1964.

————. *The Prose of William Carlos Williams.* Middletown, Conn.: Wesleyan University Press, 1970.

Wagner, Linda, ed. *Interviews with William Carlos Williams: "Speaking Straight Ahead."* New York: New Directions, 1967.

Wallace, Emily Mitchell. *A Bibliography of William Carlos Williams.* Middletown, Conn.: Wesleyan University Press, 1968.

Weaver, Mike. *William Carlos Williams: The American Background.* Cambridge: Cambridge University Press, 1971.

Whitaker, Thomas. *William Carlos Williams.* New York: Twayne, 1968.

White, Hayden. "The Value of Narrativity in the Representation of Reality." In *On Narrative,* edited by W. J. T. Mitchell. Chicago: University of Chicago Press, 1981.

Whitman, Walt. *Leaves of Grass.* Edited by Sculley Bradley. New York: Holt-Rinehart, 1949.

———. Preface to *Leaves of Grass* (1855). Edited by Malcolm Cowley. New York: Viking, 1959.

Wicke, Jennifer. *Advertising Fictions: Literature, Advertisement and Social Reading.* New York: Columbia University Press, 1988.

Williams, Raymond. "Advertising: The Magic System." In *Problems in Materialist Culture: Selected Essays.* London: NLB, 1980.

Williams, William Carlos. *The Autobiography of William Carlos Williams.* New York: Random House, 1951.

———. *The Build-Up.* New York: Random House, 1952.

———. *Collected Poems, 1921-1931.* New York: Objectivist Press, 1934.

———. *The Collected Poems of William Carlos Williams: Volume I, 1909-1939.* Edited by A. Walton Litz and Christopher MacGowan. New York: New Directions, 1986.

———. "An Essay on *Leaves of Grass.*" In Walt Whitman, *Leaves of Grass,* edited by Sculley Bradley and Harold W. Blodgett. New York: Norton, 1973.

———. *The Farmers' Daughters: The Collected Stories of William Carlos Williams.* New York: New Directions, 1961.

———. "Guitar Blues" (1937). Houghton Library, Harvard University, Manuscript collection AM 1956 [2].

———. "Hart Crane (1899-1932)." *Contempo* 2 (July 5, 1932).

———. *I Wanted to Write a Poem: The Autobiography of the Works of a Poet.* Reported and edited by Edith Heal. Boston: Beacon Press, 1958.

———. *Imaginations.* Edited by Webster Schott. New York: New Directions, 1970.

———. *In the Money.* New York: New Directions, 1940.

———. Introduction to *Charles Sheeler: Paintings, Drawings, Photographs.* New York: Museum of Modern Art, 1939.

———. *Many Loves and Other Plays.* New York: New Directions, 1961.

———. "The New Poetical Economy." *Poetry* 44 (July 1934): 220-25.

——. *Paterson.* Revised Edition, prepared by Christopher MacGowan. New York: New Directions, 1992.

——. *Selected Essays of William Carlos Williams.* New York: New Directions, 1969.

——. *Selected Letters of William Carlos Williams.* Edited by John C. Thirlwall. New York: McDowell, Oblensky, 1957.

——. *Selected Poems of William Carlos Williams.* New York: New Directions, 1969. Revised Edition, 1985.

——. *A Voyage to Pagany.* New York: New Directions, 1970.

——. *White Mule.* 1937. New York: New Directions, 1967.

Witemeyer, Hugh, ed. *William Carlos Williams and James Laughlin: Selected Letters.* New York: Norton, 1989.

Index

Credits

Acknowledgment is made as follows for permission to quote from copyrighted material:

Quotations from the letters of William Carlos Williams and James Laughlin are taken from *William Carlos Williams and James Laughlin: Selected Letters* published by W. W. Norton & Co., Inc. (copyright © 1989 by William Eric Williams and Paul H. Williams and copyright © 1989 by James Laughlin) and are used by permission of New Directions Publishing Corp., agents for William Eric and Paul H. Williams, and James Laughlin.

Passages from "A Visit" in *Random Stories* by James Laughlin reprinted by permission of Moyer Bell, Kymbolde Way, Wakefield, RI 02879.

" 'Geeze, Doc, What Does It Mean?' Reading Williams Reading *Life*" first appeared in *William Carlos Williams Review* 20 (spring 1994) and is reprinted by permission.

"The Figure of Whitman in Williams's Old Doc Rivers" from chapter 3 first appeared in the *Journal of Popular Culture* and is reprinted by permission.

Grateful acknowledgment is given to New Directions Publishing Corporation for permission to quote from the following copyrighted works of William Carlos Williams.

The Autobiography of William Carlos Williams. Copyright 1948, 1951 by William Carlos Williams.

Collected Poems: Volume I, 1909-1939. Copyright 1938 by New Directions Publishing Corporation. Copyright © 1982, 1986 by William Eric Williams and Paul H. Williams.